INDIA
BY RAIL

INDIA
BY RAIL

Royston Ellis

2nd edition

BRADT PUBLICATIONS, UK
HUNTER PUBLISHING, USA

For V. Keshav Raj
– an officer and a gentleman –
whose friendship and encouragement
helped me complete over 35,000 km of train rides
to research the first edition, and for
Gemunu Amarasinghe
who accompanied me on some great trips
in 1992.

First published in 1989 by Bradt Publications, 41 Nortoft Road, Chalfont St Peter, Bucks. SL9 0LA, England. Distributed in the U.S.A. by Hunter Publishing Inc., Raritan Center Parkway, 300, Edison, NJ 08818. **This edition published in 1993.**

British Library Cataloguing in Publication Data
Ellis, Royston
  India by rail.
  1. India (Republic) Visitors' guides
  I. Title
  915. 4'0452

ISBN 0-946983-79-8

Maps and plans by Hans van Well
Cover photographs:
Front: The Desert Queen with stewards from the Palace On Wheels. (Photograph by Gemunu Amarasinghe.)
Back: View from the Matheran train. (Anthony J. Lambert.)

Typeset by Acorn Bookwork, Salisbury, Wiltshire
Printed and bound in Hong Kong by Colorcraft Ltd.

THE AUTHOR

Royston Ellis, born in England, left school age 16 determined to be a writer. He quickly won fame as a poet, pop biographer and youth chronicler before leaving England, age 20, for a life of travel.

Under the pen name of Richard Tresillian, he has written many best selling novels, including *The Bondmaster*. He is a contributor of travel articles to magazines and newspapers world wide including *The Times*, *Sunday Times*, *Daily Telegraph*, *The Independent*, *Business Traveller Asia Pacific* and *Serendib*, the Air Lanka magazine. He writes a weekly column on hotels and restaurants in *The Sunday Observer* of Sri Lanka, and was a consultant for the *National Geographic Television Special* on the Railways of India. He is the author of Bradt Publications' *Guide to Mauritius*.

Royston Ellis first visited India in 1963, and has had a home in the Indian subcontinent since 1980. He has travelled extensively in India by rail.

The author, sketched by train driver B. S. Gill, on the Kalka/Shimla railway.

ACKNOWLEDGEMENTS FOR THE SECOND EDITION

Even after 100,000 km of train rides during more than a score of visits to India, I still find Indian Railways fascinating and enjoyable. Many of the friends I made when I was writing the first edition have remained steadfast supporters despite my constant nagging over the years for information and assistance, especially Dr S. Dandapani, Ranjit Mathur and A.P. Muthuramalingam as well as Alexander John and Keshav Raj and, of course, Neel Jayantha. For his photographs – and companionship – I am indebted to Gemunu Amarasinghe of Sri Lanka.

Since the first edition was published in 1989, letters from people around the world have brought new information, most of which is included in this edition. I was delighted to receive comments from Indians too, not just from those associated with the railways. I am most grateful for the honour shown to me when I was elected a life member of the Institute of Rail Transport, New Delhi, because of this book.

My thanks to all those who have contributed in some way to this new edition, especially to those mentioned in this book, and to Samit Roychoudhury, a design student from Calcutta passionately interested in his country's railways, Mr J. Bakthavatchalam (CPRO's office, Southern Railway), Mr N.M. Balasubrahmaniyam (Executive Director, Institute of Rail Transport), Mr G.S. Banerjee (CPRO, Eastern Railway), Mr Jai Chandra (Manager, ITB, New Delhi) and his staff, and Deccan Queen fan Dr Shirish D. Yande of Pune.

Also thanks to readers Rev J.C. Allen, Brian Edwards, Ken Donald and Vicki Ross-Weir, Ms P. Kimantas, Alan and Hazel Hall with memories of the Palace on Wheels, Roger D. Morgan, Gareth & Suzy Ralphs and Hiroaki Okamoto. To Christine Koresski, the translator of this book into French, I am grateful for her dedicated work and for pointing out ambiguities and spelling errors.

Royston Ellis
Bentota, Sri Lanka
1992.

INDIA

(SHOWING POPULAR DESTINATIONS FOR RAIL TRAVELLERS)

NORTHERN & CENTRAL INDIA

EASTERN INDIA

N

0   200   400
k m

SOUTHERN & CENTRAL INDIA

Contents

Chapter 1

Discovering India by Rail

Whether you are a first time visitor to India, or an experienced traveller there, you'll find the best way to know India is to travel her length and breadth by train. It's an adventure that will teach you a lot about yourself as well as about India, and it's no hardship since trains in India are efficient, fast, frequent and fun.

Fly in a group or tour by coach and you'll be safely isolated from prolonged contact with India. Travel by local bus and you'll certainly see more than a tourist would, but you'll be uncomfortable and will end up hating the country simply because you feel awful.

Only train travel provides a comfortable berth for you to sleep on, meals at your seat, on-board toilets (some with a shower), travelling companions as diverse as the whole of India, and an aisle along which you can walk to stretch your legs or to meet new people. All that while travelling a network so extensive it has direct trains linking stations over 3,000 km apart.

The facilities are not just for the 1st Class passenger, all classes have bunks and bearer (waiter) service of meals, snacks and soft or hot drinks to your seat. On top of that, train travel is so inexpensive, you can travel in luxury in air-conditioned 1st Class at less than 2p a kilometre.

When you travel by train you are taking part in contemporary Indian culture. It is a learning experience as well as a means of getting from, say, Madras to Bangalore. Indian fellow travellers will be kind and tolerant, talking to you if you wish, or respecting your need for solitude if you make it plain you want to be left alone. Put yourself in the right frame of mind, a positive one, and you will get far more out of discovering India by rail than a cheap train ride.

The beauty of all this is that there has never been a better time to travel in India by train. Within the past five years rail travel has been transformed until it has become an experience foreigners, as well as Indians, find convenient and pleasurable.

It hasn't always been so. Yet now you can forget those horror stories about four hours spent in a queue to make reservations, about dreadful food, over-crowded compartments and rude railway officials. The word is out in railwayland to help foreign tourists. It's easy to understand why. They bring foreign currency which the country, and Indian

1

Railways, needs. Tourism generates at least 10 per cent of India's foreign currency earnings without exporting any of the country's valuable material resources. Each new hotel room generates 12 new jobs.

In recent years the British have topped the list of foreign visitors, with US citizens in second place. About 80 per cent of the Indrail Passes sold each year are bought by Britons. The International Tourist Bureau (ITB) at New Delhi station handled over 76,400 rail bookings by foreign tourists in 1987, its first year of operation.

Improved services

It's not just because Indian Railways wants foreign tourists that services have improved. Computers have revolutionized the reservations process, benefiting every rail traveller. Meals and drinks are served more hygienically in covered foil casseroles and disposable cups. And for the foreign tourist there is a special quota of seats reserved on many trains and some stations have special counters for Indrail Pass holders, so a foreigner need not join the general queue to make reservations.

Actually, not all of India's over 7,000 stations pamper foreign tourists as a matter of course. Many of the stations I've visited are off the tourist track where some officials might be bemused by a foreigner's demands; others, though, will be exceptionally helpful to foreign tourists. You'll discover, as I did, that by following the system and procedures set out in this guide, travel problems will be few.

Facilities for foreigners

First, a word of explanation for my use of the term 'foreign tourist'. A foreign passport holder who visits India for business or leisure is termed a 'foreign tourist' by Indian Railways, as opposed to an Indian who is touring by rail. I share the dismay of those who don't like to be called 'tourists' especially as we are clearly a different breed from the average 'package tourist'. But that's the way it is!

Foreign tourists, through the special quota, can make advance reservations for berths on busy trains when an Indian might only be wait-listed. 'Foreigners are our guests,' an official said when I queried the reason for giving foreigners priority over nationals. The real reason might be commercial: foreign currency makes foreigners valuable. I mention this to salve the conscience of sensitive travellers who have qualms about being treated to special privileges. Of course, if you want to join a long line and try to make your reservation from the general quota, and travel in the cheapest 2nd Class accommodation, you can. But, remember, you are thereby depriving an Indian, who can only afford the cheapest ticket, of a place in that queue and on that train. By using the facilities developed for foreigners (such as priority bookings, travel in upper class carriages) the traveller is not only contributing much-needed foreign exchange but easing the pressure for the ordinary Indian rail passenger as well.

Don't worry about missing anything through making your reservation from the foreign tourist quota, or through the station superintendent's influence, you will still see (and smell and feel) the real India. You can't escape it when travelling by train.

Home on the rails

You can confidently make your home for a few days on the train, or simply take a train for a short trip, such as on India's 'bullet train', the Shatabdi Express which takes only 115 minutes for the 199 km run from New Delhi to Agra. The Shatabdi Express is a symbol of the changes taking place in Indian Railways. The best train to Agra used to be the Taj Express but that takes 50 minutes longer in non AC discomfort. The new train is all air conditioned with a pantry in each coach and meals included in the fare (see Chapter 11).

However, because of the distance between important stations, most train journeys in India involve overnight travel. An advantage in travelling overnight is that it saves time and the cost of hotel accommodation. Some tourists plan their itineraries around overnight trains, making the train their home. They arrive at a station in the morning, check their bags into the left-luggage cloakroom and dash off to see the sights, returning in the evening for an overnight train to the next destination on their list. If your time and funds are limited, that's probably the best way but, despite the improved comfort of train travel (the wooden bunks in 2nd Class have been cushioned), it does require stamina and a certain kind of personality to spend endless nights on a train. If there is a daylight alternative, you might like to take it so you can see India's scenery instead of sleeping through it.

Station amenities

As always with Indian Railways, there is a solution to every difficulty. A long journey can be broken at stations *en route* for a shower (most stations have them either in bathrooms attached to waiting rooms or in a separate building) or for a motionless night on *terra firma* at a railway retiring room.

Retiring rooms are one of Indian Railways' best kept secrets which few foreigners bother to discover. They are private guest rooms with attached bathrooms available at stations for rent by ticket (and Indrail Pass) holders for any period of 24 hours. They are perfect, secure bases from which to explore a town, or to recover from several nights on the rails. The station restaurants are close by and sometimes room service is provided.

Retiring rooms are usually the cheapest or the best value in town. If you only need a bed and don't worry about privacy, some stations also have dormitories, with lockers, showers and toilets (see Chapter 7).

Other facilities available depend on a station's importance. Some major ones still have loud closed circuit television (CCTV) showing US panel games, wrestling and Hindi movies chopped up between live station announcements but these have – mercifully – been reduced. There could also be a chemist and curio shops, a book kiosk with US and UK best-selling paperbacks, a fruit stall, and drinking water either from coolers or dispensed by formidable ladies with ladles. All stations will have food and tea vendors, and waiting rooms.

Password
If you have several train journeys in mind or simply want to avoid hassles, it can be more economical, and certainly much easier, to travel on an Indrail Pass (see Chapter 3).

Rail facts
Indian Railways is now the largest railway system on earth under a single management.

Origin:	1853 with 34 km of track, Bombay/Thane.
Network:	62,367 route kilometres.
Services:	7,320 passenger services operated daily.
Passengers:	10.57 million every day.
Stations:	7,100
Locomotives:	8,417 with 3,759 diesel, 2,915 steam and 1,743 electric traction.
Rolling Stock:	28,701 conventional passenger coaches, 3,142 EMU coaches and 6,668 other passenger coaches.
Running track:	Broad Gauge (BG): 1.67 m wide, most of the main line trunk routes: 72,174 km. Metre Gauge (MG): 1.00 m wide, mostly as feeder lines: 32,122 km. Narrow Gauge (NG) : 0.762 m or 0.610 m wide, on limited sections of difficult terrain: 4,562 km.
Overall average speed, including halts:	Express/Mail trains: 47.6 kph (BG), 36.9 kph (MG). Passenger trains: 28.2 kph (BG), 25.6 kph (MG).
Bridges:	116,000
Level crossings:	37,117 plus 964 canal and 3,765 cattle crossings.
Regular employees:	1,651,000 plus 145,000 casual workers.
Average cost per employee:	Rs 31,878 p.a.

Retiring rooms: At 420 stations.
Catering: Available at 3,000 stations and on 89 pairs of trains.

(Statistics supplied by Indian Railways, as at March 31 1992.)

Railway set up

The railways are run by the Ministry of Railways through the Railway Board. At board level there are six members, including the chairman who functions as the managing director. The members represent different disciplines: engineering, mechanical, traffic, electrical, finance and staff with the chairman looking after one portfolio. At Rail Bhavan (building), the headquarters of the board in New Delhi, a plethora of units and directorates function to pump information to the zones and to monitor their performance.

At zonal level, a general manager heads a small empire in each of the nine regional railways. Various managers and divisional heads serve under him including a host of chief superintendents controlling operations, commercial functions, freight, passenger traffic, catering, passenger reservations, safety and rolling stock. Belt-tightening is underway in the railways and it won't be long after you start your journey that you'll see ways Indian Railways could save money and make the service more efficient and convenient too. Suggestions to the general manager, not to me (see Complaints, Chapter 5).

The bureaucracy that runs the railways has evolved over 140 years so pruning it is very complicated. The organization devised by the British has been adapted with genius by Indian Railways and this vast, inexplicable system actually works, despite such impediments as the man (you'll meet him too) who holds a post for which he is obviously not competent.

The Railway Board in 1992 ordered a 10 per cent cut in basic administration costs; not just on the frills but with the shears snipping at posts as well. It is part of the global trim, happening in all areas of India.

According to the Board's yearbook, 'The economic, agricultural and industrial development of India is inextricably interwoven with Indian Railways' development and fortunes.'

Railwayland in India is really a country within a country. It has its own electricity service, telephone system, hospitals, colleges, bureaucracy. It is so self-sufficient it stands apart from the normal life of India, yet without the railways there would be no normal life.

The nine regional railways are listed here using the identification number which – where it appears in the first digit of a four-digit train number in the timetable – indicates which railways the train belongs to (see Train Numbers, Chapter 4).

1: **Central Railway** – HQ: Victoria Terminus, Bombay.
Divisions at Bombay, Bhusaval, Nagpur, Jabalpur, Jhansi, Bhopal, Solapur.

3: **Eastern Railway** – HQ: 17, Netaji Subhas Road, Calcutta.
Divisions at Sealdah, Howrah, Asansol, Dhanbad, Danapur, Mughal Sarai, Malda.

4: **Northern Railway** – HQ: Baroda House, New Delhi.
Divisions at Allahabad, Ambala, Bikaner, Delhi, Firozpur, Jodhpur, Lucknow, Moradabad.

5: **North Eastern Railway** – HQ: Gorakhpur.
Divisions at Izzatnagar, Lucknow Jn, Varanasi, Samastipur, Sonpur.

5: (sharing the number) **Northeast Frontier** – HQ: Maligaon, Guwahati.
Divisions at Kathihar Jn, Alipurduar Jn, Lumding Jn, Tinsukia Jn.

6: **Southern Railway** – HQ: Park Town, Madras.
Dvisions at Madras, Palghat, Trivandrum, Bangalore, Mysore, Tiruchchirappalli, Madurai.

7: **South Central Railway** – HQ: Rail Nilayam, Secunderabad.
Divisions at Secunderabad, Hyderabad (MG), Vijayawada, Guntakal, Hubli.

8: **South Eastern Railway** – HQ: 11, Garden Reach Road, Calcutta.
Divisions at Adra, Bilaspur, Chakradharpur, Kharagpur, Khurda Road, Nagpur, Waltair, Sambalpur.

9: **Western Railway** – HQ: Churchgate, Bombay.
Divisions at Bombay, Vadodara, Ratlam, Kota, Jaipur, Ajmer, Rajkot, Bhavnagar.

Steam and special trains

You will catch glimpses of steam engines, usually shunting, throughout India, but hurry if you want to ride a steam train. They are being phased out rapidly with 523 steam engines condemned in 1987/88. Since the first edition of this book was published in 1989, the number of steam locomotives has dwindled from 4,427 to 2,915. By the end of this century, they will all have gone, condemned for scrap, every one. (See Chapter 6).

In the meantime, though, there is a chance to ride not only steam engines, but also the lorry-like rail car from Kalka to Shimla, the rack-and-pinion steam train to 'Ooty' with its wooden carriages like something from an Agatha Christie movie, and the famous, but painfully slow, toy train to Darjeeling, when it is operating. But no longer does a train created out of carriages that used to belong to maharajas, the Palace on Wheels, steam through Rajasthan. It's a brand new rake now and diesel-hauled except for the run out of and into Delhi Cantt station at the beginning and end of the journey. The thrill of rail travel, though, is still to be found in modern marvels like the superfast, luxurious (in 1st AC Class anyway) Rajdhani Expresses serving New Delhi, Calcutta and Bombay, the Shatabdi Expresses between New Delhi and Bhopal, Lucknow and Kalka, and the commuter specials like the Deccan Queen and the double-deckers from Bombay and even on the newly-opened Calcutta metro. Or you can travel in your own private coach on special tours (see Chapter 11).

Give it a try

'On arrival in India my initial reaction was to get the next flight home but after 24 days I grew to like it and was very sorry to leave,' wrote Pauline Harford of Poole, Dorset when she sent in some tips. 'We had a 21 day Indrail Pass, everything went without a hitch . . . and that is saying something as we were absolute novices in our mid 50s.'

Another reader, actually writing during a temporary stay in an English prison, recalled his trip from Delhi to Agra and Varanasi and back to Delhi (a popular rail journey for the independent traveller) and said: 'I think all Brits should . . . spend six months in India. It might just make them appreciate the things in life that one would normally take for granted.'

Don't be surprised if you feel exasperated at the way things are done not only on the railways but everywhere in India. Often misunderstandings might be your fault – not theirs – since there are so many viewpoints to life and work. While you might benefit from there being more signs in English and people of competence at railway stations explaining what to do, you'll soon discover that a smile and a polite approach will keep your temper under control and lead to unexpected, pleasant adventures.

To anyone who asks me whether they should travel in India by rail – is it really fun? – I say yes, give it a try. Of course, it's not like home . . . but isn't that one of the reasons for going away?

उ.रे/N.R.

सी.एम. 257 (अंग्रेजी) (हिं.)
C.M. 257 (NR)

आरक्षण/खारिज/वापसी/आगे की यात्रा हेतु अनुरोध पत्र
REQUISITION FOR RESERVATION/CANCELLATION/RETURN OR ONWARD JOURNEY

जिस स्टेशन से Station from.............................जिस स्थान को To............ ....
यात्रा की तिथि Date of journey............................ट्रेन नं. Train No................
श्रेणी Class...............................बर्थ/सीट Berth/Seat.............................

क्रम सं. S. No.	नाम Name in Block letters	स्त्री/पु. Sex	आयु Age	कर्मचारी द्वारा भरा जायेगा To be filled in by the staff
1............				टिकट नं.·············· Ticket No./PNR No.
2............				कोच नं.·············· Coach No.
3............				बर्थ/सीट नं.·············· Berth/Seat No.
4............				प्रतीक्षा सूची नं.·············· Wait list No.
5............				ह.ई. आर. सी.·············· Sig. of E.R.C.
6............				

आवेदक का नाम Name of the applicant..
आवेदक के हस्ताक्षर Signature of applicant..
तारीख Date........................

विशेष अनुरोध
Special Request

(i) कूपा/केबिन/निचली शायिका/
मध्यवर्ती शायिका/ऊपरी शायिका
Coupe/Cabin/Lower Berth/
Middle Berth/Upper Berth

(ii) धूम्रपान निषेधयान
Non Smoker Coach

(iii) पसन्द का भोजन (शाकाहारी/मांसाहारी)
Choice of Meals (Veg./N. Veg.)

पसंद दर्शाने के लिए खाने में "√" निशान लगायें ।
Mark "√" in the block to show the choice.

पूरा पता Address in full..
....

दूरभाष Telephone........................समय Time........................

(कृ.पृ.उ./P.T.O.)

Chapter 2

Planning the Trip

PRELIMINARIES

Advance planning is essential to get the most out of travelling by train in India. Foreigners who expect a train service run the way it is at home will be annoyed to find they can't buy a ticket to travel overnight at a moment's notice. Reservations have to be made on certain day-time trains and on all overnight trains. It is to your advantage to do so as far in advance as possible.

When planning the trip, set aside at least one day after your arrival in India to make reservations. At the gateway cities of New Delhi, Bombay, Calcutta and Madras, there are special bureaux dealing with foreign rail tourist bookings as well as counters at the airports. When you buy an Indrail Pass outside India, reservations can be done at the same time but you will need to confirm them on arrival (see Chapter 3).

Maps

The first requirement for planning your trip is a map of India on which to locate the places you want to visit. Maps of India are available from good bookshops and, in England, from Edward Stanford Ltd, 12/14 Long Acre, London WC2E 9LP. Tel: 071 836 1321. In the USA, try The Complete Traveler at 199 Madison Avenue, New York, NY 10016. Tel: 212 685 9007 or Forsyth Travel Library Inc., PO Box 2975, 9154 West 57 St, Shawnee Mission, KS 66201-1357. Tel: 913 384 3440.

Free maps and lots of city and state information, as well as a leaflet about rail travel, are available from the Government of India tourist offices.

Recommended by Rob Dobson, a rail traveller I met at Delhi's Rail Yatri Niwas (Railway Inn) in 1992, is a plastic bound 64-page folder of maps which contains city plans as well as maps of individual states and lists of selected attractions. Although it's actually a road atlas, railway lines are also shown. I bought my copy of *TT Maps' Road Atlas of India* at Howrah Station for Rs30 in 1992. Publishers are TT Maps & Publications Ltd, 328, G.S.T. Road, Chromepet, Madras 600 044. They are also the producers of an excellent *Map Guide To India*, a

9

TOURIST OFFICES

The Govt. of India tourist offices are located in the following places:

IN INDIA

Agra
191 The Mall, Agra-282 001, Uttar Pradesh, Tel: 363377/363959

Aurangabad
Krishna Vilas, Station Road, Aurangabad-431 005, Maharashtra, Tel: 24817

Bangalore
KFC Building, 48 Church Street, Bangalore-560 001, Karnataka, Tel: 579517

Bhubaneswar
B-21, Kalpana Area, Bhubaneswar-751014, Orissa, Tel: 54203

Bombay
123 M Karve Road, Opp. Churchgate, Bombay-400 020, Maharashtra, Tel: 293144, 293145, 296854, 292932 Telex: 011-82922 Fax: 92-22-291585

Calcutta
'Embassy', 4 Shakespeare Sarani, Calcutta-700 071, West Bengal, Tel: 221402 225813/221475 Telex: 021-8176, Fax: (033) 22-3521

Guwahati
B.K. Kakati Road, Ulubari, Guwahati-781 007, Assam, Tel: 31381

Hyderabad
3-6-369/A-30, Sandozi Building, 2nd Floor, 26 Himayat Nagar, Hyderabad-500 029, Tel: 66877

Imphal
Old Lambulane, Jail Road, Imphal-795 001, Manipur Tel: 21131

Jaipur
State Hotel, Jaipur-302 001, Rajasthan, Tel: 72200

Khajuraho
Near Western Group of Temples, Khajuraho-471 606, Madhya Pradesh, Tel: 2047, 2048

Kochi (Cochin)
Willingdon Island, Kochi-682 009, Kerala, Tel: 340352 Telex: 0885-6847

Madras
154 Anna Salai, Madras-600 002. Tamil Nadu Tel: 869685, 869695 Telex: 041-7359

Naharlagun
Sector 'C', Naharlagun, Arunachal Pradesh, Tel: 328

New Delhi
88, Janpath, New Delhi-110 001 Tel: 3320005, 3320008, 3320109, 3320266, 3320342

Panaji (Goa)
Communidade Building, Church Square, Panaji-403 001, Goa, Tel: 3412

Patna
Paryatan Bhawan, Birchand Patel Path, Patna-800 001, Bihar, Tel: 226721

Port Blair
VIP Road, Junglighat P.O., Port Blair-744 103, Andaman & Nicobar Islands, Tel: 21006

Shillong
Tirot Singh Syiem Road, Police Bazar, Shillong-793 001, Meghalaya, Tel: 25632

Thiruvananthapuram (Trivandrum)
Airport, Thiruvananthapuram, Kerala

Varanasi
15B, The Mall, Varanasi-221 002, Uttar Pradesh, Tel: 43744

Most State Governments have their own Tourist Information Offices in their State Capitals.

OVERSEAS

Australia
Level 1, C/o H.C.I., 17, Castlereagh Street, Sydney, New South Wales 2000 Tel: 0061-2-232 1600/17961, 0061-2-233-7579 Fax: (02) 2233003

Bahrain
P.O. Box 11294, Manama Tel: 715713 Fax: 00973-715-527

Canada
60 Bloor Street (West), Suite 1003, Toronto, Ontario M4 W3 B8 Tel: 416-692-3787, 416-962-3788, Fax: 416 962-6279

Spain
C/o Embassy of India, Avenida PIO XII 30-32, 28016 Madrid Tel: 3457339, 3457340 Fax: 4577996 Telex: 22605 EOME

Sweden
Sveavagen 9-11, 1st Floor, S-111 57, Stockholm 11157, Tel: 08-215081/101187, Fax: 46-8-210186

Switzerland
1–3, Rue De Chantepoulet, 1201 Geneva Tel: (022) 7321813/1677 Fax: 0041-22-7315660 Telex: 412727

France
8, Boulevard de la, Madeleine, 75009
Paris Tel: 42-65-83-86, 42-65-77-06
Fax: 42-65-0116
Germany
Kaiserstrasse 77 (111), D-6000 Frankfurt,
AM MAIN 1 (Tel: (069) 235423, 235424
Fax: (069) 234724
Italy
9 Via-Albricci, Milan 20122
Tel: 804952, 8053506 Fax: 72021681
Japan
Pearl Building, 9 18 Ginza, 7 Chome,
Chuo-Ku, Tokyo 104 Tel: (03) 571
5062/3, (03) 571 5197 Fax: (03) 571-5235
Malaysia
Wisma HIA, Lot 203, 2nd Floor, Jalan
Raja Chulan, 50200 Kuala Lumpur
Tel: (03) 2425285 Fax: 00603-2425301
Netherlands
Rokin 9-15, 1012 KK Amsterdam
Tel: 020-208991 Fax: 003120-383059

Thailand
3rd Floor, Kentucky Fried Chicken
Building, 62/5 Thaniya Road, Bangkok
10500 Tel: 2352585, 2356670
Fax: 662-2352585
UAE
Post Box 12856, NASA Building,
Al. Maktoum Road, Deira, Dubai
Tel: 274848, 274199 Fax: 274103
UK
7 Cork Street, London W1X 2AB Tel:
071-437-3677/8 (Gen), 071-734-6613
(Direct line) Fax: 004471-494 1048
USA
3350 Wilshire Boulevard, Room 204,
Los Angeles, California 90010 Tel: (213)
380-8855 Fax: 001-(213) 380-6111

30, Rockefeller Plaza, Suite 15, North
Mezzanine, New York, NY 10112
Tel: 212 586 4901, 212-586-4902,
212-586-4903, 212 586-4904
Fax: 001-212-582-3274 Telex: 9102508316

---

folder which was issued free by the Government of India Tourist Office for the 1991 Visit India Year. Copies still turn up and since it has an insert of rail routes showing the different regional zones, it is a boon to rail travellers.

On your map, mark the places you want to visit so you can choose the most convenient airport. The typical first-time visitor to India usually wants to visit Agra and Kashmir and Rajasthan and possibly Varanasi with a side trip to Nepal, in which case Delhi is the gateway city. As the rail booking facilities at the International Tourist Bureau (ITB) at New Delhi station are the best in India, it's the ideal place for starting any rail journey.

TIMETABLES

A rail timetable is useful so you can see how long it takes to travel between cities, but if you don't have one, measure the distance on the map between the major cities you want to visit. For every 50 km, allow one hour of train time. For example, the distance between Delhi and Jammu Tawi (the station for Kashmir) is about 550 km which means a journey of 11 hours. From the journey time chart in Chapter 9, you can see that the fastest journey time between those cities is actually 10 hrs 45 mins. Other trains take from 14 to 15 hours.

The best timetable readily available outside India is the *Thomas Cook Overseas Timetable* which contains 30 pages devoted to India showing, in easy to understand format, the times of all important trains and the classes available. There is also a route map which is useful for planning the trip since most rail lines are shown. The timetable is published six times a year and is available from the Timetable Publishing Office, Thomas Cook Ltd, Thorpe Wood, Peterborough PE3 6SB, England. Tel: 0733 502568.

Indian Railways publish a timetable called *Trains At A Glance* (*TAG*) in July every year which is available outside India through the GSAs for the Indrail Pass (see Chapter 3). In India it costs Rs8. It contains most of the train times and information a visitor will need and has a map. It has a station index although it does not give the page number of every reference to each station. Also, there is no indication of what classes of accommodation are available on each train, nor all the stops the train makes.

More detailed timetables which include all the halts made by slow passenger trains are published in July by each of the nine railway zones, covering the services operated by each zone. They are only available in India, at main station bookstalls within their zone. These timetables cost Rs7 each and contain lots of extra information as well as a regional map.

Although they all follow the same format, the one published by South Central Railway has the clearest layout and plenty of additional information, including an extra map with a timetable key. A list of 'aphorisms' included has as number 13 'Diarrhoea – answer is sugar–salt solution.' The timetable of Northeast Frontier railway carries a box saying simply 'Not before twenty – never after thirty, two are plenty.' It also gives the sound advice 'Less luggage, more comfort' and the warning that 'Pelting of stones towards the train is a punishable offence.'

There is a publication that combines all the zone timetables in one, thick volume, with an index showing every station. Called *Newman's Indian Bradshaw* it is published monthly and costs Rs30. It is sometimes difficult to obtain in India although its cover lists 70 stations, including Howrah and Sealdah in Calcutta, Delhi (but not New Delhi) and Bombay (VT but not Central) where it can be bought. It is not sold in Madras. The overseas agents for this excellent if crudely-printed volume are Wm Dawson & Sons Ltd, Cannon House, Folkestone, Kent, England.

Midnight is indicated as 2400 hrs for train arrivals, and 0000 hrs for departures.

How long?

The ideal length for a holiday in India is at least three weeks, but with careful planning you can see a lot by train in just one week. I've suggested some itineraries in Chapter 9. A three week visit allows sufficient time to recover from the flight, get used to the heat, the clamour, the food, and to feel at ease. You'll be able to see enough different parts of India in three weeks to whet your appetite for further visits when you can concentrate on the areas you most enjoyed.

Planning the itinerary

It is a common mistake to try to include too much in an itinerary planned in the comfort of an armchair at home. It is difficult to imagine the distances involved, or the effect on a newcomer to India of a lot of train travelling. For instance, from Delhi to Madras is 2194 km (1362 miles), the equivalent of travelling from London to Edinburgh four times. You'll feel the strain whatever class you travel in (although you'll feel worse after two nights in 2nd Class than two nights in 1st AC Class) simply because the rhythm of train travel is bound to disturb your system. Allow time in your itinerary not just for the train journey but for extras such as delays, waiting time, and also for recovery, relaxation, a chance to see the sights, and to let things happen.

Unfortunately, the sheer volume of traffic makes delays almost inevitable. Many routes are single track only so a train has to wait on a double track section for any oncoming trains. This is known as 'crossing' and explains why a train stops in the middle of nowhere. The late running of one train extends to the train behind it and can affect the train coming towards it too.

If you are on a train that seems bound to arrive late, don't worry about missing the connection since that could be late as well. Also, because of 'cushion time' in rail schedules, even as much as an hour's delay could have been allowed for. This gives an opportunity for the train to make up time on the last lap of its journey and arrive on schedule.

Just in case, allow at least three hours to make connections unless there are plenty of alternative trains should you actually miss the one you want. Stations in India are always interesting places to wait; if you tire of watching the other passengers you could have a meal, a shower or take a walk into town. If you have to hang around a station during the night, check into a retiring room and sleep; the attendant will wake you on request (see Chapter 7). If you do miss a connecting train, you'll have lost your onward reservation and that will take time to sort out. Better to expect a missed connection and allow an overnight stop anyway.

As well as train delays, there are likely to be unexpected frustrations when you do arrive at your destination, such as a local holiday or a strike, or it could even be something nice that makes you want to stay longer. Build plenty of 'cushion time' into your own itinerary with days of nothing planned so that you have some spare days if you need them.

Plan your route to save on time. Once you've left your originating city, it makes sense not to return there unless you have to. Avoid backtracking; trains in India go across country too, not just via Delhi or the main cities. For instance, you can go from Agra to Lucknow without having to change at Delhi.

If timetables bore you, work out basically where you want to go and leave it to the Indrail Pass GSA (see next chapter) or, in India, the rail tourist guide at one of the Foreign Tourist Bureaux to suggest an itinerary. They will know the main trains but you may have to curb their enthusiasm to book you on trains leaving or arriving at impossible times.

Avoid trains that bring you to your destination late at night, especially if you've never been there before. Also trains leaving before 0600 should be resisted. Not only does that mean early rising but the passengers already on the train will be sleeping and that will make settling in difficult.

The ideal departure time is about 1000 with 1800 hours the latest for overnight journeys so you have time to size up the other occupants of the compartment before bedding down for the night. Lower berths, incidentally, are only supposed to be occupied as berths from 2100 to 0600. They are used as seats for all occupants during the day.

Not all trains have 1st or AC Class, although all do have 2nd Class of some sort. Some trains over certain routes are better than others over the same route; it's worth finding out which are faster, more convenient and have a pantry car.

Most important trains run daily but there are some superfast long distance expresses which run only once a week. You will need to study the timetables carefully, and all the little notes too, to find the best trains. I've listed some of them in Chapter 12.

When to go

The most popular time for rail tourists is November to February which is the peak of the usual tourist season of September to March. April, May and June should be avoided, not because the weather is unbearably hot (which it is), but because that's the domestic tourist season. All India takes to the tracks then to visit relatives, attend weddings, go home, make a pilgrimage or simply to ride a train because everyone else is doing it. 85 per cent of Indians on holiday travel by rail. The trains are packed, reservations are impossible to get, and it's hell on wheels.

July and August is the monsoon season and a favourite time for foreigners to take the train to Jammu Tawi on the way to Kashmir, or to head for Shimla. If you can only visit India during April to August, plan on staying in the cooler hill areas and make sure you have train and hotel reservations secured.

Although in July and August you'll be drenched with perspiration in Delhi (humidity can reach 90 per cent) in December and January the capital can be cold. If you're starting a trip from Delhi, the spring (February and March) and autumn (October and November) are best.

How to go

The four international airports of Delhi, Bombay, Calcutta and Madras are accessible by frequent direct flights from Europe and Asia. Air India have direct flights from New York and Toronto as well as from London, Paris, Frankfurt, Geneva and Rome, and from Africa and the Middle and Far East.

Flights to Delhi from London take nine hours nonstop and up to 15 hours via other points. Return fares range from £2,631 1st Class and £1,503 Business Class down to £600 for a special Economy Class fare. The same fares apply for Bombay; Calcutta and Madras are a few pounds more. There are cheaper fares available. For instance, the travel organization, Wexas International (45 Brompton Road, Knightsbridge, London SW3 1DE, England; general enquiries: Tel: 071 589 3315) quotes about £455 return to Bombay, Delhi and Calcutta and £525 to Madras.

Trailfinders Travel Centre at 46/48 Earls Court Road, London W8 6EJ, England. Tel: 071 938 3366 offers a complete service for the independent traveller, and no membership is required. They have fares by many airlines between £400 and £500 depending on the season, and can also offer great discounts on top hotels. They have an immunization centre, a travel insurance service and a library for their clients, as well as a travel bookshop. Reduced rate tickets can be bought by cash or credit card and issued on the spot.

Student and independent travellers can make their arrangements through STA. Their main UK office is at 74 Old Brompton Road, London SW7 3LQ. Tel: 071 937 9962, for intercontinental enquiries. They also have offices in Bristol, Cambridge and Oxford and at many campus cities in the USA. Their fares are competitive with the best and their staff are experienced travellers.

A novel way of flying to India is to go to Goa or Trivandrum. Inspirations East Ltd, P.O. Box 990, Windsor, Berks SL4 3UW. Tel: 0753 830883, sell a special flight/rail package throughout the season (October to April) from Gatwick to Goa and Trivandrum. Since Goa and Trivandrum are much pleasanter airports to arrive at than any of the 'big four' this seems an attractive deal. For the dedicated rail traveller, Trivandrum is preferable to Goa since there are many lines and sights within easy reach, whereas from Goa there is only one way out (see Chapter 10).

Access to Trivandrum is also possible from Colombo, Sri Lanka, by Air Lanka (recommended) and Indian Airlines as are the airports of Tiruchchirappalli (not as efficient as Trivandrum), Bombay and Madras. Sea travel by ferry from Sri Lanka to Rameswaram is temporarily suspended. Travel overland from Nepal is possible by linking up with a rail connection to Gorakhpur or Patna where onward reservations can be made.

If you arrive at Trivandrum, Goa or Tiruchchirappalli, or overland from Nepal, allow at least a day to make rail reservations since there are no special Foreign Tourist Bureaux to plan itineraries at those stations. When buying a rail ticket in Nepal, make it for the short journey to the first major station in India where you can buy an onward ticket. Otherwise you can get ripped off, paying more for the ticket in Nepal than you would in India and not getting the reservations you think you've got (see Chapter 10: Gorakhpur).

Where to go

In addition to the cities of Delhi (the top favourite), Bombay, Calcutta and Madras, the most popular destinations for foreign rail travellers are:

Agra (Taj Mahal)
Aurangabad (for Ellora caves)
Bangalore (a Raj resort)
Bhubaneswar (Temple City)
Goa (via Vasco da Gama station)
Gorakhpur (for Nepal)
Jaipur (Pink City)
Jaisalmer (desert fort)
Jalgaon (for the caves at Ajanta)
Jammu Tawi (for bus to Kashmir)
Jhansi (for Khajuraho carvings)
Jodhpur (for Rajasthan)
Madurai (Tamil culture)
New Jalpaiguri (for Darjeeling)
Ooty (Udagamandalam, for hill railway and resort)
Puri (for Konark sun temple and sea)
Quilon (for Kerala backwaters)
Rameswaram (for Sri Lanka ferry, when operating)
Shimla (hill resort)
Varanasi (Benares, ancient holy city)

Some other places worth visiting are Udaipur, the Venice of the East; Mysore, for its charm and sandalwood; Cochin, (via Ernakulam), for its maritime heritage; and the Land's End of India, Kanniya Kumari, with its sun and moon rising over three seas.

In a list supplied by Indian Railways, the following stations are also given as popular destinations for foreign tourists, but it might be the outcome of wishful thinking with some of these stations: Bijapur (for Golgumbaz Dome), Chittaurgarh (Rajasthan), Gwalior (fort), Raxaul (access to Katmandu), Sawai Madhopur (wildlife and Ranthambhor fortress), Tiruchchirappalli (historic holy city), Trivandrum (for Kovalam beaches), Haridwar (for Rishikesh), Hospet (for Hampi and Thungabhadra Dam), Hyderabad/Secunderabad, Indore (Mandu fort), Jabalpur (Kanha National Park), Lonavla (for Karla and Bhaja caves), Madgaon (for Goa) and Madurai (for temple and ancient Pandyan capital).

What to take

As little as possible. Even a flight bag weighing only 5 kg can be a strain to carry in extreme heat. You really do not need half the things you feel you should take. Anyway, if you do find you've left something behind, you can usually buy a replacement in India.

By reducing your belongings to the minimum essentials, you can probably pack everything in a bag small enough to carry on the plane with you. A duffle bag is good because its flexible shape allows it to be stuffed away or used as a pillow, but be careful of storing valuables in it since it can be ripped open. If you will be trekking or hiking, a backpack is best. It should have an internal frame as an external one can break easily and sticks into people and things. Keep it as light as possible.

Rob Robson says a good quality sleeping bag weighing about 2 kg will easily fit into a backpack and its own bag stuffed with clothes will serve as a pillow (indispensable where bedrolls are not available). Good western camping equipment and clothes are greatly valued in India as imported goods are restricted, so you could sell it before leaving.

A small suitcase, made of a lightweight, durable shell, gives you mobility, stores neatly under a train seat and is more secure because it can be locked. If you take a lot of luggage, it could be worthwhile storing it while you are travelling by train, and buying a cheap case in India (at about £4.00/$7.00) to take only what you need on your rail trip.

Books are usually the heaviest and bulkiest item in a traveller's luggage. Fortunately, you won't need many. Railway bookstalls (**Wheelers** in the north and **Higginbothams** in the south) are excellent, with a vast range of popular, and classical, paperbacks in English. If you need to keep in touch with the world, a miniature portable radio that receives BBC World Service is useful. Some travellers are inseparable from their Walkmans; it seems a shame to block your ears to India like that.

Prepare yourself for train travel in the same way that you would for a long-haul flight. Take an eyeshade and ear plugs so you can sleep if the compartment light is on and people are talking late into the night.

For sleeping on trains, a cotton sleeping bag liner from the YHA can be useful, with a blanket bought in India instead of taking a sleeping bag. Ashley Butterfield points out that cotton sheet sleeping bags can easily be made up India. In 1st and 2nd AC Classes bedrolls can be hired (see Chapter 5). If you intend visiting chilly hill stations, then a sweater and even a jacket, scarf and woolly hat could be needed.

Whatever clothes you take should be lightweight and quick drying. Cotton underwear (as long as it's loose) is the best, with a spare set for when you're washing the dirty ones. Shirts with lots of deep pockets with buttons or zips are a good idea. A cotton money belt is favoured by experienced travellers and is especially useful for keeping valuables close to your body when you're asleep. But make sure it's secure around your waist when you use the train loo.

Safari-type shirts can be made up from jazzy cotton material for about £3 each in 24 hours. A tailor will be willing to copy your favourite garments so you need not take spares but have them made there.

The light cotton shirts and pyjama-like trousers worn by Indian travellers are ideal for male and female foreigners and can be bought cheaply. A *lungi*, a floor length piece of cloth wrapped around the waist, is good for nightwear or for hiding under when you're changing clothes in a crowded carriage.

Most garments sold in Europe for wear in the tropics are a disappointment, either too hot or too fashionable to be practical. An exception are the trousers (bags) produced by Rohan Designs plc, 30 Maryland Road, Tongwell, Milton Keynes, MK15 8HN, England. Tel: 0908 618888. Rohan bags have large zippered pockets everywhere, including one that curls inside the back thigh, useful for keeping an emergency stash of toilet paper. Dark colours are best since light shades quickly show the grime from train travel. One pair is enough since you can be certain they'll dry overnight in a retiring room bathroom but they're so lightweight, you could take two in case of a special occasion. My bags were admired by fashion-conscious Bombayites and by diplomats at a cocktail party in Calcutta. Other rail travellers I met wearing them swore by them too.

A pair of sandals is essential for wearing in train toilets. Cheap plastic ones (from Rs20) can be bought at street markets. These, and a stout pair of walking shoes or good trainers, will be sufficient footwear. Socks should be cotton.

A small pocket torch is necessary for night travel, and a padlock or two, and a pocket knife for peeling fruit. You may like an air-filled pillow but this can be bought at main stations for about £1.50/$2.60 which includes an attractive woven cotton pillow case. The neck support pillows marketed worldwide have synthetic material covers and cause too much sweating in the heat. They're expensive too compared with full size pillows in India.

Take a plastic container for your special toiletries. Toothpaste and soap can be purchased everywhere but imported eau de colognes are expensive. You will need toilet paper; although it can be bought in India, it's in small rolls and you will have to hunt for it. A large plastic bag is always useful, especially when you take a shower on a train (see Chapter 5).

Bring a pack of cards, and you can make friends anywhere!

You will need a small towel, although bath towels are provided in railway retiring rooms, for drying your hands when you wash them before and after eating a meal with your fingers. No handtowel, or paper, is provided in train toilets but the bedroll you can rent at night does have a handtowel in it. A handkerchief will do in an emergency although it will soon smell of curry unless you wash it out frequently. Wet wipes or similar could help then.

An essential item is a water bottle and you can buy them at most stations. Outdoor equipment shops in Europe and the USA sell tougher ones designed for hikers. These are ideal. Carry a crown bottle opener too or, more versatile, a Swiss Army knife, for opening soft drinks and beer bottles. But if you only have hand baggage when you fly, remember the knife might be removed by airport security.

It is worthwhile taking your full quota of liquor into India since imported spirits are very expensive. Take film as well, more than you think you'll need. (Pack it in a plastic bag for hand-searching by airport security instead of letting it go through those X-ray machines.) You can buy notebooks and pens in India. Take, or buy, your own cup into which enough tea or coffee can be poured by station vendors. You pay according to the measure. The tea is delicious, milky and with cinnamon or ginger flavour.

HEALTH

I was advised to take all sorts of medical preparations but I threw out most of the ointments and pills soon after arrival when I discovered I could buy them locally. However, take your favourite headache and diarrhoea remedies and any prescription medicines you need, anti-malaria pills and water purifying tablets (available from Boots). Sometimes brand name medicines available in India are out of date but there are pharmacies everywhere. Because of the dust, you'll probably need throat sweets.

Unless a visitor arrives in India from a yellow fever area, no vaccinations are required for entry. However, they are recommended.

Cholera: If you are going from India to a country that imposes restrictions on arrivals from India because of cholera, then you need to have an inoculation and a certificate to prove it. In any case, a cholera jab is a good thing to have before you go. It is effective for six months.

Yellow fever: Do not arrive in India without a certificate of vaccination against yellow fever within six months of departing from a declared yellow fever area, such as Kenya, or by an aircraft that's transitted such areas; you'll find yourself isolated in quarantine for six days. The vaccination is effective for ten years.

Malaria: There is a risk of malaria throughout the year, so be prepared. The British Airways medical service advises Paludrin (no prescription); two tablets a day starting one day before arrival. Nivo-quine (no prescription) should also be taken; two tablets weekly, starting one week before travel. The tablets should also be taken for four weeks after leaving India. In the UK, advice on malaria precautions is available by taped message on telephone number 071 636 7921.

Diarrhoea: Non-prescription remedies are limited in variety in the UK, but don't worry, you can easily buy prescription pills (such as Lomotil) to stabilize yourself from station pharmacies in India. Take Imodium with you, just in case. The Indian Railways' medical service is excellent so if you are suffering, a railway doctor could fix you up. Since water is a cause of gippy tummy, carry purifying tablets (Iodine)

to use in it if there is absolutely nothing else to drink. A water filter is
even more effective, and may be purchased from MASTA (Medical
Advisory Services for Travellers Abroad), Keppel St, London WC1E
7HT. Tel: 071 631 4408. MASTA can also sell you a Concise Health
Brief containing up to date medical information for India.

SAFETY

Keep your passport with you (in a deep, zippered pocket, or body belt)
all the time. Not just for security but to show whenever it's asked for
by officials.

Do not display large amounts of money. Keep enough for the day's
expenses in your wallet or purse and hide the rest somewhere else.
Resist all temptation to exchange foreign currency other than with
licensed dealers. It's illegal and you stand a very good chance of being
ripped off.

Leave your most valued possessions at home; they could get lost or
stolen. Leave your address book and Filofax behind too, and only
bring copies of the addresses and information you need. Keep a record
of your credit card and passport numbers at home together with a
photocopy of your airline ticket and insurance policy in case of
emergency.

A padlock is essential, either for locking your luggage to the chain
provided under the seats of newer carriages, or to lock the retiring
room, locker or compartment door when you're absent. A combination padlock removes the risk of losing the key. There is a combination
padlock with a metre of steel wire (it's called a 'Travellers Lock
Away') that is ideal for securing luggage to a carriage fixture when
you're sleeping or leave it unattended.

A small combination padlock is useful for locking the zipper to the
ring of canvas holdalls to deter snatch thieves. Since many left luggage
offices will only accept locked luggage, a chain and a padlock (you can
buy both at most major stations) are useful for trussing up a backpack.

Keep travellers cheques, money and tickets close to you. When
sleeping on trains, have them on your body somewhere (in the pocket
of your pants or stuffed in your body belt but not under the pillow).
Keep the numbers of everything important in a separate place so if you
do lose anything you have the details. Insure to cover loss of possessions as well as for accident and illness.

Sooner or later when you tell people you are planning to travel in
India by train, someone will ask 'Are you sure it's safe?' It is, as long as
you are sensible. Train travel itself has generally a good standard of
safety, especially when the volume of passengers travelling every day is
taken into consideration. For security while on a train see Chapter 5.

MONEY

Take your money in US dollar or pound sterling travellers cheques. Many travellers find the changing process is time-consuming at city banks. The solution is to change money at the airport on arrival, or at the cashier's desk of major hotels. (You don't necessarily have to stay there but would need to be using one of their public rooms such as the coffee shop.)

You can also use travellers cheques to buy rail tickets at the ITB in New Delhi and the Foreign Tourist Bureaux elsewhere and receive the change in rupees (see Chapter 3). Tickets and reservations from the foreign tourist quota have to be paid in foreign currency or travellers cheques anyway. Credit cards can be used in hotels and shops but not for buying rail tickets unless they are local cards.

If you don't have an onward or return air ticket, make certain you have access to enough funds to leave India when you want to. Better to bring the money in some form (travellers cheques, credit cards) since having funds sent from overseas can take ages. Don't expect your consul to send you home if you get destitute.

The usual safeguard of being able to cash a home country personal cheque guaranteed by a banker's card (at your consul) or credit card, when you need money in an emergency, cannot be relied on in India because of exchange controls. If you do run out of money, you may have to borrow from friends or check into a good hotel and sign the bills until funds arrive from home.

The **currency** of India is the rupee (Rs) and there are a 100 paise (P) to one rupee. Coins are in denominations of 5, 10, 25, 50 paise and 1, 2 and 5 rupees. There are 2, 5, 10, 20, 50, 100 and 500 rupee notes.

Finding change isn't the problem it used to be. However, save coins and low denomination notes to pay the correct amount to platform vendors; the train could pull out before you get your change.

What will it cost?

It depends on you. If you intend to buy your air ticket to leave India and your rail tickets while there, then allow sufficient for those in your budgeting. The cost of Indrail Passes and train tickets are in the next chapter.

While you are on a train, expenses are easy to control: meals, drinks (no alcohol), reading matter and a bedroll for the night are all. Expenses increase when you get off the train although if you stay in station retiring rooms and eat in railway restaurants, these will still be low.

Getting to and from what you've come to see, the cost of souvenirs, medicines, laundry, beers, nights in hotels and occasional extravagance will demand a larger budget.

The cost of a day on a train and a night at a railway station, could work out as follows:

STANDARD BUDGET		ECONOMY BUDGET	
Meals			
Nonveg b/fast	Rs 9.00	Veg b/fast	Rs 8.00
Special NV lunch	25.00	Veg lunch	12.00
Std NV dinner	15.00	Std NV dinner	15.00
Snacks/fruit	25.00	Snacks/fruit	10.00
Drinks			
Tea/soft drinks		Tea (and tap water)	10.00
Mineral water	35.00		
Reading			
News magazine	10.00	Newspaper	2.00
Night			
Bed in twin bedded		Dormitory bed	15.00
room	30.00		
	Rs 149.00		Rs 72.00
(Approximately £3.00/US$5.00)		(£1.40/US$2.40)	

Thanks to the devaluation of the rupee, the cost in pounds sterling or US dollars is actually less than it was when the first edition of this book was published in 1989. But if you go off the rails, expect your expenses to be much higher. Allow plenty for those nights in luxury hotels – for when you want pampering – as their rates are in line with inflation, and not much lower than in the west.

RED TAPE

Visa

Citizens of all countries, including the Commonwealth, require visas to enter India. A multiple entry visa will be needed if you intend to visit Nepal or Sri Lanka from India and then return home via India. If you plan to go to Nepal you'll need a visa for that country (The Royal Nepalese Embassy is in Barakhamba Road, New Delhi 110 001; Tel: 3329969). No visa is required for entry into Sri Lanka. Incidentally, a multiple entry visa is not valid for re-entry if you actually return to your home country, or go on further than neighbouring countries, and then try to use it to get back into India.

A tourist Visa, whether single or multiple entry, is usually valid for a stay of 120 days in India from the date of first entry. It can be extended up to six months total by applying to the Foreigners' Registration offices in New Delhi, Bombay, Calcutta or Madras. There are also Entry Visas and Transit Visas but the Tourist Visa is the one rail travellers on holiday need.

An application form, obtainable from travel agents, tourist offices or the Indian High Commission or Embassy, requires personal particulars including Father's/Husband's name. Three passport size photographs have to be submitted with the completed form. Personal applications are usually approved for the next working day while postal applications take two to three weeks.

At the time of writing the normal price for a six-month multi-entry visa is £16. An additional charge of £10 may be added for telex fees. Allow plenty of time if applying by post. If you plan to stay less than a month and live near London or Birmingham, you can get a 30 day visa for £3.00 if you apply in person within three days of your departure. This runs *from the date of issue* not the date of departure so is only suitable for short stays. The High Commission of India is at India House, Aldwych, London WC2. Tel: 071 836 8484. In Birmingham the address is 82 New Street, Birmingham, B2 4BA. Tel: 021 6430829.

Busy people may prefer to use a visa agency such as World Wide Visas, 9 Adelaide St, London WC2. Tel: 071 379 0419. They will deal with all visa arrangements for a fee.

Photographs

Permits are required to photograph locomotives, trains and loco sheds. If you are planning extensive and serious photography, make sure you have one before you go so you can ward off the rare official who may want to hinder you. Apply to your nearest Indian High Commission or Embassy at least 90 days in advance to make sure of getting the necessary piece of paper. On the other hand, for casual photography (as long as no notice is displayed specifically prohibiting it) you can snap away without a permit.

Arrival

On the flight to India you will be given a card to fill in for immigration. A classic misprint on this seems to be asking for the name of your father's husband. Fill the card in accurately and be prepared for a long wait at the Immigration desk since your passport and the card will be scrutinized by two sets of officials in different offices.

There are red and green channels in customs but you'll be stopped, even in the green channel. Importation of personal jewellery, camera, tape recorder, binoculars, transistor radio, professional equipment, etc., is permitted duty free provided all items are taken out with you when you leave.

200 cigarettes or 50 cigars or 250 g of tobacco and alcoholic liquor up to 0.95 litres (you'll have to drink some of it if you have a full litre bottle) are permitted duty free. The interrogation can be either searching or casual; don't try to be clever.

There is no restriction on the amount of foreign currency that may be taken into India. However, more than US$1,000, or its equivalent,

should be declared on a currency declaration form. This helps if you want to take it out again. No Indian currency may be taken in.

You can change travellers cheques and cash at the airport exchange counters (open 24 hours a day). Keep the receipt of the transaction since you will need this when you try to pay a hotel bill in rupees, to prove you bought rupees with foreign currency. Don't change all your foreign currency as you might need it to buy rail tickets (see Chapter 3). Your exchange receipts will be needed if you want to exchange rupees back to foreign currency.

Departure

By the time you leave India, you will be used to queuing, but make sure you join the right queue when checking in for your flight; you might have to queue to pay the embarkation tax first. The foreign travel tax, as it's called, was raised in 1989 to Rs 150 for passengers departing for Sri Lanka, Nepal, Maldives, Pakistan, Afghanistan, Bangladesh, Bhutan and Burma. Departure for other overseas destinations costs Rs 300 in tax, payable in rupees.

Exit permits are not required by holders of tourist visas who have not stayed longer than their original visa allowed them. If you have extended your visa and hold a Registration Certificate, you will have to obtain, before departure, exit endorsements from the Registration Office of the district in which you registered. There are other hassles too, like Income Tax. Better to leave India before your time is up – Sri Lanka makes a welcome break – and then start again.

You will be given a departure card to fill in before joining the long wait at Immigration. Duty free goods such as cameras brought into India may have to be produced to customs; be prepared for questions. There will be several security searches before you eventually board the plane.

SOLO AND GROUP TRAVEL

The success of a decision to go alone, with friends or in a group ultimately depends on your own personality. Whatever you decide, you'll see the same India but your experience will be more intense if you're alone. You'll probably be adopted by friendly fellow passengers but it can be lonely too. If you travel with a companion, you'll have someone with whom to share everything, the bad as well as the good and also the luggage-minding duties.

It's only natural to want to travel with a companion in a country as extraordinary as India. However, the pairs of travellers I've met never seemed to be enjoying themselves as much as I was. They sat together, played cards, talked, ate and slept as an exclusive group of two, making no effort to speak to their fellow passengers unless to demand some information.

While there are obvious advantages in travelling with a friend, there are snags which only become apparent once you're on the train. If you don't know your companion very well, little quirks of behaviour could ruin your own enjoyment of the trip. Trains are not the place for the honeymoon stage of any relationship. Also, when travelling with companions, you may have to defer to their wishes, and thus miss sights and experiences. My personal choice is to travel alone. As a solo traveller, you will feel more at ease, especially at night, in an AC 2 tier coach or 1st Class than in a claustrophobic 72 berth 2nd Class carriage.

Children

Couples whom I met travelling with children seemed happy enough. Most western children adore rail travel and can spend hours train spotting or wandering around stations. Obviously, very young children will be a problem because of the extra care and attention they need. It is not always possible for families to be accommodated in the same sleeping compartment at night, so parents may have to make a special request to the conductor to see that their daughter is assigned a berth with at least one of them, and not separately.

Women travellers

Women travellers, alone or in pairs, face the usual problems, often through western insensitivity to Indian mores; modest dress and behaviour can help prevent misunderstandings. There is safety in numbers so women may feel more secure in a four berth cabin than in a two berth coupe. In a carriage with 45 or 71 other passengers, there would be no privacy for outright assault and other passengers would intervene at overt unpleasantness. The story about a foreign woman being raped on the roof of a moving train has become part of the rail travellers folk lore. The moral is to keep off the roof!

All trains have a separate, unreserved coach for lady passengers, usually part of, or next to, the guard's brake van. This coach has SYLR painted on it, meaning Second Class Ladies' Luggage Room coach. On trains involving a night journey, government railway police will be posted to travel in the coach. In some 2nd Class reserved carriages there is a cabin for 'Ladies Only' in which boys under 12 are also allowed as are the boyfriends and husbands of occupants during daylight hours. These compartments, although with upholstered seats/ berths, are uncomfortable for long-distance travel as they get stuffy, crowded and noisy.

Best for a woman alone is a berth in the 46-berth 2nd Class AC two-tier dormitory coach (2nd AC) since these have two attendants on duty, lots of fellow passengers to protect a lone lady, and some have a 'Ladies Only' loo. Because a berth in them is more expensive (actually higher than in 1st Class), they appeal to a different kind of passenger. An English woman I met travelling alone said she always requested the upper bunk when making her reservation as she felt safer up there than in a lower one where people might be tempted to sit.

You will find as a woman sharing a cabin solely with Indian women that conversation is difficult, unless you speak Hindi or they are very westernized. 'Indian women,' wrote one British woman traveller to me, 'are so gentle and graceful, but difficult to make contact with.'

The same correspondent travelled alone overnight in 2nd Class on several occasions. 'I chose the top bunk, although I had to crawl into it. It was OK until the early morning when on one trip I awoke to find a man sitting on the end of the bunk. He refused to move and I couldn't do anything about it as it was after 6 am. I certainly felt invaded.' (Berths are supposed to be for sitting from 0600 to 2100.)

She continues: 'I noticed how, when I did travel with a male friend, I was almost disregarded by many men – after six weeks on my own, it was amusing and gave me a break from the endless, tedious questions. I would certainly recommend any solo woman traveller to go to *southern* India – she will be an object of curiosity and good humoured questioning, but there is far less hassle and hard sell than in the north.'

There are separate Ladies Only waiting rooms at most stations. My friend writes: 'There is an excellent "Ladies waiting room" at Agra, very clean and quiet, where I managed to have a shower. Where they exist they can be a lovely respite from the chaos of platform life.' Some stations have separate counters (and thus special queues) for ladies to buy rail tickets or to make reservations, but these are not found everywhere.

Disabled travellers

Disabled travellers should be warned that the steps into and out of carriages (especially onto low platforms) are so steep that even for able-bodied passengers they can be hazardous. Wheelchairs are available at some stations for the (temporarily?) disabled with plenty of willing assistance from porters (for a tip) and from railway staff in an emergency. Rail travel for a disabled foreigner alone would be very difficult.

Group travel

The major long haul tour operators, through their High Street retailers, offer package holidays in India which include some rail travel. For the novice, this is a hassle-free way of sampling an Indian train but it is likely to be much more expensive than travelling independently. There are also specialist travel agents who arrange tours for dedicated rail enthusiasts, among them: Dorridge Travel Service Ltd, 7 Station Approach, Dorridge, Solihull, West Midlands, B93 8JA, England. Tel: 05645 776252. Some of Dorridge's tours are escorted by the renowned rail photographer, Hugh Ballantyne. One couple, Jane and Ashley Butterfield, charter their own carriage and have it attached to different trains for groups to tour India (see Chapter 11). If you fancy going with a specialist agency, do check on their guarantees before parting with cash.

IN INDIA
Public Holidays
Festivals, dry days, special events . . . there seems to be no end to disruptions to normal life, and the traveller will often arrive in a strange town when everything is closed. Further inconvenience comes from strikes, parades and demonstrations.

However carefully you plan, you will probably arrive somewhere when it's a local dry day. If it is and you are desperate for a drink, an experienced bicycle- or auto-rickshaw taxi driver should know a place where you can buy a bottle.

I tried it once. It wasn't a religious holiday but some sort of strike. We found the wine shop heavily shuttered. The rickshaw driver took my money, looked up and down the road, then banged on the shutters. A panel at the bottom of the door opened at pavement level and a hand shot out for the money. The panel closed only to open seconds later and the hand emerged holding a bottle of chilled beer.

National public holidays are January 26, Republic Day; August 15, Independence Day; October 2, Mahatma Gandhi's birthday; December 25, Christmas Day.

Time
Indian Standard Time is 5½ hours ahead of GMT, 4½ hours behind Australian Eastern Time and 9½ hours ahead of Eastern Standard Time in the USA. It's the same time in Sri Lanka and Nepal, and half an hour ahead of time in the Maldives.

Train times are listed on the 24 hour clock in timetables and at most stations, although you will occasionally see notices referring to 12.00 am, meaning 12 noon. In timetables, midnight is shown as 2400 hours for arrivals and 0000 hours for departures.

Business hours
Hours of business vary from region to region. Banks are generally open Monday to Friday from 1000 to 1400 hours and 1000 to 1230 on Saturdays. Post offices operate from 1000 to 1700, Monday to Friday and on Saturday mornings. Offices function from 0930 to 1700 and some Saturdays. Shops generally open from 0930 to 1800, except Sundays.

Reservation offices at stations have their own habits but they are generally open between 0900 and 1800. Avoid the period between 1230 and 1400 as they'll close for lunch sometime during that time, regardless of the people queuing for tickets.

Important stations are open 24 hours a day with ordinary tickets on sale, but some booking offices close 30 minutes before the departure of a train. The Station Superintendent's office is usually open 1000 to 1800; his duties are undertaken by his deputy outside those hours.

Electricity

Voltage in most places is 220 volts AC, 50 cycles, with some areas also having DC supplies. Check the voltage before using electrical appliances. Socket sizes vary, they're usually round pin.

Station retiring rooms are nearly all dimly lit so if you intend reading in bed, your own 100 watt light bulb would help. Rooms with air conditioning units often have huge boxes like disco equipment as part of their control system. Some retiring rooms have electrically-heated hot water in their showers.

Taxis

The different kind of taxis available when you arrive at a station can be bewildering. Cars in the style of Fifties saloons with yellow tops serve as standard taxis, sometimes with a meter which will probably not work. Auto-rickshaws (known as 'autos') – three wheeler vehicles with plastic canopies – are ubiquitous and generally very cheap. In some states they are metered; some even have stereo speakers and cassette players.

You'll find bicycle rickshaws too where the terrain is flat. A rare find nowadays is a rickshaw pulled by man power but these are plentiful around Calcutta's Howrah station (which also boasts river ferry access and tram transport and India's only underground Metro (see Chapter 8).) Tongas (horse drawn two wheelers) and Victorias (horse drawn carriages) can also be hired. Always negotiate the price before boarding any kind of taxi. Being a foreigner, you'll be overcharged but you can at least be prepared for the fare by agreeing it before the start of the journey instead of getting a shock at the end of it.

Drinking water

All stations have water for drinking at several points along the platform, either from standpipes, cold water dispensers or from water carts. This is drawn from the local supply so its potability is the same as that of the water drunk by the area's residents. A visitor will not have the immunity of locals so if you intend to drink it, collect it in a water bottle and dissolve a purifying tablet in it or filter it first. Like most travellers I never drink tap water, nor do I have ice in my drinks. Almost every tourist you see in India bears a bottle of mineral water in one hand. The best known water is called Bisleri, costing from Rs10 upwards for a litre bottle. To my mind the best water of all (perhaps it's the French connection) is called – and is from – Pondicherry. It costs from Rs15 for a 1.5 litre bottle.

The problem with some bottled mineral waters, according to Chris, a student who had been in India for three weeks when I met him on the Tamil Nadu Express, is that although they have sealed caps, these can be removed without breaking the seal. This means that an empty, used water bottle could be filled with ordinary tap water and resealed and sold by unscrupulous or uncomprehending vendors. You'll soon know if you've got a dud by the taste.

Chris always slashed his empty, plastic bottles with a knife to prevent their re-use. I used to cut mine neatly in half, using the bottom half as a plastic cup, ideal for drinking duty-free scotch and soda when I didn't trust the glasses in station retiring rooms.

You will only find bottled mineral water on sale at stations frequented by foreign railway travellers, since Indians prefer sweet drinks as a thirst quencher. On Southern Railway trains with a pantry car, bottled water can be bought, and plastic sachets of drinking water are provided with meals.

Alcohol

'English wine shops' are to be found close to stations; they don't sell English or any kind of wine, only Indian-made spirits and beer. Alcohol is not sold at any station or on any train (except the tourist-oriented Palace on Wheels).

Officially, drinking alcohol is illegal on trains which only encourages passengers to fill their thermos flasks with whisky and ice instead of tea. A willing bearer (steward) will see that beer is provided with meals. He adds the code words 'Bottle of Tomato Sauce' to your meal order. Sometimes an amenable bearer might produce a cold one when the train stops long enough at a station with a wine shop close by.

The names, and strength, of Indian beers are amazing, with the most blatant being HE MAN 9,000, Bullet, Knock Out and Cannon 10,000. According to a catering inspector at the Rail Yatri Niwas in Howrah, the main choice of foreigners in beers is Black Label, produced by Kalyani Brewers. Its label describes it as 'a masterpiece of the brewer's art, slow brewed for the connoisseur. Champagne carbination.' Perhaps not as strong as some beers, it tastes OK, as does Kingfisher. Look out – and enjoy – beers bearing labels that warn 'Liquor ruins country, family and life.'

At Balharshah station I was puzzled to hear a vendor calling out 'Officer *chai* (or so I thought) as he walked along the platform. *Chai* is the Indian word for tea. It was only when the vendor reached into his pocket and produced a flask, that I realized what 'officer's chai' really is: not tea, but whisky, actually named Officer's Choice.

Indian wine is not up to much, except for the notable exception of Indian 'champagne' and a new white wine, quite dry, called Riviera. Champagne India Ltd, with technical help from Piper-Heidsieck, produce a splendid sparkling wine called Marquise de Pompadour by the *methode champenoise* from grapes grown near Bombay in Maharashtra state. It is the equivalent of a good French sparkling wine but you'll have to hunt hard for it because it has become very popular with the cognescenti, and for export.

Smoking

Smoking on trains without the consent of fellow passengers is a punishable offence. It is not allowed in the AC sleeper carriages, nor on local/suburban trains. However, very few carriages are exclusively designated 'Non Smoking' but you will find one 2nd Class 3 tier non smokers coach on the following trains: Marwar Superfast Express, Grand Trunk Express, Kalka Mail, Paschim Express and the Kashi Vishwanath Express.

Food

Meals cooked in railway kitchens will be prepared from fresh ingredients since supplies are bought daily to meet the huge demand. Kitchens are run by the railway zone catering division or by licensees and there is an army of catering inspectors and plenty of guidelines on standards to ensure quality.

There are usually two restaurants at stations: the vegetarian, abbreviated in conversation to 'veg' (V) and non-vegetarian, referred to as 'non-veg' (NV). Sometimes they will be the same restaurant with a door at one end for V and an NV door at the other, although with separate kitchens. Prices are standardized throughout the railway zone, and clearly displayed.

The meals served on trains are according to a limited standardized menu. Usually they are prepared at a base kitchen and put onto the train for serving at meal times to your seat. Simple items such as breakfast and snacks will be prepared in the pantry car, if there is one.

In railway catering one sometimes means two. For instance 'one fried egg' is actually two eggs fried, and 'one boiled egg' is two eggs boiled. Boiled eggs are hard boiled but if you ask for *hard* boiled eggs you are likely to get soft boiled ones since it is believed you are asking for *half* boiled.

You will be asked if you want a veg or non-veg meal when ordering lunch or dinner. Although a vegetarian meal has vegetables with the rice and lentils, a non-veg meal actually has no vegetables at all, with curried eggs as a substitute. To get a balanced meal I order a veg meal and a special non-veg one (chicken curry).

On an increasing number of trains, meals are served in foil casseroles, with individual items wrapped in polythene bags. Other trains still use the chrome *thali* plates with compartments for different sauces around the rice. Drinks are served in disposable plastic cups although the disposable, clay teacups of old are still sometimes used by platform vendors. Some plastic cups bear the slogan 'Please deform after use.'

The variety of railway food, while well prepared and well cooked, is not very exciting unless you can get the pantry chef to cook something special. Actually, some of the best meals I've had on trains were the curries prepared for the staff which I persuaded them to let me try. For a more varied sampling of Indian food, you will have to eat outside railwayland.

Tipping

Railway employees do not expect to be tipped. However, a bearer (the railway name for a waiter or steward) will look after a passenger extra well if there is the likelihood of a tip. Since the bearer rides the train for its entire journey, your welfare will be in his hands throughout a long trip, so it will suit you both to establish a friendly relationship from the outset.

If you haven't been paying after each meal, the bill for all meals, tea, soft drinks etc. will be presented just before you reach your destination, so you can tip then if you want to; 10 per cent or more up to Rs20 according to how much extra the bearer's done for you.

At the end of the journey on prestigious trains like the Rajdhani Express, a bearer will present you with a tray of seeds on which is some money. He expects you to take a pinch of the seeds (for chewing as a digestif) and leave him some money as a tip. Whether you do is up to you. I usually don't as I prefer to tip at my discretion, not at a steward's insistence.

The attendant who brings the bedroll might hover for a tip, especially if he actually makes up the bed. It's not necessary. Sometimes you'll encounter an urchin who sweeps out the carriage and comes for a tip afterwards. That's really the coach attendant's job and the urchin shouldn't be on the train anyway. The Government of India tourist brochure says: 'Don't encourage beggars by giving them money.'

Porters, who are supposed to carry your bag for Rs 4 to Rs 5, for a head load of 40 kg depending on the station rates, will always want a tip. In hotels and restaurants a service charge is sometimes added but tip if you feel it's worth it. Retiring room attendants only deserve a tip if they have looked after you, your luggage and the room properly. But it's not essential.

Communications

Many stations have post offices within their premises or close by. For an extra fee, letters can be posted on some trains for delivery at the train's destination. Letters can be sent to passengers at railway stations and will be deposited in a glass-fronted cabinet outside the office of the station superintendent (the SS) for collection, but the system is not reliable since anyone can remove the letter.

Telegrams can be sent from Railway Licensed Telegraph Offices to passengers travelling by train in any class. The name of the station where the train stops (it must be for at least ten minutes) and the number or name of the train should be included in the address. Inland telegrams can be sent from stations. The rates are low.

It is possible to telephone from major stations, either locally or long distance. Sometimes the telephones are run by attendants who are handicapped, with their booth being sponsored by the local Rotary or Lions Club.

You will often run into unexpected difficulties in communicating with railway catering staff, especially if you ask for something that they think is odd. Getting a tea bag and a flask of hot water (which is standard issue on the Shatabdi express) to make our own tea is sometimes hard to explain, even to a college trained and English speaking catering inspector. I have a theory that this failure of communication stems from a preconceived notion of what you want, instead of actually listening to the request, or perhaps it is through a nervous desire to please which results in the reverse of what you request, in case you change your mind.

Enquiries

Do not rely on the staff at the enquiry office to give you the correct times of trains, especially if your English is heavily accented, since they might not understand your question properly. Anyway, they will be preoccupied with all the Indian travellers shouting at them. Train arrival and departure times are given on noticeboards in all stations. If you are uncertain, ask a responsible looking official face to face – you'll probably be delighted at the help you'll receive.

Language

Signs at stations are supposed to be in three languages: Hindi, English

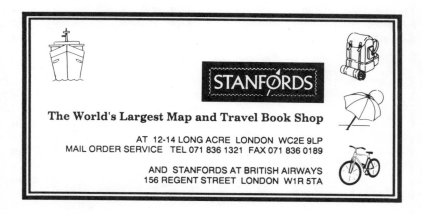

and the state language. Some stations have signs hanging above a platform and as you walk down its length they all seem to be in Hindi. Turn around and walk back and they are all in English, since the signs are double sided.

English is understood throughout India and you will get involved in some deep discussions in English with fellow passengers. The SS speaks English as do other senior station staff. In the south, English will be more readily understood among ordinary people than in the north. If you are stuck, someone will usually be around who can help translate.

Useful phrases in Hindi

Good morning/evening/day/night	*Namaste*
Goodbye/see you	*Phir milenge*
How are you?	*Aap kaise hain?*
Good	*Acha*
Bad	*Kharab*
Please	*Kripaya*
Thank you	*Dhanyavad*
Yes	*Han*
No	*Nahi*
What is your name?	*Aap ka naam kya hai?*
How much is . . . ?	*Kitne ka hai?*
Too much	*Bahut zyada hai*
Come here	*Idhar aaiye*
Go away	*Chale jaaiye*
Water	*Paani*
Cold	*Tanda*
Hot	*Garam*
Big	*Bada*
Small	*Chota*
Where is the . . . ?	*Kahan hai?*
Train	*Rail gadi*
Retiring room	*Vishramgarh*
Restaurant	*Dhaba*

Coolies (porters) playing cards at Ranchi station. (Hugh Ballantyne)
Self-catering on Bandel station platform. (Hugh Ballantyne)

The train from Mettupalaiyam to Ooty climbs across Glendale Viaduct, a mile before the principal intermediate station at Coonoor. (Anthony J. Lambert)

Chapter 3

Ticket to Ride

'What I can't understand,' said the tall Dutchman who boarded the train at Bhubaneswar and sat opposite me, 'is how to buy a ticket to travel by train.'

The Dutchman was a professor in his forties, passionately interested in medieval temples which is what had drawn him to Bhubaneswar. He explained the reason for his question.

'I have a ticket but I don't understand how I got it. I came to the station yesterday and told a clerk I wanted to travel on this train. I filled in the form he gave me then he told me to join a queue.

'I waited an hour but when I was almost at the counter, the clerk said he was going for lunch. I was very angry and left my form there and went to lunch too. When I returned, I'd lost my place in the queue so I went up to another window where no one was queuing. The clerk looked at me, took my money and gave me a ticket.'

The Dutch professor looked bemused. 'How did it happen? How did the second clerk know where I wanted to go? He didn't ask me.'

The professor's experience illustrates the good and the bad of the ticket buying process. He was frustrated by queuing at a counter that closed just as he was about to reach it, so he lost his temper and made a fuss.

Being tall and fair he was easily recognisable so when he returned, even though he went to another ticket window, the clerk knew what he wanted and helped him.

There is a policy in Indian Railways to help foreign tourists to make their reservations. However, most foreigners would rather join a line and wait their turn than demand special treatment because they are foreigners.

Indian tourists who feel themselves to be important will not hesitate to ask the Chief Reservations Supervisor (CRS) or the Station Superintendent (SS) for help if they need it. On Indian Railways, foreigners are regarded as important and are actually expected to approach officials for help. However reserved you may feel, if you want to reserve without hassles, take advantage of this.

Where to buy a ticket

Unless you have an Indrail Pass (see page 45) you will need to buy a ticket for the journey. This means a visit to the railway station. The first rule is not to join any queue until you are absolutely certain it is the right one, and don't join it near closing time.

If in doubt start at the Enquiry counter. Alternatively, a polite request to the Chief Reservation Supervisor (CRS) for help can work wonders so don't be shy to approach him. Tickets should only be purchased from station counters or from official sources. There are touts at the major stations who will take advantage of a foreigner's confusion (or frustration) to offer tickets on trains that are fully booked, or even cut-price tickets. Avoid them since trouble and complications are bound to result. These touts are not always immediately recognisable. Many railway officials dress in white. When I was approached at New Delhi station by a gentleman in white shirt and trousers who asked if I was looking for the ITB, I assumed he was an official. I was busy at the time and didn't stop to talk. Later I saw him with two foreigners in the ITB offering to change money for them. He was not a railway employee at all and quickly left when the ITB Supervisor questioned him.

Rail Travellers' Service Agents have been appointed in some areas to purchase tickets and secure reservations on behalf of passengers. They are authorized to charge a fee of not more than Rs 15 for upperclass bookings and Rs 8 for other classes.

An Australian couple told me they always use travel agents in India for their ticket purchase, usually paying about Rs20 for the reservation as the travel agent's fee. Since it saves time, they considered it worth it.

Ashley Butterfield reports that the Blue Diamond Hotel in Pune will get tickets for the Deccan Queen for a surcharge of Rs50. TAG states that tickets can be purchased at 'Railway Booking Agencies or through Railway Tourist Agent'.

Single journey ticket

At most stations, the ticket purchasing and reservations procedure has been combined (see *Making a reservation*). Tickets to travel without a reserved seat or in 2nd Class non-reserved carriages can be purchased from the booking office window labelled for the class you intend to travel, usually up to the time the train departs. The booking counters will normally be found in the station lobby, not with the counters issuing journey-cum-reservation tickets.

A passenger who has no reservation and who buys a ticket and boards the train and finds a seat may still have to pay a reservation fee if that seat is normally subject to a reservation charge (see page 58). This can be the only way of getting a seat on some trains if the unreservable seats, usually in a 2nd Class carriage at the end of the train, are all occupied to overflowing.

A passenger who intends to travel in the unreserved 2nd Class coach of a superfast train must purchase a supplementary charge ticket (for Rs 2) before boarding the train. Otherwise there is a penalty payable on the train as well as the supplementary charge.

It is possible at some stations to buy an unreserved single journey 2nd Class ticket a day in advance of travelling, to save queuing on the actual day of travel. The day of travel will be endorsed on the ticket which will only be valid until midnight on that day.

Tickets are cardboard and coloured according to class:

White: AC 1st Class
Green: 1st Class (Mail, Express or Ordinary) and AC Sleeper (2 Tier) Class
Orange: AC Chair Car
Drab: 2nd Class (Mail or Express)
Yellow   2nd Class (Ordinary)

Where printed tickets are not available, you will be issued with a coupon on which the ticket details are entered by hand.

Platform tickets

In theory, only people holding tickets are allowed on station platforms. Platform tickets are obtainable from a separate ticket window. They cost Rs 1.50 and are valid for two hours.

If you are trying to buy a ticket at the last minute and can't get one in time because the queue at the window is too long, buy a platform ticket instead. Before boarding the train present the platform ticket to the guard. He will issue a guard's certificate and charge you the full fare for the journey. A passenger trying to travel on a platform ticket without the guard's certificate will be treated as a ticketless traveller. Since the Indrail Pass is a ticket, holders do not need a platform ticket.

Ticketless travel

The penalties for travelling without a ticket are high and can include jail. Some stations have a magistrate's court within their premises for dealing with ticketless travellers and other offenders.

Travelling without a ticket is almost a tradition in India, originating during the British days when passengers did it to harm an alien ruler. After partition it was done to express a grievance against the government. The motive now, unless part of an organized protest, is simply to cheat the railways.

In the north of India especially, ticketless passengers add to the problem of over-crowding in the cheaper carriages where checks aren't so rigorous. Another problem in northern areas are those passengers who don't recognize that some carriages are for those who have paid

YOU LOSE WE LOSE

Ticketless Travellers!
You Can not Escape

● Indian Railways are a public utility service catering to about a million passengers every day Its loss is the people's loss.

● To help us serve better we earnestly seek your co-operation as responsible citizens

WHEN YOU TRAVEL, BUY A TICKET

● Ticketless travel is an offence liable to prosecution under Indian Railways Act

NORTHERN RAILWAY

more for the privilege of an upper class seat. They want to sit there too, regardless of what class of travel they have actually paid for. If a passenger with a 2nd Class ticket is caught in a 1st Class seat, not only must the full 1st Class fare be paid but a penalty too. However, it is possible for a 2nd Class ticket holder to upgrade to 1st Class by paying the difference in fares. Permission must be obtained from the guard before the passenger occupies the higher class of seat.

Ticketless travel is most prevalent in the states of Bihar and Uttar Pradesh where thousands gatecrash onto overcrowded trains daily. If the train isn't stopping where they want to get off, they have been known to pull the emergency brake cord. Ticketless travel is increasing, especially in slow country passenger trains where there are seldom any checks. In 1989 the authorities caught more than six million passengers without tickets during an eight month crackdown, collecting the equivalent of 10 million dollars in fines.

Ticket inspection

A passenger must have a ticket, even if it is only a platform ticket with a guard's certificate. Travelling ticket examiners (TTEs) check tickets, even on trains that don't have a vestibule. TTEs are sometimes in plain clothes but carry identification to show when requested. On long distance trains, few passengers are ticketless except for those hitching a lift between rural stops.

Tickets are sometimes inspected at the entrance to platforms and they will be collected at the exits after a journey. Tickets are required by people wanting to use the waiting and retiring rooms, to prove that they are genuine passengers.

Lost tickets and refunds

If you buy a ticket and lose it, there is no chance of a refund although you can get a duplicate ticket if it was for reserved travel (see later). Refunds are possible on unused tickets without reservations if presented within three hours after the departure of the train. A fee of Rs 2.00 per ticket is deducted as clerkage from the full refund. This can apply if you've bought a ticket but don't use it because you can't get a reservation or seat on the train.

Two Scotsmen travelling from Ooty to Coimbatore on the Nilagiri Express wanted to go on the West Coast Express to Mangalore that same evening in 1st Class, but they only had tickets to Coimbatore. The TTE advised them to purchase ordinary 2nd Class tickets to Mangalore at Coimbatore station and then board the West Coast Express and ask the TTE to upgrade them to 1st Class if there was space. He recommended this method because if they bought 1st Class tickets and there was no space, they would have no chance of getting a refund.

Travel restrictions

Some trains have restrictions on carrying passengers over short distances. These are usually the major expresses and will not carry passengers making journeys of less than 160 km and in some case not less than 600 km, according to the train. Indrail Pass holders escape these restrictions. The small print of the timetables reveal other restrictions too. For instance, passengers are not allowed to carry milk in cans or bottles on the 1352 Bhusaval passenger train between Kalyan and Bombay.

Breaking the journey

Passengers are allowed to make a break on a single journey ticket of more than 400 km after the first 300 km has been travelled. A break can be at any station *en route* at the rate of one day for every 200 km or part of 200 km in addition to the time occupied by the journey. The ticket should be endorsed by the Station Master (SM) where the break occurs with the station code, the date and the SM's initials. Foreign tourists travelling on an Indrail Pass can break their journey anywhere en route without the distance restriction.

If you decide to extend your journey beyond your destination, the TTE can authorize it, but only before you reach your original destination.

Fare extras: superfast trains

There is a supplement payable for travel on certain superfast expresses and mail trains. A list of the trains appears in Chapter 12. It includes the popular Taj and Pink City Expresses. The supplements are paid at the time of reservation/ticket purchase and are the same for children and adults. Indrail Pass holders pay nothing extra. The rates are:

AC Class	Rs 25
AC Sleeper	12
1st Class	12
AC Chair Car	12
2nd Class Sleeper	6
2nd Class sitting	2

Sleeper charge

In 2nd Class there is a surcharge for sleeper accommodation levied according to the distance of a passenger's journey:

Up to 500 km	Rs 15
More than 500 km	20
More than 1000 km	25

Indrail Pass holders are exempt from this surcharge; the sleeper fee is included in 1st and AC Class reservation fee.

FARES

Carrying passengers is not lucrative for Indian Railways, according to a DRM who told me that it is a public, not a profitable, service. He seemed to regard passengers as a necessary evil. The carrying of freight was his main interest since that is profit generating and actually subsidizes the passenger services. Attempts to raise fares are resisted by the travelling public who consider they pay enough already. They were actually raised on April 1, 1992, by 20 percent for 1st AC Class and 15 percent for other upper classes and by up to Rs25 for 2nd Class on mail and express trains. At the lower end of the scale, fares are cheap; at the upper end – for Indians – they are not. The top fare on the Rajdhani Express in AC Class for the 1384 km overnight ride from New Delhi to Bombay is more than ten times the lowest fare by mail or express train in 2nd Class sleeper on the same route.

Throughout the Indian Railways' network, fares are calculated on a fixed price per kilometre from station of origin to destination, according to the class travelled. The timetables show the kilometres between stations so it is possible to work out the approximate cost by reference to the fare table produced in the zonal timetables and in TAG. Examples of standard fares between stations cannot be quoted with complete accuracy because every fare depends on the route taken. For instance, there are four different routes between Delhi and Calcutta and three between Delhi and Jammu Tawi, all with different fares. In addition, there are various supplements according to the train actually travelled on, as well as reservation and sleeper fees.

The minimum cost of travel by train is Rs 1.50 which buys up to 10 km of train ride in ordinary 2nd Class. The most expensive minimum cost is Rs 122 which will give 9 km of air conditioned 1st Class travel. A sample of fares from 1 to 5000 km appears on page 44, in Indian rupees.

Discounts

Even though 2nd Class fares are low for foreigners they can represent an obstacle to rail travel for low income or no-income Indians. Concessions are made to certain groups with reductions up to 75 per cent on fares for 1st or 2nd Class travel. The list of groups includes sportsmen, professional entertaining parties, students up to 25 years old on studies, articled clerks, research scholars, blind or deaf and dumb people; TB, cancer and leprosy sufferers; the orthopaedically handicapped; nurses, midwives and war and police widows.

Free rail travel is given to MPs and former MPs, to nearly 100,000 Freedom Fighters as well as to serving – and former – railway employees and their families. No wonder the trains are crowded!

The only discount for foreigners is the Indrail Pass. However, foreign students under 25 who are resident in India (and therefore not eligible for the Indrail Pass) can qualify for a 50 per cent reduction on 2nd Class fares for approved journeys, such as to attend a government organized seminar or to visit places of historical or other importance during vacations.

Km	1st AC Class	2nd AC (2-tier) Class	1st Class	AC Chair Car Class	Mail/ Express (Non AC) 2nd Class Sleeper	Ordinary (Non AC Non Sleeper) Passenger Class
1	122	89	25	25	7	1.50
50	144	113	63	44	13	9
100	231	151	97	60	22	14
200	350	221	156	95	42	24
300	490	294	218	134	57	33
500	741	417	327	194	87	46
1000	1212	670	534	296	143	67
2000	2039	1072	891	481	201	101
2500	2438	1232	1065	569	225	117
5000	4432	2019	1934	999	347	200
Per 50km block over 5000km	40	22	21	11	5	3

Children between five and 12 years of age travel at half fare but are subject to the same minimum fares as for an adult. Children age five and under travel free.

Kilometre distance

As with air fares, the price per kilometre drops the further a passenger travels so it makes sense to buy a ticket to the furthest point on your journey and take advantage of the rules about allowing a break in the journey on the way. To help arrive at an estimate of what it might cost, the following is a list of the kilometre distance between selected stations. However, different distances may be used in fare construction and there are also the various supplements.

New Delhi to	Madras Central	2188 km
	Howrah (Calcutta)	1441
	Bombay Central (with WR)	1384
	Bombay VT (via Bhusaval)	1538
	Trivandrum	3054
	Agra Cantt	199
	Bangalore City	2491
	Jammu Tawi	589
	Patna	992
Howrah to	Bombay VT	1968
	Jammu Tawi	1967
	Madras Central	1662
Bombay VT	Madras Central	1279

Adjusted fares

The fares to many destinations are posted on the walls of station booking halls. They are the basic fares without the addition of supplements, reservation fees and sleeper surcharges.

On some routes, the fare per kilometre is adjusted in order, according to one official source, 'to avoid losses as the cost of construction and maintenance on certain sections is considerably heavy.' These routes provide spectacular journeys which are often undertaken by tourists. They are listed below.

RAILWAY	CHARGEABLE DISTANCE
Neral–Matheran	63 km
Khandwa–Hingoli	Distance plus 33⅓ per cent
Ambala–Kalka	1⅓ times distance
Kalka–Shimla	3 times distance
Pathankot–Jogindernagar	1½ times distance
Mettupalaiyam–Wellington	2¾ times distance
Wellington–Udagmandalam	Twice actual distance
Kottavalasa–Kirandul	1½ times distance
Fatehpur Shekhawati–Churu	Twice actual distance
Udaipur–Himatnagar	1⅓ times distance

THE INDRAIL PASS (IRP)

If you intend making more than two trips by train, consider buying an Indrail Pass: it may not always save you money but there are other advantages, mainly of convenience. Some of them, compared with the purchase of several single journey tickets, are listed on page 46.

The Indrail Pass can be bought in India or abroad from GSAs (General Sales Agents). The cost is calculated in US dollars and payment in foreign currency is based on the dollar price. Passes purchased in India must be paid for in dollars or pound sterling; credit cards are not accepted.

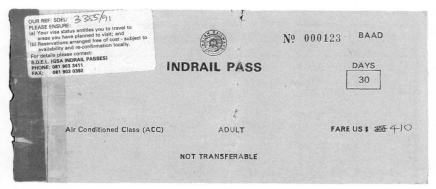

Indrail Pass	Single journey tickets
Unlimited kilometres	Distance restriction
Network freedom	Travel restricted
Separate ticket purchase not required	Ticket must be purchased for every journey
All reservations can be made at the same time	Separate reservations must be made for every journey
Reservations can be made by mail through home country GSA	Reservations must be made at stations in person
Reservations can be made 360 days in advance	Reservations can only be made 60 days, or less, in advance
Reservation priority	No priority
Eligible for foreign tourist quota	Only eligible for foreign tourist quota at some stations if pay in foreign currency
No restrictions in travelling short distances on any train	Restrictions
Can break journey anywhere	Restrictions
Can use waiting and retiring rooms anywhere any time	Can only use rooms if holding day's ticket
No supplements payable	Supplements payable
No surcharges payable	Surcharges payable
No reservation fees payable	Reservation fees payable
No sleeper charges payable	Sleeper charges payable
No minimum distance charge	Minimum distance charge
No need for platform ticket	Platform ticket needed for platform visit if not travelling
Can board any train	Must buy a ticket before boarding any train
Recognized as a Very Important Traveller	No special recognition
Reduced queuing	Frequent queuing

Where to buy the Indrail Pass outside India

	Telephone	Telex
Australia		
Adventure World, 37 York Street, Sydney.	2903222	22680
Penthouse Travel, 5th level,		
72 Pitt Street, Sydney, 2000 NSW.	2311455	10718892
Canada		
Hariworld Travels Inc,	3662000	062 3918
Royal York Hotel, 100 Front Street West,		
Arcade Level, Toronto, Ont M5J 1E3.		

	Telephone	Telex

Finland
Intia Keskua Ltd
Tarkk Amopujankatu, 8A
00150 Helsinki 9.

France
Le Monde de L'Inde et de L'Asie,   46340320   202221
15 Rue Des Ecoles, Paris 75005.

Germany
Asra Orient, Kaiserstrasse 50,   (069)253098   413451
D-6000, Frankfurt M1.

Japan
Japan Travel Bureau,   81-(031) 284-7391   28648
Overseas Travel Division,
1-6-4 Marunouchi
Chiyoda KU, Tokyo-100

Malaysia
M/S City East West Travels, Sdn. Bld. no. 135-A,   293 0569   33526
Jalan Bunus, Opp. Jalan Masjid India, 50100
Kuala Lumpur, Malaysia

Mauritius
Mauritius Travel & Tourist Bureau
Sr W. Newton & Royal Rd,
Port Louis.

Thailand
S S Travel Service   2367188   87450
10/12–13 S.S. Building,
Convent Road, Bangkok 10500

UAE
M/s Sharjah National Travel & Tourist Agency (Pvt)   351411   68021
Ltd, P.O. Box 17, Sharjah, UAE.

UK
S.D. Enterprises Ltd,   081 903 3411   94012027
103, Wembley Park Drive,
Wembley, Middlesex, England HA9 8HG   Fax: 081 903 0392

USA
Hariworld Travels Inc,   212 957 3000   4952383
30 Rockefeller Plaza,
Shop 21, North Mezzanine,
New York, NY 10112.

In India

Indrail Passes can be bought at the following stations: Ahmadabad, Agra Cantt, Amritsar, Aurangabad, Bangalore City, Bombay, Calcutta, Chandigarh, Gorakhpur, Hyderabad, Jaipur, Madras, New Delhi, Rameswaram, Secunderabad, Trivandrum, Vasco de Gama, Vadodara, Varanasi. In 1992 they could not be bought at Tiruchchirappalli even though the city has an international airport.

Indrail passes are also available at Delhi, Bombay, Calcutta and Madras airports and from some travel agents.

The ticket doctor

If you can get to London during the planning stage of your trip, there is a remarkable man who will answer all your questions and help plan the itinerary. He is Dr S. Dandapani who has his office in a corner shop near Wembley Park station, on the underground Metropolitan and Jubilee lines. The full address is: S.D. Enterprises Ltd, 103, Wembley Park Drive, Wembley, Middlesex HA9 8HG, England. Tel: 081 903 3411, Fax: 081 903 0392; telex: 94012027 SDEL G. Dr Dandapani is the GSA in Britain for the Indrail Pass and for the Palace On Wheels but he does much more than that.

'Selling a ticket is child's play,' he told me. 'I'm preparing people to visit a great country and come back happy.' Dr Dandapani overflows with sound advice, not just on places to visit, but how to make the most of the trip and even what underwear is best (cotton; jockey shorts for men).

He is a sociologist who worked for Indian Railways for 25 years and for 15 years as a UN adviser, as well as being an author of more than a dozen books on business management.

Dr Dandapani is the ever-cheerful pioneer of promoting the Indrail Pass. Even if you can't get to London to meet him, a phone call or fax will bring immediate advice on your trip. Whenever you buy an Indrail Pass or a ticket from him you will be able to benefit from his years of experience, and be deluged with tips on what to take, how or where to go and on how to get what you want out of India.

If you have a specific reason for wanting to visit India, tell Dr Dandapani. It's amazing what he can arrange. The parents of a friend of mine wanted to visit a small town named after my friend's grandfather who had lived in India. Dr Dandapani not only plotted the whole rail itinerary, he also arranged for the station superintendent to greet the couple on arrival and for a surprise civic reception for them.

Should you have doubts about travelling by train, even after reading this book, discuss them with Dr Dandapani. His desire is for passengers to be satisfied with their train travels and he has thousands of letters of appreciation to prove they are. He likes to say that he has two million railwaymen working with him and when he promises something, you can depend on him.

'Everything is possible with Indian Railways,' he once told me, 'but you must allow adequate time.'

To help travellers who have a vague idea of where they would like to go, but have neither the time nor the inclination (nor the right timetable) to plot their own itinerary, Dr Dandapani's staff have prepared over a dozen itineraries. These are based on the kind of journey the majority of visitors to India want to experience, including visits to Agra, Rajasthan, Khajuraho, Shimla, Darjeeling, Goa, Ooty and Mysore from either Bombay or New Delhi, utilizing trains with practical departure and arrival times.

Dear Doctor –
What an absolutely fabulous
county India is !! Our week in
Goa was quite wonderful (though
eventful - will tell you ● of it some
day) and the Lalitha Mahal and
Mysore itself everything you
promised. Your arrangements for
the Railway Passes have gone
perfectly - thankyou for all your
help and advice !
Happy New Year.
Michael Simkin (the Actor)

DR DANDAPANI
S.D. ENTERPRISES LTD
21, YORK HOUSE.
EMPIRE WAY.
WEMBLEY
MDDX
ENGLAND

Dr Dandapani sells more Indrail Passes than anyone else in the world. If you can't visit him, give him a call or write with your itinerary and purchase the pass by post since he mails them wherever required.

In the USA, the pass is available through New York travel agency, Hariworld Travels, in Rockefeller Plaza. They also have a branch in Toronto, Canada.

British travellers form the vast majority of purchasers of the IRP followed by French, Australian, Japanese and German. The most popular is the 30-day 1st Class pass which also permits travel in AC Sleeper. Next in demand come 21-day and 15-day 1st Class passes.

Pass details

The pass looks like an airline ticket and is issued for three different classes of train travel:

1) Blue or White Ticket	AC 1st Class
2) Green Ticket	AC Sleeper (2 tier), 1st Class, AC Chair Car
3) Orange/Yellow Ticket	2nd Class

The front cover bears the pass number and indicates its total validity period: 7, 15, 30, 60 or 90 days. There is also a 24 hour pass which is mentioned below. The pass is valid for one year from the date of issue and its validity period starts from the day the first journey begins to midnight on the final day.

The terms and conditions, kept very simple, are outlined inside the front cover. Journey and reservation particulars are noted by carbon duplicate on what is called the 'passenger foil'. There are two of these with the second one forming the back cover of the ticket. The GSA keeps the original of the ticket's 'foils' on which he has entered the passenger details. Also recorded on the foil are the passenger's name, nationality, passport number, fare paid, signature and stamp of the GSA, and the date of issue. The validity of the ticket showing the first and last day of usage is noted in a space at the foot of the ticket. There is space on the rest of the ticket for endorsements showing the train number, date, from/to and remarks concerning every train trip included on the itinerary.

Armed with this you have a permit to travel 'wherever you like, whenever you like and by whatever train you like' within the period of its validity. The words are those of Indian Railways: a remarkable concession. However the pass does not guarantee reserved accommodation, unless you confirm all your arrangements with the GSA at the time of purchase. Even so, onward reservations should be confirmed in India by verifying them at the reservation office on arrival at each destination.

The Indrail Pass can be purchased up to 360 days before travel, and reservations can be made at the same time. Reservations by local travellers within India can only be made up to 60 days in advance, so a foreigner requesting a reservation between 61 and 360 days before a journey, is competing only with other foreigners for a seat or berth. Even within the 60 day period before travel, a foreigner booking from overseas gets priority. The reservation (for which there is no charge) will be confirmed by telex to the GSA within seven days.

In India, the process of making a reservation is greatly simplified by the pass. It entitles you to berths from the foreign tourist quota, and will also bring out the best in station staff willing to help. There are none of the reservation charges, supplements or sleeper surcharges that are levied on single journey tickets.

The Indrail Pass can be bought by foreign nationals who are not resident in India and by Indians residing outside India. A foreign national resident in India is regarded as Indian for the purpose of train travel and is not entitled to reservations from the foreign tourist quota. Correspondingly, an Indian resident abroad, with passport to prove it, is regarded as a foreign tourist.

When buying an IRP (or seeking a reservation from the foreign tourist quota) in India, take along your passport to prove that you have not been in India longer than six months and are not officially resident in India. The IRP issued in India is a folded card with holder's name entered on the front together with country of passport origin and passport number. There is no space on it to enter reservations so it is more flexible than a pass purchased overseas that has an itinerary scrawled on it.

A pass can be purchased out of India by mail with accompanying draft for US dollars sent to the International Tourist Bureau (ITB), New Delhi Railway Station, New Delhi 110055, India, (fax: New Delhi 343050). However, if you are going to purchase by mail, I suggest you do so through Dr Dandapani who is accustomed to sending passes by registered airmail to most countries of the world.

To quote the SR timetable, 'the Indrail Pass ticket will also be issued for: (1) a foreign tourist demanding an Indrail Pass for his Indian wife; and (2) a foreign tourist preferring to take a guide instead of depending on local assistance.' The reference to a guide means someone officially recognized by an Indian tourism authority, so you can't take along an Indian chum, unless he's licensed, of course.

The pass is not transferable and the traveller should be prepared to show passport as proof of identity.

What it costs

This tariff came into force May 1, 1992, with fares given in US dollars. The one day pass is only sold out of India.

Period of Validity	1st AC Class		2nd AC Class (AC 2-tier) 1st Class AC Chair Car		2nd Class Non AC	
	Adult/Child		Adult/Child		Adult/Child	
1 day	78	39	35	18	15	8
7 days	270	135	135	68	70	35
15 days	330	165	165	83	80	40
21 days	400	200	200	100	90	45
30 days	500	250	250	125	110	55
60 days	720	360	360	180	165	83
90 days	960	480	480	240	210	105

A child is between the ages of five and 12 years. Children below five can travel free on the Indrail Pass of their parents.

One day pass

The one day pass was introduced to help people who want to make only a short journey, perhaps to Agra and back from Delhi, or overnight from one city to another and would like to have their ticket and berth reserved before they arrive in India.

All passes, including the one day pass, are valid for the class for which they are sold, except on Rajdhani Express trains where the one day passes are only valid for the class below what you've paid for, since that's a special train, with meals included. The AC 1st Class one day pass entitles the holder to travel in AC 2-tier on the Rajdhani, while the holder of an AC 2-tier pass can travel in the AC Chair Car. I once used my 30-day AC 2-tier IRP to travel in the luxury of Rajdhani 1st Class but I had to pay the difference on the single journey AC 2-tier fare and the AC 1st Class fare in US dollars to get the upgrade.

Pass refund

The regular passes have to be used within one year of date of issue. The cost can be refunded, less 15 per cent of the face value, if it is returned to the office of issue unused at least eight days before the commencement of its validity. There is a deduction of 20 per cent after that period, and also of any cancellation charges for abandoned reservations. There is no refund possible after commencement of the pass's validity; if it is lost or stolen; or if the journey is undertaken in a lower class of accommodation.

The pass holder with a pass purchased outside India who decides while in India not to use it, should present it to a Station Master to have it cancelled and to obtain a dated cancellation certificate. The cancelled pass and the certificate should be kept to claim a refund eventually from the overseas office that sold the pass.

An Indrail Pass can be revalidated to commence on a different date by the overseas office of issue on payment of US$10.00. Cancellation of confirmed reservations and substitution of new ones incurs a penalty of US$10 outside India, or Rs 10 per change (up to a maximum of Rs 50) if changes are made in India.

Extension of the validity period of the pass can be made in India by the nearest Area Officer or gazetted Station Superintendent if it becomes necessary due to circumstances beyond the control of the pass holder, such as train delay.

Pass value

Is buying an Indrail Pass worth it? The answer is a big YES, but you have to take more than the cost per kilometre into consideration. On a straight comparison of costs (distance travelled on single journey tickets versus distance travelled on a Pass) there is little financial advantage, unless you spend all your time in India on trains just to clock up excess kilometres. It is being able to avoid the boring rules and surcharges that give it real value.

There is no financial advantage in buying a 2nd Class pass. Anyone who is prepared to travel at length in 2nd Class is likely to be young (in mind if not in age) and not impressed by the convenience and prestige that make an Indrail Pass worth having. The financial savings come with the 1st Class pass with its entree to superior accommodation in 1st or AC coaches. Its value is not only in kilometres travelled but also in the (free) nights spent on board in comfortable berths. The pass pays for itself in a few nights from the savings made on hotel accommodation alone.

WP 4-6-2 between Daund and Manmad (east of Bombay), specially embellished for VIP passenger the Minister of Railways. (Anthony J. Lambert)

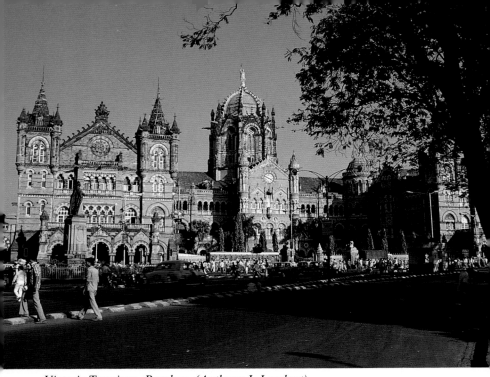

Victoria Terminus, Bombay. (Anthony J. Lambert)

The Gothic Madras Central station was designed by George Hardinge and built between 1868 and 1872. (Anthony J. Lambert)

The most expensive pass of all, the AC Class (ie: 1st Class Air Conditioned Sleeper) Indrail Pass, brings a greater saving on buying single journey tickets since those tickets are themselves much more expensive. There is also the bonus of privileged accommodation in the luxury of 1st AC Class. Unfortunately, only about 60 trains (listed in Chapter 12) have 1st AC Class, so only buy that pass if most of your long journeys will be on trains that do.

I was taken to task by Rendell A. Davis, an attorney in the USA, for seeming to lack enthusiasm for the AC 1st Class Indrail Pass in the first edition. He wrote: 'I suggest you might want to recommend AC 1st Class more highly. By western standards, it is not very expensive. The cost difference between a three-week AC 1st Class pass and a three-week ordinary 1st Class pass was about the cost of staying in certain '5-star' hotels for one night. Yet the comfort of AC 1st Class can make an enormous difference.

'I took a two-night and a day rail trip from Madras to Calcutta on the Howrah Mail. At the end of that trip, I got off the train totally rested and ready to go. If I had spent two consecutive nights sleeping in a lower class, I would probably have wasted my first day in Calcutta recovering from the rail trip. For that trip alone, the extra cost of AC 1st Class was worth it.

'AC 1st Class is also more widely available . . . For example, I rode AC 1st Class between Jaipur and Delhi on the Pink City Express . . . Similarly, the various Shatabdi Expresses now carry an airline-seat style of AC 1st Class that is much more comfortable than the ordinary AC Chair Car seating on those trains.'

Having used a 30-day AC 1st Class pass in 1992 (when it cost about US$8 a day more than the ordinary 1st Class/AC 2-tier sleeper IRP) I can vouch for what Rendell A. Davis says. It is by far the less stressful way of train travel with the extra attention of beds made up with clean linen, stimulating travel companions, civil service, showers in the loos and access to any part of the train. The food, however, is the same as in all the other classes.

The ordinary 1st Class long period passes represent the best bargain financially. With a pass for 21 or more days you don't have to travel day and night to get full value from it. You can linger in different places and still be able to travel more kilometres than if you'd spent the same amount of money on single journey tickets.

With an Indrail Pass you will have freedom of the Indian Railways network. It is important, though, to remember that because of the demand for space on Indian trains, it is not always possible to jump on a train at random and expect to find a berth. You *have* to make a reservation, usually a few days in advance, if you want to be sure of travelling on a particular train, no matter what class of rail pass you have.

A fixed itinerary is what many rail travellers are keen to avoid, but

the Indrail Pass helps the impulsive traveller too since, with it, you can
turn up at a station four hours before a train's departure and try to get
a reservation. Or you can simply find the conductor when the train
comes in and try to arrange everything with him. The authorities hate
these last minute arrangements, and so will you if there is no berth
available, but you stand more chance with an Indrail pass than without
it.

RESERVATIONS

It was raining when I arrived in Secunderabad. My train from New
Delhi had been delayed and I had missed my connection so the
itinerary, painstakingly prepared for me by the staff of the ITB, was
now useless. The SS sent me out of his station into the dark, wet night
and I carried my two cases past the bus stand to the reservations office
600 metres away around a corner.

After a day of travelling, I felt dreadful; I was soaked to the skin and
fed up. The prospect of queuing for a reservation made me feel worse,
but I had to leave for Madras the next day. The reservations office was
like a council hall with rows of seats in which people were waiting.
There were no queues. I asked at the enquiry desk what I should do.
The clerk told me to fill in a requisition slip.

The slip was headed 'Requisition for Reservation/Cancellation/
Return/Onward Journey' and contained spaces for 'Station from . . .
to . . . Date of Journey . . . Train number' and for the names of up to
six passengers with age and sex columns. The name of the applicant,
address and signature with date were also needed.

I returned the slip to the clerk and was given a number and told to sit
and wait. I sank into a chair gratefully and composed myself for a long
wait. Looking around I saw numbers flashing above the different ticket
counters; to my amazement my own number was being displayed. The
clerk at the counter took my Indrail pass, scribbled 'R' on it and some
numbers, and gave it back.

My reservation had been made and it was not the exacting process I
feared. I was in a strange city, without friends and at my lowest ebb,
expecting the worst. Yet the system worked perfectly, and I can only
guess it was because I had an Indrail Pass.

Making a reservation
If you don't have an Indrail Pass you must buy a journey-cum-
reservation ticket. In the Advance Reservation Centre fill in a requisition slip with details of when you want to travel, by what train and in
what class, adding your name, age, sex and address. This has to be
handed in at the appropriate reservations counter. When the reservation is confirmed, the journey-cum-reservation ticket issued by a man-
operated reservation counter is endorsed on the reverse with the

reservation details. It is only valid for the particular train and day for which it is endorsed. For a 1st Class booking it will have the letter 'R' written on it and the actual allotment of seat/berth will be done on the day of travel; you will see your allotted number on the lists posted in the station lobby and on the platform of your departing train. In the case of a reservation in 2nd Class, the seat/berth number will be quoted, such as S3-45 which means seat 45 in Coach S3. If the reservation office does not have a quota for the journey you will have to buy a ticket and wait at least three days for messages to be sent and replies received to confirm the reservation. If it can't be confirmed, the ticket cost can be refunded, as detailed under 'Refunds'. When the advance booking is done at a computerized reservations centre, a single coupon instead of a cardboard ticket is issued by the computer and this serves as your ticket.

If you have an IRP, details of your itinerary will be entered on it for your information but the journey-cum-reservation coupon is what will get you your berth when you are on the train.

John Gleeson, writing from Cork, commented: 'While any station can theoretically make a reservation on any train, they can only give you a confirmed reservation while you wait if the station has an allocation of seats on the train. If it doesn't have an allocation then a message must be sent to the originating station to secure a seat from there.

'I found, when I arrived at the originating station, that on four out of five occasions, no message had been sent by the station at which I made the reservation. Thus no seat!

'On the one occasion that a message was sent, it was only because I went directly to the CRS (at Siliguri) and begged him to ensure that the message was sent.

'For example, Bombay VT does not have an allocation on the Gomantak Express from Vasco Da Gama to Miraj. We were assured that everything would be OK but when we got to Vasco to confirm, no message had been received.

'I think it would be a good idea if you advised travellers to ascertain if the situation mentioned applies in their case and to ensure (perhaps by going to the CRS or SS) that the required message is sent.'

What happens if you can't get the reservation you want? Rob Dobson tried and says he was 'bounced from reservation desk to supervisor, in the end I had to go and see the Assistant Commercial Superintendent. The quota system has gone crazy if you have to go so high up the tree to get a seat. It took an hour to get a ticket to Madras.'

His experience proves that the system does work – but start at the top. If there is a foreign tourist counter at the reservations centre, the clerk there will advise you on what to do. If you actually want to buy a ticket and have no foreign exchange – or there is no counter especially for foreigners – you will be competing with everyone else for space.

Even so, being a foreigner, you can still ask the CRS for help or the SS or the officials who control the Emergency Quota, usually the Assistant or Divisional Commercial Superintendent. Buy a Wait List ticket, so you've got something to show, and ask them to sort it out.

If the worst comes to the worst and you simply have to travel that day and you don't have an IRP, buy a 2nd Class ticket at the current (trains departing that day) counter. You'll have to try your luck when the train comes in, paying the TTE or the train conductor the extra fare for any upgrading, reservation fee, supplements, etc. If there is no space at all, you'll have to squeeze into the general, non-reserved 2nd Class carriage. An official at the ITB told me: 'Share with our problems like others. The capacity of the train can't be increased, you must avail yourself of the existing capacity.'

Don't despair though! Pat Moynihan, also of Cork, wrote of her trip using single journey tickets: 'I had to buy a 2nd Class ticket at Cuddalore as they had no 1st Class quota to Bangalore. When I got on the train, I was able to upgrade to 1st Class, and had a two-berth coupe to myself.'

Chris Smith with a 15-day IRP was on the last leg of his journey when I met him on the Tamil Nadu Express. He said that he wondered about spending so much money on rail travel but he found his pass absolutely worth it. He travelled only between the major cities (with a side trip to New Jalpaiguri from Howrah for the toy train to Darjeeling). He spent lots of nights on the train 'because I found the sleeping accommodation much cheaper and safer than in cheap hotels.'

He was amazed at the efficient running of the trains and so impressed by the system he wished he had taken a longer pass to travel more. Since he wanted to travel without an itinerary, he used to turn up at the foreign counter of the main station's reservations office on the day of a train's departure and get put on the waiting list. 'Somehow,' he said, 'berths were found from some quota.'

Computer coupons

The computer-generated ticket/reservation coupon is approximately 15×9 cm in size, white and blue in colour and contains several numbers. The most important is the PNR (Passenger Name Record) number as this identifies the passenger. The passenger's name does not appear on the ticket although it will appear on the reservation chart pasted on the side of the train and on the station notice board showing berth allocations.

The coupon contains details of the class of travel (in English and Hindi), the train number and date. The boarding and destination stations will be indicated together with the distance between them in kilometres. It will state whether the ticket is for an adult or child and the sex and age of the passenger are also shown (to prevent fraudulent use) as well as the seat/berth number if allocated in advance. Additional information, such as where the train comes from and the journey routing will appear at the bottom of the ticket.

Types of reservation

There are two kinds of reservation: (1) Confirmed and (2) RAC. Confirmed passengers are allocated berths/seats at the time of booking and the details are endorsed on the tickets. RAC (Reservation Against Cancellation) provides a limited number of passengers, only at the train's originating station, with seats on the train in all classes. A berth is promised if one becomes vacant due to a cancellation or no-show.

RAC passengers are entitled to board the train at its originating station and to occupy the seats assigned to them. If an RAC passenger is actually provided with a berth, the sleeper surcharge and the difference in reservation fee is collected by the TTE.

If all berths and the RAC quota have been filled, the name of passengers with journey tickets are entered on the Waiting List. Wait List passengers are accommodated in the order in which their names appear on the list, subject to space being available, within the ten minutes before the departure of the train. Sometimes, extra carriages are added to a train, so it is worth having your name on the waiting list.

Check the computer reservation coupon carefully when you receive it to see that you understand what it means, so then you can ask what to do if it says RAC or WL. Rob Dobson thought that WL on his coupon meant he was seated in coach WL for his journey from Agra to New Delhi. When he turned up for the train in the evening, he found he was wait-listed (WL) and had no right to travel on the train at all. So he stayed in the retiring room and got a seat on a less popular train the next morning.

Wait List (WL) does not mean you can board the train and hope to find a seat in the manner that RAC gives the right to travel. You can only board the train with the knowledge and consent of the train conductor or TTE (and then you'll have the various surcharges to pay unless you have an IRP). If you do have an IRP, the chances of you getting a berth even though you're wait-listed, are increased since you qualify for accommodation from the Emergency Quota (see page 61).

If you purchase a journey ticket and are assigned to the RAC quota or Wait List and then decide not to travel, you can claim a refund on your ticket. No cancellation charges will be levied unless a confirmed reservation was actually provided before you cancelled. A clerkage charge of Rs 2.00 will be deducted though.

Return reservations

Return journey reservations can be made at the originating station by filling in the requisition slip and purchasing a return journey (card or blank paper) ticket which will cost twice the single journey. A telegram is sent, at no charge to the passenger, to request accommodation

from the return journey station. Some return journey quotas have
been set aside on popular mail/express trains and berths can be
allocated from the originating station.

With the expansion of the computer system, you can make return,
and onward reservations, from anywhere that is connected to the
computers, without relying on non-sent telegrams.

Space

Stations have Advanced Booking counters, sometimes in a separate
building adjacent to the station, where reservations are made. Many of
these buildings are agreeable places in which to wait, and have coffee
counters and magazine stalls. The availability of space on the train will
be indicated by coloured discs or lights so you can see if there are
berths available on the train you want. The colour indicates the
following:

Green:	Space available
Yellow:	RAC space available
Pink:	Wait List available
Red:	No space, fully booked.

If the train of your choice is shown as fully booked, don't despair.
As a foreigner you have access to seats issued under different quotas
(see page 61) and should apply at the separate counter for foreign
tourists or to the CRS.

If you leave making your reservation until the day of departure,
requests at the reservation counters are usually accepted up to four
hours before the scheduled departure of a train. After that you must
try the ticket collector (TC) or Conductor at the train's originating
station during the hour before the train's departure.

Reservation charges

Where computerized reservation facilities are available, there is an
extra charge to pay for reservations. The fees (but these are not
applicable to IRP holders) are:

Reservation fee:	Manual	Computerized
AC 1st Class	Rs 12	20
AC 2-tier/1st Class	6	10
AC Chair Car	5	10
2nd Class Sleeper	5	7
2nd Class Sitting	2	3
2nd Class Sleeper		
Surcharge up to 500 km	15	
from 501–1000 km	20	
above 1001 km	25	

The fees and surcharges are the same for adult or child.

Refunds

For single journey tickets, minimum cancellation charges are:

1st AC Class	Rs 30
AC Sleeper (2-tier)	20
1st Class	20
AC Chair Car	15
2nd Class	10

The original reservation fee is not refunded; the journey cost will be refunded less deductions according to when cancellation is made. Cancellation charges are not levied if an alternative reservation is made.

Cancellation charges of 50 per cent are levied on refunds when the cancellation is within two days before, or three hours after, the departure of the train. Refunds can also be sought on partially used tickets or due to the failure of a train's air conditioning equipment (if the ticket is for AC accommodation).

NB Foreigners who have reservations from the tourist quota should always cancel them if they cannot travel, as this releases the berths for other tourists who may be on the waiting list.

Lost reservation

It could be useful to record the number and date of your ticket in a safe place in case it is needed for future reference, as well as the number of the train, berth allocation (if any) and date of travel. However, if you lose a reserved berth ticket and there is a record of your name as being its purchaser, you can still travel on the same reservation. A payment of 25 per cent of the original fare paid will be levied for this duplicate ticket.

Special requirements

Reservations can be made only up to 60 days in advance of departure for all classes and on all trains except for some special expresses on which the advance reservation period is reduced to 15 days or even less. This restriction does not apply to Indrail Pass holders.

An individual can book only up to four berths in the case of a party or a maximum of six berths for a family on the same train travelling to the same destination. It is sometimes possible to request a particular berth or seat: for instance, an outside lower berth or a berth in the ladies compartment, subject to availability. Reservations are not transferable.

For reservations from an intermediate station, the passenger must apply at least 72 hours before the departure of the train from its starting station. Reservations are not accepted by telephone. They are done in order of receipt of requisition slips.

Boarding the train

To make sure your reserved berth isn't given to someone on the RAC or Waiting lists, be at the station at least 30 minutes before the train is due to leave. This will give you time to find the platform, the train and your berth.

Passenger lists are posted in prominent places in a station before a train's departure, and on the side of carriages themselves. The lists show the passengers' names, sex and ages with numbers of allotted berths and carriage number. Each carriage has its number painted on its side and also an indication of where numbered berths are to be found.

If you are confronted with a passenger list that's only in Hindi, you could find your berth by checking the list for your ticket number. Don't be surprised to see your name written in some novel forms. I've been listed as Ston Elli and a friend of mine called Christine invariably found she was travelling as Christ.

If you are boarding the train at an intermediate stop, arrive there with enough time to find out from the passenger lists which is your carriage and where it will be when the train pulls in. Some trains have 21 carriages so you will need to position yourself properly for boarding as there won't be time to run the whole length of the train searching for your carriage before it leaves.

Gary, an Australian I met at Karjat, was puzzled about how to find out where to stand on a platform so he was near the carriage in which his berth was booked. This is especially important when the train only stops for a few minutes and has no vestibule. The helpful assistant station master at Karjat explained that 1st and AC coaches are usually located near the pantry car which is usually in the centre of the train.

To find out the exact location for Gary's train he consulted a booklet that every SM or SS has that shows the composition, marshalling order and accommodation of every mail, express and passenger train. Gary's ticket indicated FC3 (1st Class, third coach) so the ASM counted down the coach order until he found the position of the relevant coach, in this case number eight from the engine. Gary waited under the sign (they exist at most major stations) which showed where that particular carriage would be when the train stopped. The system worked and he boarded the train without panic. So, if in doubt, ask the SS or SM where your carriage will be.

Reserved sleeping accommodation is provided between 2100 and 0600. During the day (0600 to 2100) overnight passengers must make room for seating passengers in the compartment, up to the number it is marked to carry.

The quota system

Many foreigners wonder why accommodation can be found for them on trains which are shown as fully booked. They suspect some inefficiency or corruption. In fact it is due to the miracle of the quota system.

Railway officials turn coy when you ask them about the various quotas and how the system works. Basically, it is an arrangement which enables a reservation clerk at a station to allot berths on a particular train without reference to the headquarters controlling the sale of berths on that train. This is done by headquarters assigning the station a specific number of berths, more than which cannot be sold by that station.

Lists of berths available at various stations appear in all the zonal timetables. For example, from the South Central Railway timetable, we discover that Aurangabad has a quota on Train 7552, the Ajanta Express from Manmad to Kacheguda, to sell up to 10 AC Sleeper berths, up to 95 2nd Class 3 tier berths.

Foreign tourist quota

Trains which are popular with foreign travellers have a foreign tourist quota set aside for reserving at tourist-frequented stations. Any foreign traveller can request a berth from that quota, where it exists. If there isn't one, the foreigner must try to get a berth out of the general quota which is open to all passengers.

What happens if the general quota is sold out, as is often the case? That is when the system gets interesting and the officials get coy.

There are over a dozen different quotas formulated over the years to cover the needs of special passengers. As well as the General, Return Journey and Foreign Tourist quotas, there are the Parliamentarian, Defence, VIP, Outstation, Railway Employees and Emergency quotas. (Outstation means a station – or a town without a station – where the train does not stop, usually because it is on another line.)

Berths from all quotas which haven't been taken up by the time the train departs are released to the conductor to allocate according to priority on the RAC and Waiting lists. Where there is no foreign tourist quota, the SS or the CRS can apply (to the area manager) to have the foreign tourist accommodated on the Emergency quota. Preference is given to Indrail Pass holders over purchasers of single journey tickets and even over railway officials.

A Reservations Guide is published in some daily newspapers showing the earliest date on which berths are available on trains from major stations. Trains are listed with class of accommodation alongside and the dates from which there are vacancies. Some trains, such as weekly expresses, are very popular and are likely to be fully booked from the day reservations open.

With the introduction of computers, even though you may be among the first in the line at one counter on the day reservations open, you may still find all berths from the general quota have been allocated, since people queuing at other counters with access by computer to the same quota, have already reserved all the berths.

Reservation assistance in India

If your itinerary, arranged weeks in advance by Dr Dandapani or another GSA out of India, changes, or you are setting up your journey in India, you will need assistance from competent, trained personnel. Fortunately, many reservations offices are geared to dealing with foreign rail travellers. The best service is provided by the ITB (see page 64) and by reservation offices with foreign tourist guides, whose authority is required by reservations clerks to seek reservations from the foreign tourist quota.

Northern Railway (which actually administers the IRP) has offices with foreign tourist guides at New Delhi station (ITB on the first floor), Jodhpur (first floor), Varanasi (off the main lobby) and at Jaisalmer (off the main platform). Central Railway has a counter in the Bombay VT station reservations complex. Western Railway has a desk and an expert guide on the first floor of the reservations complex at Churchgate, Bombay.

At Madras, there is an efficient, separate foreign tourist 'cell' on the first floor of the reservations complex alongside Madras Central station. In Calcutta, foreign travellers can make reservations at the complex on the first floor of the Fairlie Place building, Calcutta. At other stations, according to their importance, there are counters dealing specifically with foreign tourists. Where there is no dedicated counter, deal directly with the Chief Reservations Supervisor (CRS). If the station is too small to have a CRS, then introduce yourself to the station master.

Computerization

The recent introduction of a computerized reservation system has dramatically improved the booking process. Computers are now inter-linked so reservations can be done instantly on trains leaving stations other than the one from where you are making your booking. Where there is no computer link up (even if the station actually has its own computer) reservations will have to be made by telex or the dreaded telegram.

Stations where reservations are fully computerized are Agra, Ahma-dabad, Allahabad, Amritsar, Bangalore, Bhopal, Bhubaneswar, Bom-bay, Calcutta, Coimbatore, Cuttack, Delhi, Dhanbad, Ernakulam, Gorakhpur, Guwahati, Jaipur, Jammu, Jodhpur, Kanpur, Lucknow, Madras, Madurai, Nagpur, Patna, Pune, Puri, Secunderabad, Surat, Tiruchchirappalli, Trivandrum, Vadodara, Varanasi and Waltair.

Stations where the computerized reservation facility will be in oper-ation by the end of 1993, are: Bilaspur, Chandigarh, Gwalior, Indore, Jabalpur, Ludhiana, Mangalore, Ranchi, Shimla, Tatanagar, Tirupati and Vijayawada. Eventually computerized reservations will be possi-ble in at least 70 per cent of the rail network.

Computerized railway reservation terminal in Calcutta.

In anticipation of this, new reservation centres are being built at many stations, and the whole reservations process is being streamlined. Since computers require careful maintenance in a dust-free, air-conditioned atmosphere, passengers are benefiting too with climate controlled, clean and comfortable areas in which to sit and await their turn. With less harassing conditions in which to work, the booking clerks have become customer-friendly too.

The computerized reservations system switches off automatically at the stipulated closing time, usually 2000 hours. So it's no good hoping to complete a complicated itinerary by starting just before 2000 hours since the operator, however helpful, can do nothing about it when the computer has closed down.

The International Tourist Bureau

The International Tourist Bureau (the ITB) is the flagship of Indian Railways' bureaux for dealing with foreign tourists. It is located on the first floor of New Delhi station, opposite the restaurant, and was opened in 1987 to cater for foreign travellers who no longer have to go to Baroda House to make reservations. It sells single journey and point to point tickets and reservations as well as the Indrail Pass.

The ITB, sometimes known as Central Space Control, is the nerve centre of the Indrail Pass scheme which is coordinated by the Northern Railway. When a pass is sold by an overseas GSA (or by an agent in India) the GSA telexes the name, nationality and passport number of the purchaser, with the Indrail Pass number, class, itinerary and reservations required. A file is opened for the passenger at the ITB.

Apprehensive foreigners just arrived in Delhi who visit the ITB with their foreign-bought Indrail Passes are delighted to discover not only are their reservations confirmed as promised, but their full itineraries have been carefully recorded. This is possible because each GSA has an experienced reservations officer at the ITB who looks after the GSA's clients. When the telex containing the reservation request is received it is processed swiftly and confirmed by telex within seven days. Even if your Indrail Pass itinerary doesn't take you to Delhi, the details are recorded there.

The ITB is a brightly lit, cheerful office, open from 0730 to 1700 every day except Sunday. The staff take a break of 30 minutes for lunch from 1330 but tourists can wait in the pleasant conditions of the office during that period.

Two tourist guides are available at a separate desk in front of a showcase of books about India. If in doubt, start there either for help with your itinerary or advice as to whether point to point tickets or an IRP is best for you, and which counter to go to. The counters opposite the entrance, with chairs in which to wait your turn in comfort, deal with point to point reservations and are equipped with computers to issue the coupons. Payment is accepted in dollars or pounds (in which case change is given in the same currency) or in rupees against the original and photocopy of your foreign exchange encashment certificate. If you have only rupees and no exchange certificate, you'll have to buy your tickets from the general quota at the reservations complex next to New Delhi station. (The reason is that foreign tourist quota tickets should be purchased with foreign currency.)

A notice indicates that 'foreign students studying in India or Indians studying abroad are not dealt here.' Your passport and visa will be checked to see you have not been in India for more than six months, since the ITB facility is only for genuine tourists.

If you want to buy an Indrail Pass it can be done swiftly here, at a dedicated counter. Payment for this has to be in dollars or pounds. So if you plan to buy an IRP at the ITB do not change all your travellers cheques in advance as you'll need them to buy the pass. Actually this is a pleasant way to cash your travellers cheques as the rate is calculated at the day's bank rate and the change is given in Indian rupees. Credit cards are not accepted 'because the card companies require commission which is not built into the existing cost of the IRP,' according to an ITB official. This comes as a shock to sophisticated tourists used to paying with plastic.

Another counter deals with travellers who have bought their Indrail Passes overseas and it has signs indicating the countries represented. The staff, who are delightfully helpful, speak Japanese, German and French as well as English. If you have arranged your itinerary in advance through a GSA, you will be able to pick up the reservations coupons, have your IRP endorsed and be on your way.

Whenever I go to ITB I always have a new and complicated itinerary, changing the one I'd first thought of. With computer link up throughout India, most bookings can be made promptly, other requests are telexed. It's amazing what the staff can achieve. Since I usually spend three or four days in Delhi, I call in at ITB on the first morning and then call back on my last evening and find all the reservations are confirmed. It's the same for all IRP holders, since we are VIPs on Indian Railways.

A word of advice: if you've just stepped off the plane after an overnight flight, you'll be exhausted by the time you get to ITB – the heat, the crowds, India generally, will be overwhelming. So know what you want before you get to ITB; it will make everything much smoother and you won't test the clerk's patience too much. There is a snack trolley with mineral water and cold drinks on sale, a call box for local and internatinal calls, a left luggage office was due to open in 1992, and there is even a tape recorder if you want to sound off. Or pop into the manager's office. On my last visit the manager was Mr Jai Chandra whom I watched dealing with bewildered travellers with the calm assurance of a man who knew everything was going to be all right.

SS: The Sensible Solution

If something does go wrong while you are travelling, what to do? The office of the Station Superintendent (SS) is a haven for the troubled traveller. He is the man to resolve whatever travel problems you have. Travellers who barge into his office in high dudgeon are urged to sit down in one of the many chairs in front of his desk. A glass of water is offered immediately, followed by tea if the agony looks like being prolonged.

Station superintendents are usually men of great charm and personality who use tact and wisdom to soothe the irate traveller. Any foreign tourist who is bothered by an aspect of rail travel should go straight to the SS first. Shuttling around from one junior official to another will only compound your dissatisfaction. Save your temper and from the outset seek out the SS: he's the Sensible Solution.

Every station has a Station Master (SM) who deals with the operation of trains, while the SS is responsible for overall supervision. Smaller stations will only have an SM.

In colonial times station masters were considered as very important personages. One retiring Viceroy is said, either at Bombay or Delhi (there are several versions of this story) to have thanked the station master for his courtesies over the years, to which the man replied: 'Not at all, Your Excellency, it has always been a pleasure to see you go.'

1. THIS IS YOUR OFFICE PLEASE HELP US TO CLEAN IT.
2. PLEASE DO NOT PUT YOUR LUGGAGE ON THE SOFA AND CHAIRS PLEASE DONOT SLEEP IN THE OFFICE THANKS.

M.M. PUROHIT
INTERNATIONAL TOURIST BUREAU

Chapter 4

Class Distinction

'You must,' said my publisher, 'travel 3rd Class. That's all that many rail travellers can afford and they'll want to read about it.'

The good news is that there is no '3rd Class'. 1st Class is being phased out too. A Divisional Railway Manager told me this is being done as part of a scheme to create a classless railway. It's not true, I discovered, but it sounded right.

There are, in fact, six classes defined by ticket cost, with variations in style and comfort depending on the age and status of the train and whether it's day or night travel. In rising order of expense, the classes are:

1. 2nd Class Ordinary (Passenger train seating)
2. 2nd Class (Mail/Express 3 tier sleeper)
3. Air Conditioned Chair Car (ACCC)
4. 1st Class (Non air conditioned sleeper)
5. Air Conditioned Sleeper (2 tier) (AC2 or 2nd AC)
6. Air Conditioned 1st Class (sleeper) (AC1 or 1st AC)

In India, any class that's not 2nd Class is referred to as Upper Class. If the list seems complicated, it's going to seem worse as you read on.

Train type

Trains are either express/mail or passenger. Main line express/mail trains will include 2nd Class accommodation and one or more of the other classes on the list, unless they are 'Janata expresses' when they have only 2nd Class (non AC) carriages. Passenger trains are slower, sometimes steam hauled, stop at every station and village halt and will generally have ancient 2nd Class carriages with wooden seats but usually with 1st Class accommodation even if its only two compartments in a combined 2nd and 1st Class coach. Incidentally, what I call a carriage or coach is also called a bogie in India.

For fast travelling, you need an express or mail train, preferably a superfast one since there are few expresses that manage to go very far – or fast – without stopping at a station. Broad gauge trains are capable of greater speed than metre gauge ones and, indeed, most metre gauge lines are being converted to broad gauge for more convenient travel.

FIXED UPPER BUNK

ATTENDANT'S SEAT

CHAIN TO SUPPORT MIDDLE BUNK

BACKREST BECOMES MIDDLE BUNK

TYPICAL INSIDE COMPARTMENT

FIXED UPPER BUNK

BACKREST BECOMES MATTRESS

TYPICAL OUTSIDE COMPARTMENT

W.C.

W.C.

w.h.b.

w.h.b.

LUGGAGE SHELVES

Ladies' Comp.ᵗ

w.h.b.

w.h.b.

W.C.

W.C.

2nd. CLASS   3-TIER COACH

~ Typical 72·berth layout

CLASS STRUCTURE

Sometimes it is difficult to tell from the timetables just what the accommodation consists of. The daily Delhi/Howrah mail is shown as having: 'One AC 2 Tier, one AC I, two I and five II 3 tier sleeper car and three II.' The Tinsukia Mail from Guwahati to Delhi has 'one air conditioned II Class 2 tier sleeper coach' while a sister train runs from Dharmanagar to Guwahati with 'one II Class 3 tier cum 2 tier sleeping coach and one II Class coach.'

In those examples 'II Class' means 2nd Class. 'Air conditioned II Class 2 tier' is AC Sleeper. Some timetables call it AC II 2 Tier. Really you can only consider it as 2nd Class because it is the second most expensive way of travelling by train.

(1) 2nd Class Ordinary

The reference to 'II Class coach' means a 2nd Class carriage without sleeping accommodation, often called the general (ie: non reserved) coach. Passenger trains are composed of similar carriages; in other words the old style 3rd Class accommodation.

These carriages usually have a side aisle giving access to the open sided compartments of two wooden benches facing each other, and seating four (or many more) people on each bench. The luggage racks, of wooden slats, hang from the ceiling, giving extra space for passengers to sit or sleep (although signs say they are only for luggage). The luggage racks block out the light and add to the gloom of the compartment, as do the horizontal iron bars across the windows. Each compartment has two fans. On trains with a vestibule running its length, the linking door from the general carriage to the rest of the train is kept locked to prevent passengers slipping into the reserved carriages.

(2) 2nd Class Sleeper (see plan)

Long distance expresses and mail trains have 'II 3 Tier Sleeper Coaches' which means 2nd Class carriages with sleeping berths in three tiers: lower, middle and upper. There are 72 berths; the day time seating capacity is supposed to be 75 but usually expands beyond that.

The windows are always open in hot weather and closed tightly as soon as it begins to rain, hence the carriage gets stuffy. The windows have bars across them, like a mobile jail, although both doors at both ends of the carriage are usually left open so anyone can jump in, or out, as the train stops. There are three fans to each compartment (no AC) and they can be airy in the cooler months. In hot weather, nothing tempers the heat, and the dust billowing in through the open windows adds to the swelter.

The carriage is divided into nine open sided compartments. Each one has bench type seating for three people facing another bench for three people. On the other side of the aisle is one single seat opposite

DROP-DOWN UPPER BUNK

TIP-UP SEAT

BACKREST
FORMS
MATTRESS

4·BERTH CABIN
(seats 6 in daytime)

W.C.   W.C.

CABIN

CABIN

COUPÉ

COUPÉ

COUPÉ

CABIN

CABIN

CABIN

TIP-UP SEAT

W.C.   w.c. &
shower

1st. CLASS (Non AC Sleeper)
— Typical 36 seat /26 berth layout

another. The seats and benches have been converted from the old wooden ones and have been firmly padded and upholstered in rexine.

The padded back of the lower bench is raised to become the mattress of the middle berth, supported there by chains hanging down from the upper bunk. This upper bunk is a fixed, padded ledge suspended by permanent supports from the ceiling. The bunks formed in this manner have a width of 55 cm and a length of 184 cm.

Across the aisle are the 'outside' berths, converted out of the two single seats facing each other. The cushioned backs of these seats drop forward flat across the seats themselves to touch in the middle and form the lower bunk. The upper berth is fixed. These berths measure 55 cm in width with a length of 166 cm.

Thus, '3 tier' refers to what are known as the inside berths, while the outside berths (those parallel to the outside of the carriage wall) are two tier. This makes eight berths per compartment, all open to the aisle that splits them. Sometimes passengers hang clothes and towels as curtains but with so many people in a small space, there's not much privacy.

Each compartment has nightlights and clothes hooks. Access to the upper bunks is by scrambling up the metal hoops by the aisle; these also serve as handholds for people passing through the coach.

There are two toilets at each end of the carriage, but no shower. There are also mirrors and wash basins in the lobby by the entrance doors. At one end of the carriage there is a seat for the attendant and shelves for luggage. On a long trip the inside of the carriage gets dirty when people throw their rubbish on the floor instead of out of the open windows or in the bin at the end of the carriage.

Because the top bunk is fixed, it is frequently used for passengers' luggage. A family or friends travelling together might keep the middle bunk in place too during the day which adds to their lack of headroom and comfort.

The choice of where to sleep usually depends on the luck of the draw at the reservations centre. The lower bunk, being used as a seat, is only available for sleeping when the other passengers have retired to their own bunks. Similarly, the middle bunk can only be used when the seated passengers have finished sitting since it is their back rest. The upper bunk is available all the time, but requires agility to climb in and out and it's close to the fans and the lights. This is where an eye mask helps for sleeping.

Women travelling alone can request accommodation in the ladies' compartment which is a separate cabin, with a sliding door, at the end of some 2nd Class 3 tier carriages. It sleeps six. While men are not allowed in, they often spend time there during the day. Boys, up to the age of 12 if accompanying a lady, are permitted. On expresses with a train superintendent on board, the ladies' cabin closest to the 1st Class is reserved for him as his quarters.

There are some odd combinations in 2nd Class such as 'II class 3 tier cum 2 tier sleeping coach'. This is a composite coach with both three and two tier sleeping berths but in separate compartments. The word 'tier' is frequently pronounced 'tire'.

(3) Chair Car Class

Chair car class has many variations and is usually encountered on day time journeys. Only some cars are air conditioned (the AC Chair Car class) with a separate fare structure, while others are non AC at 1st or 2nd Class fares.

AC Chair Cars seat from 56 to 73 passengers in a 2 × 3 layout. Some operate on overnight routes and a list of trains with AC Chair Car accommodation appears in Chapter 12. As well as the AC unit there are plenty of fans; the windows are sealed and the glass is tinted a sunset bronze. These carriages are a bit claustrophobic. The seats have tables which fold down from the chair back in front and a magazine pocket; they recline slightly. Be careful in locating your seat since when you think you've found, say, seat 45, because it says so above the fold-down table, you are actually in seat 40 because that's the number on the back of the seat you're sitting in. Western and Indian style toilets are available.

The 1st Class non AC version has 60 reclining seats in a 2 × 2 layout, with the aisle passing between the two pairs. There are fans and the windows open. Curiously, a seat in such a carriage can cost up to 60 per cent more than one in the newer AC chair cars.

Seats in the 1st Class, non AC coaches have a width between armrests of 44 cm and a cushion width of 50 cm. The armrest dividing the seats is broad and fixed. Leg space (pitch) from the back of one seat to the back of the one in front is 55 cm. There is a footrest, a pocket for papers in the seat back, and an ashtray at the side. All seats are forward facing except for a pair either side of the aisle at the end of the coach which face the others.

Seats in non AC 2nd Class are likely to be of wood in bench sections of 3 × 3, facing each other. There could be a total of 108 seats, plus two jump seats by the centre doors. Seats can be cramped when more than three people squeeze onto them and leg room is limited when there are passengers on the facing seat. There are Indian style toilets at both ends of this kind of coach.

(4) 1st Class (Non AC Sleeper) (see plan)

Forget the glamour and luxury associated with 1st Class travel; on Indian trains those comforts are now only to be found in the air conditioned coaches. It is hard to know what to call 1st Class when it ranks third in expense after AC 1st and AC 2nd.

Where possible, 1st Class carriages are being replaced by the AC sleeper 2nd Class coaches since 46 people can be accommodated at night in those two-tier coaches, compared with 26 in the same amount of carriage space in 1st Class. As a result, many 1st Class coaches are being allowed to deteriorate. They are often shabby with hard, bench type seats covered in grimy, patched grey rexine.

Passengers who don't like travelling in air-conditioned isolation, or in the cramped conditions of 2nd Class, have only these neglected carriages to ride in. However, the situation may be improving as a number of these coaches have recently been rehabilitated and others are being rebuilt. This is not because of passenger demand (although this is acknowledged to exist) but because there are certain routes where 1st Class cannot be replaced by AC coaches for technical reasons, and also because insufficient AC coaches are being built each year to replace all the 1st Class rolling stock.

Unless it's a Chair Car, all 1st Class coaches have sleeper accommodation. A typical 1st Class carriage is split into five compartments with four berths in each, and three two-berth 'coupé' cabins. There are four fans in the four berth cabins and two in the coupés. The glass windows open upwards and there are metal screens which can be lowered at night while the window remains open to let in air. There are bars across the windows, as in 2nd Class.

There are window screens that can be raised on the aisle side of the cabin too, and a sliding door which can be double-locked by bolts from the inside to keep out intruders. There is a metal loop fitted on the aisle side of the door (at its base) that enables the door to be secured with a passenger's own padlock. Some doors have a name card holder on them, a relic of the style of the old days.

The upper berths in these cabins can be raised during the day and bolted flat against the compartment wall. Many passengers keep them lowered though which obscures what little light there is, reduces the space available and becomes an obstacle when getting up from the seat below. (Mind your head.)

There are two foot rests that flip down from the cabin wall to help the passenger get into the upper bunk. A reading light and a pocket for personal items are fixed to the wall just above the bunk, and there is a shelf over the window.

The main disadvantage of being assigned an upper berth, apart from the process of getting in and out, is that it is close to the fans, fine in hot weather but they are noisy, and to the ceiling lights. Although these aren't very bright they can be annoying if the passenger in the lower bunk doesn't switch them off. There is a blue night light over the door.

The lower berth is formed by unbolting the cushioned back rest and letting it drop forward to make a wider mattress than the seat of the bench. At the aisle side it has a ledge for personal belongings and a holder for glasses or bottles, to which suitcases can be chained. There are also coat hooks, ashtrays, a pocket attached to the wall above the

AIR-CONDITIONED SLEEPER

(2 tier) – Typical 46 berth layout

bunk and a reading light. There is a small table between the two lower berths, under the window.

The lower berth is easier to use but the occupant may feel obliged to wake early if the person in the upper bunk wants to sit on it, or to go to sleep late if the upper berth occupant stays up.

During the day the bench seats can accommodate three sitting passengers, which raises the total complement in the carriage to 39. The upper berth is 64 cm wide and 188 cm long, with the lower berth being 57 cm wide and 192 cm long.

The advantage of 1st Class travel, despite its recent deteriorations, is its spacious privacy. The cabins have enough room for four people to spend nights together in security and for six to travel companionably in the day. The coupés, while being perfect for a couple or loner who gets one for sole occupancy, are a bit depressing with only the cabin wall to face. 1st Class is as hot and dusty as 2nd Class, as the windows are always open, but it's not so dirty or noisy.

There are two toilets at each end of the carriage. At least one of these is western style. A marvel is that one of them will have a shower, such a boon on a long, hot journey. At one end of the coach is the attendant's seat, positioned so he has full view of the aisle. There is shelf space there too for meal service.

Many older carriages are still in use which is bad news for 2nd Class travellers since the seats are the old style wooden slats. But 1st Class passengers benefit from older coaches which have larger compartments than those built in the 1960s. They have wooden fittings, such as latches to keep the windows open, and a lime green interior instead of a grim grey. Toilets, too, are bigger with only one at each end but one is western style, and the other has a shower.

(5) AC Sleeper (2 tier) Class (AC2 or 2nd AC) (see plan)

This kind of accommodation is also known as 'AC II class 2 tier' and shares with II class (2nd Class) a dormitory style accommodation. Its air conditioning, cleanliness, facilities, fixtures and fittings have made it superior to 1st Class (and more expensive). It has become the most popular with Indian upper class travellers.

The coaches have 46 seats/berths. Entrance is by doors at either end into a lobby which is cooled by a ceiling fan. At one end there are two toilets, a wash basin, the control panel for the AC unit in a glass fronted cabinet, shelves for storing meal containers and flasks, and a jerry can of drinking water and a seat for the attendant. A shelf drops down to serve as the AC unit technician's bunk. At the other end of the carriage there are two more toilets, a wash basin, more electrical controls and a cupboard for the storage of bed linen, which also serves as the attendant's cabin.

Self-closing doors lead into the air conditioned dormitory part of the carriage which has an aisle running its length. On the outside of the aisle are single seats, facing each other in seven pairs. Bunks hang down above them from the ceiling, although they can be raised and bolted back to the cabin wall.

Each pair of seats converts, with the lowering forward of the chair back, into a lower bunk. At one end of the carriage there is only one lower bunk and no upper, making a total of 15 'outside' berths. One of the seats used to make this sole lower berth is actually an extra one. The worst berths are numbers 5 and 6 which are by the door and number 46 by the other door and under an ever-humming AC unit.

At the other side of the aisle are the 'inside berths' grouped in compartments of four each (two upper, two lower) with a curtain that can be pulled across to close the open space to the aisle. The upper bunks can be raised and bolted back flush to the wall to give greater space and light, but most passengers prefer to keep them down for day-time sleeping.

The lower berths are formed by letting down the cushioned back rest. The seats/berths are covered in a blue-grey rexine and are comfortable even on long journeys. A prominent sign says: 'Please pull up the backrest-cum-bed during 6 am to 9 pm to avoid inconvenience to sitting passengers.' Few people bother.

There is a shelf serving as a table, and two glass holders, below the windows. The windows have curtains; they are sealed and double-glazed and tinted, sometimes yellow, adding to the gloom within the carriage.

There is a strip light with push-buttons to switch it on or off by the window, and another strip light above the aisle, controlled by the passenger in the lower outside berth. Reading lights above each bunk are switched on automatically when the covering shade is raised. There is a fan above the aisle for each compartment, with a switch under the mirror on the inside wall.

Carriages have seven four-berth compartments with one having only three berths; two lower and one upper. Berths have different measurements. The outside lower one, converted out of two single seats, is 186 cm long and 53 cm wide. The berth above is 184 cm in length and 54 cm wide. Inside, the upper berth measures 184 cm long and 61 cm wide while the lower berth is shorter, at 173 cm long but wider at 65 cm.

Of the coach's four toilets, at least one is western style and one might be for ladies only. The 'Ladies' has side as well as full-face mirrors. Newer models of these carriages have fans in the toilets too, but there are no showers.

Carriages built since 1988 have several improvements over the original models. The end side seat, number 5, has a partition wall by it that protects its occupants from the ceaseless opening and shutting of the access door. Curtains have been added to the side bunks giving privacy and since each one is curtained off individually, the bunks adjoining the aisle are actually more private than those in the four berth compartments. Chains to which luggage can be padlocked have been fixed under the seats too.

These AC coaches have two attendants (one is the technician who looks after the AC unit) so they are usually well-maintained. Some passengers like the AC unit set at maximum, perhaps feeling that if they are not cool, they are not getting their money's worth. The usual temperature is around 72°C.

Attendants have different views on keeping the carriages clean. I've been in one carriage where the attendant was scrupulous in his job, crawling around on his hands and knees with a dustpan and brush and a damp cloth, and in another where rubbish was allowed to accumulate until passengers complained. There is a rubbish bin in the lobby at the end of the carriage, under the wash basin. The toilets are generally kept clean. Each AC carriage is issued an Opinions Book in which the attendant will try to get two entries every trip, preferably complimentary ones.

I've noticed in this class of coach that Indian passengers tend to spend the day lolling in their bunks in apparent boredom, whereas they seem livelier and more friendly in the 1st and 2nd Class carriages. I was curious to see several fellow passengers were very old men, with companions of equally advanced years. They turned out to be Freedom Fighters, pensioners who have been given an annual pass by the Government of India to ride free in 1st or AC 2nd Class with a spouse or companion.

There are no separate compartments for ladies in this class although women can request to be accommodated with other women. An appeal on board to whoever is in charge of berth allocation will usually be successful in achieving any necessary change. In theory, a woman travelling alone in this class is safer with 45 other passengers and two attendants than she would be alone in a 1st Class coupé.

Smoking is prohibited in the AC part of the coach: smokers congregate in the lobbies at either end.

The main appeal of this type of accommodation is the air conditioning. With the windows permanently closed, the dust and noise are kept out as well as the heat. However, you also miss much of the scenery since you can't see through the tinted windows clearly.

There is no spare space in the compartments and I personally find them claustrophobic and a bit dismal. However, if you can't stand the heat, this is an ideal way to travel. But if you want the windows open so you can see, feel, and smell, the India you are passing through, then a non AC coach is better.

(6) AC 1st Class (Sleeper)

Since it costs about double the price of a berth in AC 2nd Class (and about eight times the price of one in 2nd Class), you expect something splendid in AC 1st Class. I wasn't disappointed. The difference was apparent the moment I set foot in the carriage, with attendants eager to help and inordinately proud of their jobs serving in the best accommodation available to passengers on Indian railways.

The division of cabins and berths in this class differs according to the carriage and route. Where demand is small, berths are limited to ten; two cabins of four berths each, and one coupé.

The floor of each cabin is carpeted and the upholstery is a soothing brown. The upper bunks are bolted flush to the cabin wall during day time, with the lower berth serving as a comfortable rexine-covered seat for two. The seat converts into a berth at night by lowering the cushioned backrest down over it to serve as a mattress.

This mattress has been ingeniously designed with flaps down the length of its sides forming an envelope into which the bedding can be tucked. (This refinement, incidentally, is also to be found in the new generation of AC 2 tier coaches.) Freshly laundered bedding – and a hand towel – is included in the ticket price and the bed will be made up by the attendant.

Cabins have a wash basin under a small table top and a collection of switches for lights, fans and summoning the attendant. Bed tea (the early morning cuppa) is usually served at 0700 and other meals served to the cabin throughout the day. While the accommodation is vastly superior to other classes, the food is not; it's the same in every class. Service in AC 1st Class can be amateurish or lethargic, the same as in other classes, unless an 'old school' bearer is on duty or tips are in the offing.

The toilets (two at each end, one western, one eastern) aren't too clean, although some might have toilet paper tucked behind the water pipe (or available on request). In this class, both kinds of toilet have showers and fans. A sign in some loos says: 'To stop train, pull the chain.' It refers to the emergency cord, not the toilet flush.

Each cabin has a sliding door, which can be locked from the inside, with a curtain to hide it. The windows, also with curtains, are sealed shut because of the air conditioning which is kept at an unobtrusive level, there are fans as well. Cabins have a drop-down table; some coupés have a miniature washbasin. There are ashtrays and a rubbish bin, a pocket for papers, and holders for glasses which are provided. Cold water is available.

A narrow, shallow closet contains a ladder to be removed for reaching the upper bunk, and some coat hooks, but no coat hangers. There is a range of buttons for putting on or switching off the strip lighting and night lights, or for summoning the attendant.

The only disagreeable feature of this cosy accommodation is a sign which says: 'Drinking of alcoholic drinks prohibited' which tends to spur all but the devout to disobedience.

AC 1st Class is only available on some 60 trains, not all of them daily, and only on major routes (see Chapter 12). Despite the cost, it is popular. Fellow passengers, if they have acquired their tickets in advance, are likely to be men of stature: politicians, military officers, businessmen. Since upgrading from 2AC to 1AC is possible on the train, others not on the passenger list may turn up. For the less adventurous tourist, this is the best way to travel by train, especially if using an Indrail Pass which makes this top class a low cost bargain.

Double decker carriages

A novel feature in some trains operating to/from Bombay are the double decker carriages introduced in 1978 for 2nd Class travel. The Panchavati Express running daily between Manmad and Bombay VT, a five hour journey, has some of these.

By deft design, 144 to 148 people are accommodated in two decks of a single coach. The lower deck to which passengers descend by a few steps after entering by a door at the end of the carriage, holds 69 people. They sit on bench type seats, some of which are upholstered, with space for four on each. There are single seaters at the other side of the aisle.

The upper deck has seating in a 2 × 3 layout as well as singles, like thrones, and pairs, at the top of a tiny flight of stairs. When these carriages are empty, the clever use of space is impressive. When they are full, they are chaotic, hot and stuffy despite the fans. There are two toilets at both ends of the carriage.

Metre gauge accommodation

There are many combinations of berths and seats on MG trains which, like the Pink City Express, have had carriages custom-built for them. You will come across 2nd Class two tier sleeper coaches (non AC) with 16 upper berths and 64 seats and even three tier sleeper coaches with 48 berths and 64 seats. The MG Vaigai and Pallavan Expresses are all 2nd Class chair car but with one new AC chair car with 40 seats, and eight non-AC seats. In AC class the layout differs from that of BG trains. For instance, the Pandyan Express (see Chapter 11) has 1st Class AC cabins in a carriage which also has 2nd Class AC (two tier) berths in cabins, instead of in the usual BG dormitory layout.

Metre gauge trains are renowned for their leisurely pace. There is a story about a travelling ticket examiner on an MG passenger train who asked an old man with a beard for his ticket. The old man gave it to him.

'This is a child's ticket', said the TTE in surprise. 'You can't travel on that'.

'Believe me', the old man replied, 'when I started on this train journey, I *was* a child'.

Rolling stock

Many trains on Indian Railways are very long, sometimes longer than the platform, and consist of at least 20 carriages. A major express will be made up of one AC 1st Class carriage (sometimes combined with AC Chair accommodation) and an AC sleeper (2 tier) carriage next to it. This will be joined to the pantry car with a 1st Class carriage the other side. The remaining carriages will all be 2nd Class 3 tier sleepers with two unreserved passenger coaches, one at the front and one at the rear making up the rest of the train.

Individual carriages on long distance mail and express trains are manned by railway staff. They will close and lock the doors five minutes before a train is due to depart, leaving one door open on the platform side of each coach so they can check late-comers. Doors open inwards.

The worst long distance trains are those without a corridor. It's difficult to know in advance whether a train will be vestibuled or not. Even when they do have a linking corridor, the attendants seem to delight in locking the doors so people can't walk up and down.

Why should you need a vestibule? Precisely so you can walk the length of the train to stretch your legs and to meet new faces in different carriages. And if the train stops in the middle of nowhere for 20 minutes you can get out and walk its length and not worry about hurrying back to your compartment when the train moves off, since you can board it anywhere and walk back along the corridor at your leisure.

When getting off a train, do remember to face the engine so if the train moves suddenly, you'll be able to recover your balance. Of course, never get off a train when it is moving, and always make sure the tracks are clear if you are clambering down on to them.

Train numbers

Train numbers were changed in November 1989 to four digit numbers so that each train has its own number which the computerized reservation system can understand. The first digit indicates the zone that operates the train, unless that digit is '2' which indicates the train is one of the 70-odd Superfast ones where a surcharge is levied and the numbering is controlled by the Railway Board.

The second digit indicates the division where the carriages for the train are maintained. In the case of Superfast trains only, the second digit shows the zone that operates the train. The last two digits correspond to the last two digits of the train's previous number.

Thus, the 131/132 Madras-Jammu Tawi Express became 6031/6032 which shows it is a Southern Railway's (6) train based at Madras (0). The 125/126 Kerala Mangala Express became 2625/2626 because it is a Superfast train (2) operated by SR (6) with its last two digits 25/26 corresponding to its former number.

There are no more 900 series of Superfast trains. For instance, the 931/932 Secunderabad/Rajkot weekly express is now 2731/2732, meaning a Superfast train (2) operated by South Central Railway (7). The Rajdhani Expresses are now 2301/2302 Howrah–New Delhi and 2951/2952 Bombay Central–New Delhi. The Shatabdi Expresses, being new, have not changed their numbers: 2001/2002 New Delhi–Bhopal; 2003/2004 New Delhi–Lucknow and 2005/2006 New Delhi–Kalka.

The Key

First Digit

1 = Central Railway
2 = Superfast
3 = Eastern Railway
4 = Northern Railway
5 = Northeast & Northeast Frontier Railway

6 = Southern Railway
7 = South Central Railway
8 = South Eastern Railway
9 = Western Railway

Second Digit

Central Railway (1):
0 = Bombay
1 = Jhansi

2 = Bhopal
4 = Others

Superfast Trains (2):
In the case of these trains only, the second digit shows the railway zone (see first digit key above) that operates the train.

Eastern Railway (3):
0 = Howrah
1 = Sealdah
2 = Danapur

3 = Dhanabad
4 = Malda

Northern Railway (4):
0 = Delhi
1 = Allahabad
2 = Lucknow
3 = Moradabad
4 = Others

5 = Ambala
6 = Firozpur
7 = Bikaner
8 = Jodhpur

Northeast & Northeast Frontier (5):
0 = Lucknow (BG)
1 = Varanasi (BG)
2 = Samastipur (BG)
3 = Lucknow (MG)
4 = Varanasi (MG)
5 = Samastipur (MG)

6 = Lumding (BG)
7 = Katihar and Alipurduar (MG)
8 = Lumding (MG)
9 = Tinsukia (MG)

Southern Railway (6):

0 = Madras (BG)   4 = Not allocated
1 = Madras (MG)   5 = Bangalore
2 = Mysore (MG)   6 = Palghat
3 = Trivandrum   7 = Others

Southern Central Railway (7):

0 = Secunderabad   5 = Hyderabad (MG)
1 = Others   6 = Not allocated
2 = Vijayawada   7 = Guntakal (MG)
3 = Hubli (BG)   8 = Hubli (MG)
4 = Guntakal (BG)

South Eastern Railway (8):

0 = Kharagpur   4 = Khurda Road
1 = Chakradharpur   5 = Waltair
2 = Bilaspur   6 = Adra
3 = Others

Western Railway (9):

0 = Bombay Central   5 = Others
1 = Vadodara   6 = Ajmer
2 = Bhavnagar (BG)   7 = Jaipur
3 = Ratlam   8 = Bhavnagar (MG)
4 = Kota   9 = Rajkot

UP or DOWN Trains

Railway staff refer to a train as being an UP or DOWN one, a familiarization too complicated to fathom as it seems derived from different reasons in different zones. A helpful assistant station master at Karjat tried to enlighten me by saying that, in Central Railway, a DOWN train (one with an odd number) has departed from Bombay; UP trains (those with even numbers) are bound for Bombay. A commercial inspector based at Calicut agreed that even numbers are usually UP trains, and odd numbers are DOWN. Trains, he said, heading to and terminating at divisional or the zonal HQ are even numbered (ie: UP) unless they are only touching their HQ and terminating at Delhi in which case they are odd numbered (ie: DOWN). In Calcutta I was told it depends on the route of the train compared with the flow of the Ganges.

Chapter 5

On the Move

There's an air of excitement on the platform as the train's departure time draws close. You've found your name on the passenger list, together with the names of those in the compartment with you so you already know your fellow passengers' names, ages, sex and destination. People are pushing past you to get on as you show your coupon to the conductor and he tells you to board.

Your fellow passengers are settling in, staking out their claims to territory with too much luggage. A bell clangs but there is no slamming of carriage doors, no blowing of whistles and no shout of 'All aboard!' as in the States. The train simply draws out of the station while people stroll alongside and, with studied nonchalance, clamber on one after the other through the still-open doors.

You claim your own seat, pleased to be on the move. Since you have a long journey ahead in the company of strangers, what happens next will govern your enjoyment of the trip. You can start up a conversation and make friends, allies, quickly, or be anti-social and lonely for the whole of the journey. Of course, it depends on your personality but if you are travelling alone you'll need an ally, someone you feel you can trust to watch your luggage when you go to the bathroom. You can't isolate yourself completely on a train so if that's your style, train travel isn't for you.

I get a thrill out of the start of every train journey in India. It's not just the excitement of moving on to a new place, there's the anticipation of what's going to happen on the journey; the pleasure at the new acquaintances I'm going to make; the dissolving of city skyline into lush, rural landscape beyond the windows; and the heightened emotions of everyone on board. Indians love to travel by train; they are used to it and prepare properly so it becomes a picnic on wheels. I get a charge out of being part of it; you will too.

With Indian Railways, like everything else, you get what you pay for. In India, though, there is a bonus. If you choose the unreserved carriage on the slowest passenger train, you can be sure of an unpleasant overnight ride. In retrospect, it may provide you with amusing anecdotes at the expense of your Indian fellow travellers. But you're not seeing any more of the 'real India' than if you reserved a berth in affordable 1st Class on a superfast express with meals served at your seat and fellow passengers who are lively, intelligent company. That's the bonus.

Part of the excitement of train travel is meeting new people who will pass on tips. However, some will regale you with their horror stories, seldom realizing that the fault could be theirs, or that of their guide books.

According to an article in an Indian journal, 'Travel guides dish out advice: when in India, think cheap, dress cheap, travel cheap, eat cheap and count on local hospitality and kindness of strangers to get you through.' The article urges foreign rail travellers to 'try to balance their experiences of cheap travel, and do themselves a favour, by travelling in a more comfortable class.'

For a foreigner, India is cheap but that doesn't mean you have to choose the cheapest and miss the best. Do the opposite. If you can't afford 1st Class in your home country, give it a try in India. You'll meet a cross section of the 100 million Indians who travel in upper class from time to time. Never stayed in a 5 star hotel? Now's the chance, since some of the world's best are in India.

Signals

The thrill begins with seven sharp rings struck on the warning bell (or sonorous piece of pipe) hanging outside the station master's office. That means Only Five Minutes Before The Train Leaves. At Bombay Central, though, seven bells indicates Ten Minutes To Wait. Two strokes on the bell means Departure Time.

The guard will wave a green flag, or a green light at night, and the journey begins.

When the train is passing through a station you will see a railway man on the platform holding out a green flag horizontally (at night he waves a green light). This signal tells the driver and guard that the train is 'proceeding in a safe and proper manner.' If the watcher notices anything unusual about the train, he will hold out a red flag so the driver or guard know to stop it immediately.

If you need to stop the train in an emergency there is a communication cord. It is activated by pulling down a handle very much like the end of an old fashioned toilet chain and seems to be a relic of the Raj. It is placed close to where a standing passenger is likely to grab if the train jolted and he lost his balance. Be careful, especially in the toilet where it is tempting to pull the cord to flush the loo. There is a penalty of Rs 1,000 and/or imprisonment for improper use.

Train end

LV displayed at the end of a train means 'Last Vehicle' (at night there is a red light). This indicates to those monitoring the train's progress that the entire train has passed them. If the last carriage does not have

LV or a red light, then the train watcher will know that the rear section of the train has become detached, so he will flash a signal to the driver. On the other hand the sign, or the watcher, might have dropped off.

Passenger rules

Compartments contain many notices advising passengers how to behave, such as 'Switch off lights and fans when you don't need them,' and 'Discourage beggars,' and 'Smoke only if other passengers don't object.'

There is a rule about alcohol on trains. The Western Railway timetable says 'No passengers should consume alcoholic drinks in II AC Sleeper, II Class and AC Chair Car Coaches or be in a state of intoxication in any railway carriage.' The inference is that in 1st Class carriages, drinking is OK. But I've seen signs in 1st Class that state alcohol is prohibited there too. In practice, if it is done discreetly and without causing offence to other passengers, alcohol is consumed and even sold to passengers by trackside vendors, especially on the line to Goa.

Central Railway has a rule saying 'Case of transistor radios in an air conditioned chair car is not allowed except with an earphone'.

Train staff

Some expresses are under the command of a Train Superintendent (TS) who travels from the originating station to its destination. He is the train's manager and will take a keen interest in foreign travellers requiring help. His office is likely to be a requisitioned Ladies Only cabin in the 2nd Class carriage near the pantry car.

A conductor travels in the 1st Class coach and joins the train only for the few hours it is in his railway zone, not for the entire journey. At wayside stations he helps joining passengers in all classes with their accommodation. He carries a reservation list as well as a complaints book.

He ensures that passengers are evenly distributed and prevents over-crowding. He has been instructed to 'exercise tact and firmness in dealing with passengers occupying more than their fair share of space in I and II class compartments either for themselves or for their luggage.'

A conductor's duties also include checking on the train's cleanliness, waking passengers who have to leave the train during a night halt, and taking orders from upperclass passengers for meals where these have to be ordered in advance. Conductors usually wear black jackets with a white shirt and a tie, and often with white trousers too. They are supposed to have a name badge.

Corridor Coach Attendants are less smart although they do have a khaki uniform of shirt and trousers, and name badge. They act as support for the conductor in 1st Class and have a passenger list and can help with berth location and check tickets if the conductor or TTE aren't available. They are supposed to 'keep a good lookout on the corridor of the coach from the attendant's seat, particularly during night time' and to see that everything is in order. Whereas the conductor will have a seat in a compartment, the attendant uses the tip up seat in the corridor of the 1st Class coach.

There will be several travelling ticket examiners (TTEs) on a train in 2nd Class who join at different stations for a few hours. As well as the obvious duties of checking passengers' tickets and assigning vacant berths, they also take orders for meals, see the carriage is kept clean, and 'look after generally the comfort and convenience of passengers'. They are supposed to see that upper berths are folded up and locked during the day.

TTEs usually wear uniforms of dark jacket and tie, and will sit in the coach they are in charge of. Travelling ticket inspectors in plain clothes will also be encountered occasionally. Since they are looking for fare dodgers, they are unlikely to be as affable as the TTEs or conductor.

The *Indian Bradshaw* contains hints for travellers, one of which says: 'Civility on the part of railway travellers to the railway staff who have frequently unpleasant duties to perform will, as a rule, command civility in return. Discourteous conduct on the part of railway servants should be reported to the authorities'.

Other train people you will meet are the pantry car staff. Bearers will come through the corridors with meals, snacks and drinks for sale. They are usually dressed in a drab grey uniform and tend to look scruffy. Since they have to live on the train in cramped conditions while it travels to its destination and back, this is not surprising.

The pantry car is under the control of a catering supervisor who has a white uniform but he sometimes wears his own clothes because of the difficulty in keeping the uniform clean.

The effectiveness of train staff differs by railway zones. Some trains do not seem to have enough TTEs to cope. In the north especially, 1st Class can become just as crowded as 2nd Class with ticketless interlopers and bogus free-pass holders. There are no restrictions on the beggars, pedlars and shoe-shine boys who invade the train and push their way through a carriage seeking money.

Loo lore

Perhaps what most puts potential passengers off train travel in India are tales about the toilets. I've got good news: they are not as bad as the anecdotes of travel writers and horror stories of tourists pretend them to be.

There are usually four toilets to each coach, a far better ratio of loo per passenger than on a jumbo jet. Some coaches have Ladies Only toilets, and there is no graffiti. At least one of the toilets in the upperclass coaches, and many in 2nd Class, will be western style. This means a flushable commode. Indian style is an aluminium trough with foot stands and a hole over which one squats.

For hygienic reasons, the Indian style lavatory is preferable to the western one. Often the western one won't have a seat and when it does you'll hardly want to put your bottom on it. At least the Indian version does not demand bodily contact. You will have to learn how to hang on while the train, as well as you, are in motion. There are strategically placed bars and handles for that purpose.

I am not advocating that, as a westerner, you abandon your personal toilet training and do it all Indian style. Carry your own toilet paper. (Contrary to popular belief, this can be bought in India.) There is a tap at knee level for personal hygiene and a lever to flush the trough.

If you are not sure how to use an Indian toilet, glance out of the train window as it goes through a town in the early morning and you will see people squatting with their backs to the tracks in the recommended position.

You will probably find train loos pleasanter to use than station ones. An article in *The Guardian* by Jugs Suraiya recalled the days when trains had no toilets and a passenger wrote in the complaints book: 'Beloved Sir, I am arrive by passenger train and my belly is too much swelling with jack fruit. I am therefore went to privy. Just as I am doing the nuisance that guard making whistle blow for train to go off and I am running with *lota* in one hand and *dhoti* in next when I am fall over and display all my shockings.'

You need your own soap for handwashing and the basin will have cold water from a self-closing tap. There is a hand towel provided in every bed roll but this is small. If you are going to take a shower, you will need your own, larger towel. There are no showers in 2nd or 2nd AC Class so if the train has a vestibule you'll have to use the one in 1st Class.

In the toilet, be careful where you hang your clothes since the hooks are so positioned that water from the shower will soak whatever is hung on them. Take a plastic bag and bundle your clothes and valuables in it so they can be hung safely from the handle that flushes the latrine. The water isn't heated and comes from a rose set into the ceiling.

Keeping clean

You'll be amazed at how dirty you get on a train, especially if you travel in a carriage where the windows are open. You can wash, and shower, in the toilets, but doing your laundry is not practical because of the drying process. That has to be done during overnight stops. Clothes dry quickly in India. Laundry is cheap and you can usually find someone at the railway retiring rooms who will arrange to have your clothes washed, pressed and returned before you move on.

When a train stops for a long period, you could even have a shower on the platform. Station waiting rooms have showers attached to them and there are also separate shower cubicles on many platforms, for which no charge is made. Take with you your own soap, and towel, and valuables in a plastic bag to place where you can keep your eye on them.

The cleanliness of the carriages themselves is fairly good although it depends on the attitude of passengers. The AC Sleeper Class coaches are usually the cleanest while 1st Class is somewhat shabby with compartment walls that are in need of a good scrub since repainting seems unlikely.

Freelance cleaners will hop on board some trains and make desultory sweeps with a broom of twigs and then pass around for tips. On the Tinsukia Mail from Patna to Malda Town there was a railway cleaner who swept out the carriage twice and then produced a book for passengers' comments, instead of asking for a tip. Since most people when confronted like that are unlikely to put down anything critical the cleaner was pretty safe. However, someone had the courage to write 'foul'.

SLEEPING

Many foreign travellers sleep in their clothes, seeing this as the best way of keeping all their possessions intact as well as avoiding the confusion and embarrassment of undressing in a crowded compartment.

Indians sleep with their briefcases under their heads, using them as a pillow. They might change into a cotton pyjama-style suit on the train, or wear a *lungi*. On one occasion when I shared a compartment with an Indian lady (and two men, all strangers to each other) I noticed she dived under her blanket every night still swaddled in her sari.

In the 2nd Class 3 tier coaches, you have little option but to sleep in your clothes with your valuables close to your skin. This is where your own blanket will come in useful. One regular rail traveller from England told me that he buys a new blanket every time he arrives in India. He uses it as a seat cover during the day since he wears shorts and the rexine gets uncomfortable, and to cover himself at night. He takes the blanket back to England after each trip as a colourful souvenir.

Air pillows with a choice of attractive woven pillow cases can be bought at major stations. Without air they do not take up much luggage space and they can be blown up very easily. They are useful as cushions for padding hard seats during day time travel as well as being better than a briefcase for resting one's head on at night.

When travelling in areas where nights are cold, it may be warmer in the AC carriages than in 1st Class. This is because the temperature in AC is controlled, usually around 72 degrees, and there are none of the draughts which can chill you to the bone overnight in 1st Class during cold spells.

Another irritant to sweet dreaming will be fellow passengers. On a recent trip I began to believe the same man was at the other end of the carriage on every train I rode. He always spoke at the top of his voice far into the night, and woke me in the morning with his raucous hawking. You'll probably encounter him too, so don't forget the ear plugs.

An Englishman told me he prefers to share a bay of four berths in the 2nd AC compartment with women passengers. 'They don't snore, they don't play music, they talk less and are less likely to be rogues.'

Bed rolls

Travel bags, more popularly known as Bed Rolls, can be hired for overnight journeys in AC 2nd Class and in 1st Class if there are any spare. They are also available on some trains in 2nd Class 3 tier coaches. In AC 1st Class and on the Rajdhani Expresses they are provided free.

Bed rolls have to be ordered in advance, when making the reservation is the best time, and they cost Rs 5. For this you get a large canvas bag containing two bedsheets, one blanket, one pillow with pillow case, and one hand towel. The linen is crisply laundered and the blanket clean.

From October to March bed rolls hired from Northern Railway have an extra blanket, and cost Rs 6. The charge is per night and you have to pay double if you keep the bed roll for a second night. Get a receipt listing the contents which will be checked by the attendant when he collects the bed roll the next day. There is no deposit payable but there is a charge for anything missing.

If you forget to order one when you make your reservation, apply at the station at least three hours before the train's departure. Some zonal timetables show where bed rolls are available and there are about 100 trains which provide this facility.

Christine and Mike Wadsworth of Cumbria, UK, have become old hands at the bed roll game. They find it works only when you join the train at its starting station, not if you board during the journey, despite requesting bed rolls in advance. 'We travelled on the 6028 Mangalore–Madras from Cannanore, an excellent journey but no bed rolls despite requesting them from the SS that morning who promised to relay the request,' they wrote in 1990. In 1991, they wrote: 'Yet again there were no bed rolls in a sleeper, this time on 6202 Vasco–Bangalore from Margao.'

Both trains are run by Southern Railway whose timetable says: 'Passengers travelling in 1st Class will be supplied with bed rolls . . . if requisition is placed two hours in advance before the scheduled departure of the train at the station from where reservation is obtained.'

एक बिस्तर नं........................प्राप्त हुआ, जिसमें निम्नलिखित वस्तुएं हैं :—

Received One Bedding Set No..................
Consisting of

1. दो चादर/Two Bed Sheets.

2. एक तकीये का गिलाफ़/One Pillow cover

3. एक कंबल/One Blanket

4. एक गद्देदार तकिया/One Foam Pillow

5. एक तौलिया/One Towel

6. केनवस/रेक्ज़ीन बैग में पैक किया हुआ ।
 मैं बीच के कोई स्टेशन पर यात्रा विराम नहीं करूंगा ।
      (कुल सात वस्तुएँ)

Packed in Convas/Rexine bag.
   (Total Seven Articles.)

 I do not intend to break Journey at any
Station en route.

दिनांक/Date   यात्री के हस्ताक्षर पत सहित ।
     Signature of Passenger with Address.

Berth control

If you have a lower berth in either 1st Class or AC Sleeper Class, you will have to fold down the back rest over the bench seat to form the bunk's mattress. By laying your trousers and flat valuables on the seat before lowering the backrest mattress on top of it, you can keep them safe during the night, and your trousers get pressed too.

In full compartments you will have to develop an economy of movement in making up your bunk without disturbing other passengers. The upper bunk is the most difficult. In hot weather, the blanket can be used to sleep on. However, the temperature of the AC coaches is usually so cold you'll need the blanket on top of you instead of underneath.

Is it possible to get a good night's sleep on a train? When you think of the jolting, the constant stopping and starting of the train, the sudden shrieks of engines passing in the night, the insistent shouting of platform vendors when the train halts, the disturbance caused by passengers getting in and out during the night, and the worry about the safety of your belongings, it seems unlikely. Ear plugs and an eye mask will help. Since there are less people in AC Sleeper or 1st Class you stand a better chance of sleeping in them than in 2nd Class. This is another argument in favour of not travelling the cheapest way but going for the best value.

Incredibly, after a day sitting on a train doing nothing very much, you will still feel tired at night. After a couple of night's practice, you'll be able to fall asleep easily, shutting out the noise and ceasing to worry about your belongings. I got so accustomed to sleeping on moving trains that occasional nights in a retiring room bed were sleepless ones because it was stationary.

Rob Dobson comments that 'Indians love to travel *en famille* so they may request that you change your berth with another member of their party; the attendant may also make this request to accommodate travellers.' He advises you to check the alternative berth before agreeing to move. You do have the right to refuse, especially if you've requested a lower berth and they are trying to shunt you off to an upper one.

When this happened to me and I declined to budge, the atmosphere in the cabin was frostier than the AC, but at least I was spared the round of interrogation about my private life that is customary with fellow Indian rail passengers upon first acquaintance.

SECURITY

The possible theft of belongings is a worry to foreign travellers but it need not occur if you take sensible precautions. Luggage in compartments should be padlocked to the chain under the lower berth or to a fixed fitting so it can't be removed if you leave it for a few minutes. On platforms, never leave bags unattended. Carry valuables, whether money or documents, on your person, and sleep with them too.

If you're in a compartment with a door to the corridor, lock it on the inside at night but check there's no one already in the cabin hiding under the seat who'll wait until you're asleep and then disappear with your unchained luggage. The four external carriage doors can be fastened and double locked from the inside to prevent unauthorized entry. The doors linking carriages on vestibuled trains are also locked at night.

A German traveller told me he felt safer on a train at night with his luggage locked and secured under his seat than he did in a cheap hotel room, having lost a camera from one hotel room when he was asleep.

Don't leave anything of value by open windows. Busy stations have gangs of urchins who cluster around trains as soon as they arrive. Many of them carry long sticks with hooks on the end with which they fish out discarded plastic cups from under the train. They could also catch your purse or bag if you're careless.

You will see notices on stations warning people not to accept food or drink from strangers. There are stories of passengers being given drugged food or drink and then robbed. It is hard to refuse an invitation to share a picnic lunch with a friendly Indian fellow traveller without causing offence. But if you are suspicious then plead an upset stomach.

Fellow travellers are just as likely to be thieves as urchins are, especially in the 3 tier carriages where you are sharing sleeping accommodation with 71 strangers. There is no need to become neurotic about losing things; if you do, your attitude could attract the very calamity you are anxious to avoid. Good sense will save you from most awkward situations.

Delia Rothnie, writing in *The Independent*, reported: 'Barely five minutes into the journey, we fell victim to an immaculate conman. We had booked a 1st Class sleeper on the train from Bombay Central to the little station of Sawai Madhopur. There were the trains, but which was the right platform? Five queries elicited five different answers from porters and bystanders. At last a smart chap in white shirt and trousers bustled over.

'"You are wanting your carriage?" Indeed we were.

'"Please to be following me this way." In minutes he had shown us to a berth.

'"And you will be requiring lunch and dinner also?" inquired our saviour. Yes, most certainly.

'"Please give me money for purchase of coupons. I will bring menu." So we handed over Rs200 (then about £10) and off he went never to be seen again!

'When our fellow passengers heard the tale, they chortled. "You are in India, my dear sir and madam," they expostulated. "Never must you give away your money without first having seen your purchase!"'

If you are robbed while on a train, contact the conductor or guard immediately you discover it. They have forms for theft reports so it is not necessary for a passenger to leave the train to lodge the report at a police station.

Some trains have police travelling on them, especially when they are going through areas notorious for *dacoity* (banditry) or demonstrations. The responsibility of providing security is undertaken by two agencies, the Government Railway Police (GRP) and the Railway Protection Force (RPF). The GRP works under the various State Governments and looks after the security of passengers and their belongings. There are about 32,000 railway police and a further 64,000 in the RPF, which concentrates on the protection of railway property.

An Indian newspaper carried an article in late 1988 about ticket collectors with canes trying to drive away young beggars who have made the railway stations their homes. Periodically these urchins are rounded up and despatched by lorry to an unknown destination.

'But lo', said the newspaper, 'the brats make a stormy entry into the station like homing pigeons before even the lorry comes back'.

Kids are attracted to the station because of the new packaging used by railway caterers. The discarded silver foil, casseroles and plastic cups can fetch their finders as much as Rs 40 a day. Consequently passengers are urged to crush their cups before disposing of them to prevent them being used again.

MEALS ON WHEELS

The use of foil casseroles for different dishes instead of serving meals on the traditional tray-dish, *thali*, is spreading throughout the railways and enhances the hygienic serving of food. The method of preparation, too, has undergone changes in recent years. Only in occasional circumstances are entire meals prepared on a train, even when there is a pantry car.

Orders for meals are taken from passengers and a message is sent to the base kitchen scheduled to supply them. Meals are cooked in base kitchens on demand, and according to strict standards, under the supervision of a catering inspector.

Many kitchens have been modernized with machines to churn dough and other innovations to make them capable of cooking the thousands of meals required daily. Major base kitchens are equipped with mobile heated cabinets in which the foil dishes are kept hot for delivery to a train's pantry car. If there is no pantry car, the meals are brought to each individual carriage and distributed to those who ordered them.

A long haul express of 21 carriages would probably carry about 1,100 people. At least a third of them will want meals every meal time. Others make do with food brought from their own homes, which is what many Indians prefer. They will also buy from vendors on the platform.

There is a variety of snacks on offer at the major stations and omelettes can be cooked in seconds over a kerosene stove on a trolley outside the train window. The platform vendors are either railway catering department employees or they work for a licensee. They are subject to inspection and food handlers have a regular medical check up.

Platform vendors sell on commission. In trains with a catering staff many of them are paid on a commission basis too, which is why there are frequent offers of refreshments by bearers passing up and down the aisle of every carriage. On trains without a pantry car, or a vestibule,

Bearer serving casserole meals in a moving train.

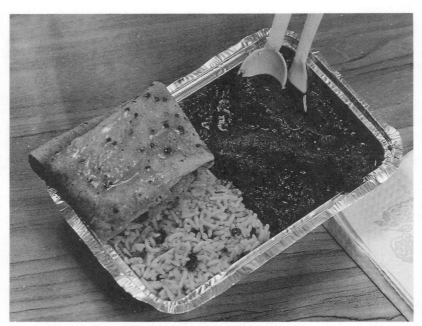

A typical non-veg meal: chicken curry, rice and chapati.

unlicensed hawkers will board the carriage to ride it to the next stop selling snacks, or tea from a huge kettle.

Mike Wadsworth recalls how the conductor on the Nandi Express from Bangalore to Mysore used the bottom of the passenger list computer printout to note his tiffin order. 'He then tore it off, rolled it into a ball and threw it out when passing through a station. Obviously it was picked up and telegraphed ahead as usual, because when we next stopped there was a man waiting with the meals, flasks and glasses.'

Special meals

If you are keen on food, you could meet the catering supervisor of the train and discuss special requirements with him, and be agreeably surprised. After a surfeit of standard base kitchen fare, I fancied chicken curry on one long journey. It was prepared in the pantry car and was delicious. Then it occurred to me to ask how they had managed to store the chicken since there was no freezer.

'We didn't,' said the supervisor. 'When we stopped at a station this morning, I bought a live chicken and we killed it especially. '

Bearer service

Where meals are put on the train from base kitchens, they will be served late if the train is late at the scheduled pick up station. On some journeys, the train stops long enough for bearers from the station restaurant to bring meals to passengers' seats. A typical vegetarian lunch served in that manner, as a *thali* meal, would be helpings of four vegetable curries (such as cabbage, potato, ochra and dhal) chapati and rice with curd in a chrome dish. A spoon could be provided on request if you haven't got your own cutlery, or you can use your fingers like Indians do.

The bearers who serve on trains come in all shapes and sizes. One I encountered was especially proud of the hygienic packing of the food he served me, pointing out the advantages of the foil casseroles for foreigners with sensitive stomachs. Having laid out the dishes on a table made up of my briefcase across my knees, he dug deep in his pocket and produced a plastic spoon. With a flourish, he polished it on the collar of his grubby uniform jacket before handing it to me.

His concern to give good service was impressive but it did make me wonder what sort of training he received.

'On-the-job training.' I was told by a top railway official. 'The bearer may not be sophisticated but he does know how to serve on a moving train'.

A superfast express with a pantry car could have 20 bearers/vendors on board with two cooks, two kitchen helpers/cleaners, a supervisor and an inspector. Breakfast and snacks are cooked in the pantry over charcoal or gas stoves. If possible, pick a train with a pantry car (some are listed in Chapter 12) to get food at meal times.

Pantry car panorama

Trains to avoid are those with a pantry car but no vestibule. The bearers have to wait for the train to stop, at a signal or station, and then run down the outside to serve. Consequently meals arrive less than fresh and the service is unreliable since it depends on the train stopping and on bearers who have to work under impossible conditions.

Some trains which have a railway-staffed pantry car can also have a contractor service. This explains why nondescript vendors appear on trains alongside railway uniformed bearers offering coffee, soft drinks and snacks.

On a train with a pantry car the day starts with morning tea brought to the compartment about 0630 hours, as long as you've ordered it the night before. If, like me, you find the tea too strong when a bag has stewed in a flask of hot water for a long time, request the flask of hot water and the tea bag to be served separately and make the tea to your own strength. Indians prefer tea strong and milky and very sweet.

Breakfast is served about 0800 to order. On the Jhelum Express to Pune I was even asked if I wanted my eggs single or double fried. They were served in a casserole with tomato ketchup in a small polythene envelope, buttered toast and chips. Two hours later, cups of tomato soup were on offer while women with sacks of oranges sold them, one by one, to passengers.

Tariff

The price of meals served on trains is not the same in all railway zones, although the difference is slight. The menus are similar, with a choice: either vegetarian or non-vegetarian. In the south there are the special breakfasts which are a popular part of South Indian cuisine, such as Iddli and Vadai and Masala Dosal.

Typical meals and prices as at January 1, 1992

(Rates are inclusive of taxes)

Breakfast (Vegetarian)		Breakfast (Non-Vegetarian)	
2 potato chops	100gms	1 Omelette	2 eggs
Tomato ketchup	20gms	Tomato ketchup	20gms
2 Bread/Butter slices		2 Bread/Butter slices	
Potato rounders	25gms	Potato rounders	25gms
Price: Rs8.00		Price: Rs9.00	

Lunch/Dinner (Veg)

Rice	200gms
Vegetables	100gms
Dal	175gms
Roti/Chapati/Paratha	100gms
Curd	90gms
Salad	20gms
Price: Rs12.00	

Lunch/Dinner (Non-Veg)

Rice	200gms
Roti/Chapati/Paratha	100gms
Egg curry (2 eggs; with 125gms gravy	215gms
Salad	20gms
Price: Rs15.00	

Special Meal (Veg)

Mixed veg pullao	150gms
2 stuffed parathas/ 2 Roomali roti	100gms
Dal/Rajmah	100gms
Muter panner/vegetable	150–165gms
Malal kofta with 90gms gravy	75gms
Pickle	5gms
Price: Rs12.00	

Special Meal (Non-Veg)

Rice	200gms
2 Roomali roti/chapati paratha	100gms
Chicken curry	225gms
Salad	20gms
Price: Rs25.00	

Beverages

Tea in pot (285ml)	Rs3.00
Tea in cup (150ml)	Rs1.50
Instant coffee in pot (285ml)	Rs4.00
Coffee in cup (150 ml)	Rs3.00

Service times

Meals are normally served on trains and in refreshment rooms and restaurants on stations during the following times:

Morning Tea	0600 to 0800
Breakfast	0800 to 1000
Lunch	1200 to 1430
Afternoon Tea	1500 to 1730
Dinner	1800 to 2100

As well as the normal beverages available on board, fruit juices are sold in cartons, the most popular being mango which costs about Rs 5 as well as soft drinks, fizzy sweet ones, and sometimes bottled mineral water.

Generally, train food is perfectly safe for foreign stomachs, so do not be nervous about eating it. The problem is lack of variety, especially on a long journey when curried eggs for every meal can become boring. Meals can be brightened by fruit and other regional delicacies sold at wayside stations. If you do suffer from problems caused by food (or drink) while on a train, at least you are close to a toilet and being taken ill on a train will result in speedy attention.

OTHER SERVICES AND FACILITIES
Medical aid
There is a first-aid box on every passenger-carrying train and guards have some training in first-aid. If you're in need of assistance, ask the coach attendant or TTE to summon help. While it is not obligatory on the part of the railways to provide medical aid to passengers, it is invariably rendered. A simple scheme has been introduced to help staff find out if there is a doctor on board. On the reservation requisition form doctors are asked to indicate if they could be of help in an emergency. An asterisk is then marked against the doctor's name on the passenger list so train staff can find who and where the doctor is whenever necessary.

In an emergency train staff can arrange for a doctor to meet the train at its next stop. The doctor will supply medication or arrange for the patient to leave the train. The Northeast Frontier Railway has published a list of the charges a doctor is entitled to recover from a passenger:

Consultation fee for the doctor	Rs20.00
Dose of mixture and tablet	.50p
Dose of higher antibiotics	Rs 1.00
Sterile dressing of wound	Rs 1.00
Injection, including price of common drug	Rs 4.00

In the guardsvan for emergencies will be a box containing a telephone which can be plugged into wayside posts in the event of an emergency stop so that master control can be informed. There is also a high-power battery for energizing lights, and a couple of stretchers.

Station facilities
Most stations have upper class and ladies waiting rooms. These are usually kept clean and have a zealous attendant at the door who will only allow entry to authorized ticket, or Indrail Pass, holders. The rooms have fans and most have attached bathrooms, often with showers, and luggage racks to which you could padlock your suitcase. The waiting area for other passengers is sometimes a spacious hall or a room with an enormous table (used as a bed at night).

Facilities vary according to a station's status. Main stations have closed circuit TV (CCTV) with train announcements transmitted live in colour from a studio actually on the station. CCTV is very popular with waiting passengers, but adds to station noise when sets are at full volume. Another feature of big stations are the juice bars selling canned and bottled apple juice from Kashmir. Some pasengers warn that if the juice is made with apple concentrate, beware of the water it is made with.

Some stations have wheelchairs available for disabled passengers, and also self-help luggage trolleys.

The Railway Board has defined the basic amenities which should be at every Regular and Flag station as: 'adequate seating arrangements; a drinking water supply, minimum of two hand-pumps at wayside station; sanitized latrine with water arrangements nearby for hand washing purposes; electric light; proper booking facilities; shady trees'.

At Halt Stations: 'rail level platform of suitable length; a small waiting shed which will serve as a booking office; electric lighting where trains stop at night; shady trees'.

The following facilities are being provided, where justified as a priority: 'waiting halls; pucka platform surface for whole or part length; platform covers for adequate length; raising of platform from rail level to medium level/high level; coolers where piped water is available'.

A second priority programme is for stations to have: 'retiring rooms as required; upper class waiting rooms; bathrooms as per yardstick; enquiry office; refreshment rooms'.

As well as these improvements, some stations in each railway zone have been designated as Model Stations, which means they are being rebuilt to cope with rail users demands in the 1990s. As well as improved passenger comforts, the booking facilities are being upgraded to match the sophistication of the computer age.

Station nameboards are located facing the end of the platform, perpendicular to the track so they can be read with ease from passing trains. As well as the station's name, they show the station's height above sea level.

Small stations, halts, are let out to contractors who can earn as much as Rs1,000 a month on commission from ticket sales and for this they must maintain the station and booking office.

Luggage

Main stations have 'cloakrooms' which are not toilets but where passengers may leave luggage for up to a month. The charge starts at Rs 1 or more per 24 hours for the first two days, then rises in day-stages according to the total time of deposit. There are also safe deposit lockers at some stations. A typical locker, such as those at Bombay Central station, is 90 cm wide, 52 cm in height and 42 cm deep; big enough to take a small suitcase. An advance payment of Rs 3 or more has to be made and the cost begins at Rs 5 per 24 hours for the first two days, rising each subsequent day.

There are regulations about the weight of luggage that may be carried into a train's compartment, but since the 2nd Class free allowance is 35 kg and the 1st and AC Class is 50 kg (it's 20 and 30 kg in an aircraft) this won't affect many foreign tourists.

From Western Railway comes the following information: 'In the case of air-conditioned First Class passengers with tiffin baskets including small ice boxes, small handbags or attache cases (not suit cases), walking sticks and umbrellas, are allowed free and will not, therefore, be weighed. In the case of Second Class passengers walking sticks, umbrellas and such articles of food as may be required on the journey are allowed free and will not, therefore, be weighed'.

Excess luggage should be booked and an excess fee paid. The luggage of upper class passengers exceeding $100 \times 60 \times 25$ cm should be carried in the brake van, not in the compartment. The maximum size allowed in AC Chair Car is $63 \times 37 \times 20$ cm. On the Pink City Express between Jaipur and Delhi, passengers are prohibited from carrying heavy luggage in the compartments. Maximum permitted size is $62 \times 37 \times 20$ cm.

Regular train travellers are emphatic that the least amount of luggage you carry, the better off you'll be. One told me, 'the lack of luggage helps you to conserve energy, then you won't feel a need to drink so much water'. Another believes that his small, tatty bag indicates that he has nothing worth stealing.

Porters

Luggage you can carry yourself means you won't need a 'coolie', as porters are called.

Porters are licensed by the station authority and pay a fee for the privilege of carrying people's luggage. They are supplied with a uniform red shirt and with a brass armband showing their licence number. A system was devised for the porter to give a token with his number on it to a passenger in exchange for the passenger's luggage. Then the passenger would have proof of who was the porter if the luggage and porter disappeared. Instead, the token disappeared.

If you do have a porter, keep an eye on him. He is adept at loading your luggage into a taxi you don't want. On the other hand, although a porter's uniform of red shirt and red scarf tied around his head, makes him look like a brigand, he can be useful in locating the right train, or even to guard your luggage. He'll want at least Rs 5 from you because you're a foreigner, but the normal carrying charge is from Rs 2 to Rs 4 a head load depending on the station's rates, even if it's only one bag.

Complaints

Complaints, or compliments, can be made easily and effectively while actually on board the train. 'Suggestion-cum-Complaint' books are carried by the guard/conductor of mail, express and passenger trains, and also in the dining or pantry cars.

A request for the complaint book can cause great consternation among the train staff because all entries are investigated and can result in disciplinary action. The complainant is required to record full name and address and ticket number as well as the train number and date.

As a foreigner, you may be asked to write down your comments if the train or catering staff think you are likely to be appreciative.

Complaint books are available at large stations in the station master's office, in the goods shed or in the parcel office. Refreshment rooms and restaurants also have books. Suggestion-cum-Complaint Boxes are available at major stations for passengers' letters.

Many stations have 'Public Grievance Booths' where passengers can let off steam or register formal complaints to a railway employee. Letters of complaint can also be sent direct to the DRM or General Manager of the zonal railway.

It is worth using the complaints machinery. Some foreigners keep their complaints to themselves, then malign the railway system when they return home. Only if they make their comments known to the railway management can there be any improvement. An Indian once urged me to complain because 'a complaint from a foreigner can improve the system for all of us.'

Complaints relating to bribery and corruption are investigated by a special vigilance squad run by each zonal railway. The complainant should be prepared to give evidence before the investigating officer and the original complaint should be sent by mail to the Chief Vigilance Officer at the HQ of the railway concerned.

A traveller from the UK recently rooted out several instances of bribery and wrote to tell me, instead of the railway authorities. He claims his cabin mate (an Indian) on the Howrah Mail paid Rs750 above the ordinary ticket price to secure a berth, bidding against seven others. 'Corruption underscores the importance of purchasing an Indrail Pass,' he said. 'In some ways the pass can be viewed as a legal pay off that gives westerners many of the benefits that Indians can get only through bribery.'

In *Expression*, the American Express magazine, I saw the following advice: 'Tipping is unusual among Indians but it is still practised by and often expected of visitors. Tipping, or *baksheesh*, is often done in advance. For example, Rs10 given to a train conductor will help you get a seat on a packed train. Porters are usually given about Rs5 per suitcase.'

Travellers' tips

Most foreigners you meet will be happy to share their tips. One told me that since local trains are slow, he actually prefers bus for short trips, only taking superfast trains on major trunk routes for long distance journeys. He travels 2nd Class, unreserved, during the day, not in the general coach but in a reserved carriage in which there are seats, and he pays the extra reservation fee, and surcharge, on the train (see Chapter 3 for how to do this). He travels during the day to see the scenery rather than at night. He was amazed by the number of

SOUTH CENTRAL RAILWAY APPEALS
DO NOT DETAIN TRAINS

RAIL ROKO & RASTA ROKO are resorted to by organisors of agitations to press their demands.

SOME INSTANCES

1. "DATE: 15.7.88 PLACE: ONGOLE. Severe dislocation of rail traffic caused by agitators squatting on the track ... to highlight the grievances of Cotton Growers of Prakasam District!

2. "DATE: 27.7.88   PLACE: SECUNDERABAD.   VIJAYAWADA, NANDYAL Trade Union Organisations squatted on track as part of RASTA ROKO.. to press withdrawal of proposed changes in Industrial Disputes Act. etc.,

"PLEASE   DO   NOT   DETAIN TRAINS"

* Detained trains set off "CHAIN REACTION" by causing other trains to be detained.
* Thousands of passengers get detained at locations far away from their homes.
* Goods trains carrying essential commodities such as foodgrains, coal can not reach destinations affecting the Public Distribution System, power generation etc.

**ISSUED IN PUBLIC INTEREST
BY
SOUTH CENTRAL RAILWAY**

rail routes in the eastern, Ganga, region where, he said, they probably only have a pair of trains a day.

Pat Moynihan wrote: 'In the south of India, I used the local bus service quite a lot. They have the advantage of not needing advance booking, covering more destinations, and being very cheap. The disadvantages are obvious – overcrowding, discomfort and confusion. Often I was the only westerner on the bus, and therefore the object of much curiosity. This can get wearying but I certainly felt I was getting in touch with ordinary Indian people (often literally!)'

An English couple told me: 'We travel by bus as well as train, but we don't like it. Not that it's crowded but it leaves you tired at the end of the day, and emotionally wrecked. The frenzy of driving, and the horror of watching near-misses the whole time, destroys whatever pleasure there could be'.

Another traveller said: 'To help avoid that feeling of lethargy that can be demoralizing on a long haul trip, I make a list from the timetable of all the scheduled stops and times of arrival and departure of the train I'm going to take.

'If the train leaves late, as often happens, I list my own idea of the ETA based on the amount of delay. In a third column I list the actual times of arrival and departure. It's amazing how some trains make up time despite inexplicable delays in the middle of nowhere'.

He added: 'I try to stick to a timetable of my own on a long journey, listening on my shortwave transistor radio to BBC World Service at 0730 and 1630 (Indian time) every day. A shower and a change of clothes works wonders for the self-esteem. The shower is usually empty during the hour before lunch or dinner since those passengers who use it at all are likely to do so in the early morning or late evening'.

Another tip: 'Conversing with fellow passengers really helps to pass the time, and relieves the isolation of being of no fixed abode. An eyemask (Gulf Air give them out free in economy class), is useful when you've had enough conversation and want to meditate or sleep without being disturbed. Indians usually respect such an extreme desire for privacy'.

Someone else told me: 'Earplugs are absolutely essential if you want an after lunch nap. It's not the noise of the train, which at least has a regular rhythm, that is disturbing, but the shrieks and caterwauling of the free-range children whose troublesome activities seem to be encouraged by their parents'.

Other tips I've gleaned from travellers met in India:

- When arriving by train at a station you've never visited before, make for the station restaurant, not the exit, and relax over a cup of tea while the rush to get out of the station subsides and the touts take off. The local passengers you'll meet there, and the restaurant manager, will give better advice on where to stay than the touts will.

- The best seats, or berths, are those in the centre of the carriage where they are not over the wheels.

- Use timetables as a guide rather than as a guarantee of departure time or train accommodation. A check at the station in advance is vital since departure times can even be brought forward.

- If you have problems with officials at a station at night, head for the nearest hotel, check in, sleep, and wait for the next morning to resolve matters. Getting a good night's sleep is important if you are going to be quick witted enough to deal with Indian bureaucracy. Besides, in the morning, there should be different officials on duty who'll be more helpful.

- Try to adjust to the Indian tendency to make everything as complicated as possible. Remember there is no way to rush the system. You are the guest and don't have the right to dictate anything.

- Don't expect to get the right answer; you are told what people want you to hear. Nobody wants to be the one to tell you bad news.

- Whenever you hear 'No problem!' watch out – something is sure to go wrong.

The best advice I had was from a young Indian navy officer who wrote to me after our meeting on a train: 'Things may be difficult but you will encounter many people, many things, which will linger in your memory for long. Everything has a bad side – you must take them as a bad experience. I can assure you that definitely with time you will love this country'.

Chapter 6

Past Trains and Present Steam

To Madras goes the credit for the first plan to have a railway network in India when, in 1831, a parliamentary committee discussing the affairs of the East India Company, proposed the introduction of rail roads to improve the deplorable communications. Although the idea was considered again in 1836 nothing happened for 20 years.

Instead, Bombay did something about it in the 1840s with the result that the formal inauguration of the first railway line in India took place on April 16, 1853, when a train carried 400 passengers from Bombay to Thane. Actually, it had taken only 28 years after the start of the world's first commercial train service, between Stockton and Darlington in the UK, for India to have her own passenger trains.

Calcutta followed swiftly, inaugurating a 24 mile line from Howrah to Hooghly in August 1854. It would have happened sooner but the ship bringing the locomotives went to Australia instead. In South India, the first line opened in June 1856 for the Madras Railway Company: 65 miles of track (built in three years at a cost of £5,500 per mile) from Madras to Walajah Road.

Meanwhile, in the north, a length of 119 miles of line was laid from Allahabad to Kanpur and opened in March 1859. Three years later, a line between Amritsar and Lahore opened for traffic.

Engineering feats
The achievements of the 19th century railway engineers are remarkable. The laying of a rail line from Bombay across the Bhore Ghats to Pune and the Thal Ghats to Bhusaval was the most difficult then undertaken anywhere in the world. Work began in 1860 with 40,000 men labouring for four years. The average daily consumption of gunpowder was 2½ tons. The two lines were opened in 1864, having been built without dynamite, pneumatic tools or any of the equipment used today.

More remarkable was the construction in 1874 of the 55 mile long metre gauge line at Godspeed from the left bank of the river Ganga to Darbhanga, forerunner of the present day North Eastern Railway. Major F.S. Stanton, Superintendent Engineer of the Rajputana

Malwa Railway carried out the survey, acquired the land, moved material to the other side of the river, laid the track, commissioned the locomotives and opened the line for traffic, all in 65 days.

The government was anxious to attract private capital to develop the railways but private companies were cautious about the potential for their investments so a guarantee system was devised. After 1870, railway development became rapid.

For centuries, the growth of roads had radiated from the interior, from centres such as Delhi, Lahore, Allahabad and Agra, to the coast. With railways, the communications expansion was reversed with lines commencing at the major sea ports and penetrating inland. The line over the Bhore Ghats to Pune, for instance, was to serve as a connecting link with South India and the line over the Thal Ghats to Bhusaval went on to Delhi and Calcutta.

Rail fever

As well as tracks being laid throughout the country when rail fever took hold, stations were being constructed. The railway companies were the patrons of new architecture in the 19th century. Stations, big and small, were constructed in different styles: Classical, Gothic Arabic, Indo Arabic, Traditional and 19th century Contemporary. The stations are still in use while the early locomotives have disappeared.

One such station is in Madras, at Royapuram, one kilometre by suburban train from Madras Beach, where there are a few remnants of the grandiose building opened in 1856 as the terminal station for the southern link by rail of India's east and west coasts.

None of the three locomotives used on the first line from Bombay, they were called Sindh, Saheb and Sultan, exist now. Sindh did survive the two world wars and was kept on a pedestal at Matunga only to be sold for scrap. The first locomotive which hauled passenger trains on the East Indian Railway between Howrah and Raniganj is still preserved, however, at Jamalpur.

Travel by steam train in the early 20th Century was the height of luxury with the Grand Indian Peninsula (GIP) the forerunner of Central Railway, the pioneer. A postal express ran weekly between Bombay and Calcutta providing sleeping and dining accommodation for 32 1st Class passengers. Another GIP venture was the running of hotel trains complete with sleeping cars and restaurants vestibuled together from Bombay to various tourist spots. The weekly P & O ship from London to Bombay was met by the Special Boat Express which, with the opening in 1911 of the shorter route to Delhi, enabled the BB and CIR to run its boat specials in 24½ hours while the GIP Postal Expresses did the journey in 28½ hours.

In the 1920s, the railways entered a new phase of development as the state began to take over the management of the various railway companies. A period of prosperity followed, including electrification which was introduced in 1925 by the Great Indian Peninsula Railway and in 1928 by the suburban section of the Bombay, Baroda and Central India Railway (BB and CIR – which was also known as the Bloody Bad and Can't Improve Railway). The Madras suburban section was electrified in 1931.

The Second World War brought a setback to the railways when some rolling stock and materials were shipped out for the war effort, and some lines were dismantled and workshops used for ammunition manufacture. After Independence, the entire network of 42 separate railway systems came under State control. They were reorganized into six zones in 1951/52, which eventually became the nine zones in operation today.

Since the reorganization there has been a phenomenal growth in usage. In 1950/51, there were 1,284 million passenger journeys; in 1986/87 the figure was 3,580 million. The average distance travelled by a passenger in 1986/87 was calculated as 71.6 km (compared with 51.8 km in 1950/51) while the average per upper class non suburban passenger was 528.4 km. The route kilometres of the railways now is over 62,000; almost twice the length of the national highways, with over 10 million people travelling on the fleet of over 8,000 locomotives every day.

As Indian Railways prepares for the 21st Century and the colossal increase in passenger and freight traffic, expansion is being planned at the same time as streamlining takes place in an effort to control runaway expenditure. There are plans to import new rolling stock including electric locomotives (some from Japan, Sweden and Europe have been put on trial on the Kirandul–Kottavalasa section of South Eastern Railway) as well as to increase indigenous production. Essential to expansion are new tracks as existing railroads already work to capacity. The railways are speeding up the conversion of all metre gauge (MG – one metre wide) lines to broad gauge to keep pace with India's rapid industrialization, as a unified system is seen as a must for development. MG lines carry about 20% of passengers and have been described by a railway official as 'the white elephant of the railways.' Of the existing 32,000 km of MG lines, 6,000 km are to be converted soon. A recent conversion was the 114 km MG line between Manmad and Aurangabad, a tourist and pilgrim centre, at a cost of Rs70 crore.

Railroad gauges throughout the world vary due to 19th Century political or economic decisions. Broad gauges support heavier trains, narrow gauges are cheaper. India's trunk lines are mostly broad gauge (1.676 m, 5 ft 6 in wide) which is also common in Bangladesh, Pakistan and Sri Lanka. The original British 'standard gauge' of 1.43 m (4 ft 6 in) is used in North America, most of Europe and China; Finland and Russia use 1.5 m (5 ft) gauge.

The "Family Tree" of the 9 Railway Zones

1853–1872	1873–1892	1893–1912	1913–1932	1933–1951	1958
Eastern Punjab E.I.R. (Lucknow Moradabad & Allahabad Div.)	Rajpura Bhatinda Jodhpur: Bikaner state: B.B.C.I. (Delhi Rewari Fazilka section)	Ludhiana Dhuri Jakhal Kalka Simla	Hosiarpur Doab Branch Jind Panipat Sirhind Rupar Kangra valley	Rupar Nangal Dam	Northern Railway
	Assam Bengal B.B.C.I: Kanpur/ Achnera section Bengal & N.W. Tirhut. Lucknow Bareilly Rohilkund. Kumayon Darjeeling Himalayan	Coochbehar State	Chaparmukh Silghat Katakhal–Lalabazar	Assam Bengal Assam	North Eastern Railway North East Frontier Railway
East Indian Eastern Bengal	Tarakeswar Dildarnagar Ghazipur State	South Bihar			Eastern Railway
	Bengal Nagpur	East Coast Northern Rupsa Talband Naupada Gunupur Purulia Ranchi branch Raipur Dhamtari Satpura	Central India Coalfields		South Eastern Railway

Madras Railway Southern Mahratta Rly. South Indian South Indian (MG)	Madras Railway Southern Mahratta Rly. Kolhapur State Pondicherry Branch French Mysore State	Kolar Gold Fields Shoranur Cochin Sangli State Nilagiri M&SMR. Travancore Peralam Karaikka	Bangalore–Chick Ballapur Light	Cochin Harbour Branch	Southern Railway South Central Railway
Great Indian Peninsula	Scindia State Bhopal Itarsi Nizam State	Bhopal Ujjain Bina–Goona Baran Nizam State Dholpur State Matheran Hill Scindia	Dhond Baramati Ellichpur Yeotmal Pachora Jammer Pulgaon Arvi		Central Railway

B.B. & C.I.
Holkar State (MG)
	Petlad Cambay
	B.B.C.I.
	Gaekwars Mehsana
	Bhavnagar State
	Gondal
	Porbandar State
	Junagadh State
	Gaekwars Baroda
		Tapti Valley Nagda–
		Ujjain
		Ahmadabad Dholka
		Branch
		Ahmadabad Prantij
		Palanpur State
		Jetalsar Rajkot
		Jamnagar. Morvi.
		Drangadra State
		Jaipur State. Rajasthan
		Gujerat–Champaner
		Rajpidla State
		Morvi Tramways. Cutch
			Boriavi Vadtal
			Jamnagar Dwarka
			Okham Andal
			Bodeli Chotaudaipur
			Gujerat–Godhra
			  –Lunavada
			  –Nandad
			  –Kapadbhan
			Piplod–Devgod. Baria
			Bhavnagar–Talja
			Mahuja Tramways
				Jodhpur–Marwar
				Phulad Section
					Western Railway

Rail museums

The history of Indian Railways can be traced in the excellent Rail Museum in Delhi (see page 133). A lesser-known museum exists at Mysore, and this is described on page 194.

STEAM IN INDIA – 1992
by Hugh Ballantyne

For convenience this brief guide to current steam working on India's vast railway system is divided into the nine railway zones. Trains from two or more different railways serve some places such as Agra with Northern, Central and Western trains, Varanasi with Northern and North Eastern, Lucknow with North Eastern and Northern and Pune with Central and South Central Railway.

India once had a bewildering variety of locomotive types but the variation has been simplified. On the 1.67 m broad gauge (BG) and metre gauge (MG) lines there are only standardized classes to be seen and it is left to the narrow gauge (NG) lines to provide the variety, mainly laid to .762 m gauge but a few at .610 m.

The main BG types are the WG class 2-8-2, WP class 4-6-2 and a few light WL class Pacifics. No less than 2,450 WGs were built between 1950 and 1970, with the first 100 being built in the UK by the North British Loco Co., and the others in India (at the Chittaranjan Loco Works in West Bengal) plus some small batches built in France, Germany, Austria, Italy, USA and Japan. Built for freight traffic, they are used on passenger trains as well. They are large, impressive and very functional machines and with an 18½ ton axle loading have the route availability to be found all over India where steam still remains in use.

The WP class Pacific contains many standardized parts with the WG and was designed just after the Second World War as a passenger locomotive with the same axle loading as its WG goods counterpart. However, their appearance is quite different as the WP has a bullet nose smoke box door and semi-streamlined casing along the boiler, making it a very distinctive and attractive locomotive. A total of 755 were built between 1947 and 1967 with the original 16 coming from Baldwin Locomotive Works in the USA. The WL class Pacifics were designed for use on routes restricted to a 17 tons axle load and a total of 104 were built, the first ten in England by Vulcan Foundry in 1955 and the remainder at Chittaranjan between 1966–68.

The MG railways have two standard types which at a quick glance look almost identical. These are the YG class 2-8-2 for goods and the YP class Pacific 4-6-2 passenger locomotive, so the same wheel arrangements are found on both BG and MG railways. 1,076 YG class were built between 1949 and 1972 and 871 YPs between 1952 and 1972. Until recently another standard post war class in use was the YL 2-6-2,

For the independent traveller keen to explore some of India's remoter and less visited parts, the narrow gauge railways provide some interesting routes. Particularly recommended is a journey on the Satpura Express south from Jabalpur which passes through some delightful country in Madhya Pradesh. Another pleasing though shorter railway is the Parlakamidi Light Railway from Naupada to Gunupur, which follows the border between Andhra Pradesh and Orissa for much of its route. Motive power used to be provided by these little 0-6-4 tank engines built in Stoke-on-Trent. (Anthony J. Lambert)

an attractive and efficient all purpose engine for branch line use, and 264 were built between 1952 and 1956.

Finally there is the WD class 2-8-2 which is the wartime American designed and built 'MacArthur' and were obtained from the USA Transportation Corps after the war, or later built new in 1948, and eventually totalling 304 engines in India. Some are still at work and one was station pilot shunting stock at Agra Fort station for many years.

Of the four principal Indian cities only New Delhi sees steam regularly and Calcutta occasionally.

Taking the railways clockwise from New Delhi:

Northern Railway   Care needs to be exercised on this railway to the north of Delhi in view of the political situation in the Punjab. This is unfortunate as for BG this is now the best steam area in India. At Firozpur the light WL class Pacifics were still operating with excellent centres at Firozpur, Ludhianu and Jalandhar, and stopping trains on the Jalandhar route in 1992. Nearer Delhi Saharanpur is a busy place and its shed has an allocation of eight WGs and 32 WPs, with steam working to Delhi via both Meerut City and Shamali, south east towards Moradabad, which has an allocation of 23 WGs and 15 WPs, and north to Ambala.

There is also steam working from Bathinda and Laksar JCT, the latter being home to about 40 WGs (with some outstationed at sub-sheds). However, note that Lucknow broad gauge shed closed in 1992, so this once busy place with its impressive station only sees MG steam in any quantity with Lucknow Charbagh half round-house having 10 YG and 31 YP locomotives. At Bareilly steam on both gauges remains active, WGs working the Aligarh line and towards Lucknow and North Eastern Railway YG/YPs, well kept, running on the MG to Kasganj, Kathgodam and Mailani.

North Eastern Railway   This railway mainly operates on MG but there is some conversion to BG in hand. It is probably the best railway in India overall for concentrated steam activity. On BG Sonpur is the busiest shed with an allocation of 19 WP and 13 WG in 1992 plus its MG shed alongside. On the MG, Gorakhpur has about 24 MG steam hauled trains at its station every 24 hours, other good centres are Bareilly, Kasganj, Gonda, Varanasi, Lucknow (Charbagh), Samastipur and Darbhanga.

North East Frontier Railway   This operates mainly in a security area and is difficult to visit. The world famous Darjeeling–Himalayan Railway is a .610 m gauge line in this region and if it is operating you are strongly recommended to travel on it. This railway suffers frequent washout damage nearly every year during the heavy rains which closes the railway to through workings. When this happens enquire if the Kurseong to Darjeeling school train is running as this is not usually affected. With its spirals and zig-zags, this amazing railway climbs to a summit of 2259 m at Ghum before descending by means of a double loop into Darjeeling, all steam worked with its beautiful B class 0-4-0STs. On the plains, connection is made at Siliguri with the MG, and at New Jalpaiguri with both MG and BG (see Chapter 11). Steam types to be seen at the latter are YG, YP and WD on MG and WG on the BG. Finally Katihar is also a good MG centre and with a new BG connection now opened sees WG class as well.

Eastern Railway   BG steam is still very active with plenty of WG and WP to be seen but mainly in deplorable condition. Best centres are Patna, Asansol, Andal, Sitarampur, Dhanbad, Burdwan (now known as Barddharman) and Jamalpur. On the NG the Burdwan–Katwa–Ahmadpur NG (.762 m) gauge line has Bagnall of Stafford built 0-6-4T and 2-6-2Ts, although there are railcar workings on the Burdwan–Katwa section.

South Eastern Railway   A BG railway with numerous NG but no MG at all. On BG a little work for WG class but rapidly being phased out. NG has six separate systems all .762 m gauge. From east to west: Bankura–Rainagar uses CC class Pacifics dating from 1906. Ranchi–Lohardaga is now diesel. The Kotshila–Purulia railway uses ZE class 2-8-2s as does the Rupsa to Bangraposi branch. The Naupada–Gunupur line further south has some attractive PL class 0-6-4T built by Kerr Stuart of Stoke-on-Trent. The Raipur and the extensive NG lines around Gondia and Nagpur are all diesel operated.

Southern Railway   Broad gauge steam engines have been eliminated in the SR zone. However, there are many MG routes which are served by steam-hauled trains. Some of the stations where you can catch a steam train are Tiruchchirappalli, Madurai, Rameswaram, Dindigul, Villuparam, Pondicherry and Thanjavur. There is also the popular steam loco ride on the rack and pinion line between Mettupalayam and Udagamandalam (Ooty). This MG line is operated by X class compound 0-8-2T built by Swiss Loco and Machine Works from 1920.

South Central Railway   Much reduced on BG but in the Rajamundry area (south of Waltair on the main south east coast line) WG and WP are still at work. On MG, Hubli and the lines to the west have been extensively worked with steam haulage as have the branches off the main line going east towards Guntakal. There are no NG lines on this railway.

Central Railway   A very large BG network, nominal MG mileage but eight NG lines, six of .762 m gauge and two of .610 m. Except in the

Bombay area, steam does local work from some main centres and junctions on the BG. Sheds that have traditionally always had big allocations are Bhusaval, Jhansi, Jabalpur, Amla, Bina and Wardha but the main line between Delhi and Jhansi is now electrified. On the NG the Daund–Baramati no recent reports, but is expected to go diesel soon. The Kurduvadi system known as the Barsi Light Railway is diesel. The Pachora–Jamner has ZE class 2-8-2, Murtajapur Fard ZD class 2-8-2 and Arvi-Pulgaon some ZP class 4-6-2. Both the narrow gauge lines at Gwalior and also the Dhaulpur system are now diesel operated.

Western Railway   A large and busy railway with important BG and MG main lines plus some NG branches. On the BG, Vadodara, Ratlam, Kota and Gangapur have busy sheds and one or two locos can usually be found if staying in Agra, at the small shed of Agra Idagh (which also has an MG shed on the opposite side of the running lines). The MG network is extensive and the two standard classes can readily be seen at such places as Ahmadabad (main shed is at Sabarmati), Mahesana, Rajkot, Ajmer and Jaipur. There are regular steam work-ings to Agra Fort but numerically not many locomotives to be seen. All the NG is .762 m gauge and the biggest system centred on Dabhoi, just south of Vadodara is now diesel operated. The remaining steam operated NG lines are the Nadiad system to the north of Vadodara and three little lines to the south, Bilimora to Waghai, Kosamba to Umarpada and the Ankleswar system, all four now using the attractive standard class ZB 2-6-2's.

Permits

It is possible to visit locomotive depots but a permit has to be obtained first. Applications, stating the name of the sheds to be visited and when, should be sent to the Indian High Commission or Embassy in your home country. It will be forwarded to Delhi for official approval so allow at least three months for a reply. Often replies are delayed or permission refused for unexplained reasons. Applying before you go saves having to spend time coping with bureaucracy in India. Some of the smaller sheds can be visited on the spur of the moment without a permit, if you are lucky. Permits are also required for photography (see Chapter 2).

Chapter 7

Where to Stay

Retiring rooms

Guide books for the budget-conscious tourist and the travellers' grape-vine concentrate on low-cost hotels and guest houses in most towns in India yet usually overlook the perfect place to stay within metres of the station platform: the railway retiring rooms.

From Rs 50 for a double room with twin beds here is the best, cleanest and most secure accommodation you'll find at the price. It's also the most convenient since you don't have to traipse around town with your luggage looking for a place to stay.

Don't be put off by the term 'retiring room'. These are nothing less than comfortably furnished guest rooms, nearly all with attached bathrooms. The most luxurious are suites with sitting room, bathroom, pantry, TV, fridge and air-conditioned bedroom. Rooms are usually located off the main platform or on the first floor above the booking office. .

Railway accommodation conforms to minimum standards that include adequate bedroom furniture and a rule that the bed linen be changed after every occupant. If you find the sheets are grubby when you arrive, ask for them to be changed. It will be done without rancour.

Towels are also supplied on demand. The bathrooms will have a shower (sometimes with hot water) and sometimes a western toilet, but no toilet paper. You will usually be given a padlock with a key to lock the door, or you can use your own. Many of the attendants are eagle-eyed women (wearing light blue saris) who won't let a miscreant near your door, so security is good.

The rooms in British-built stations are large and airy, with fans. Many of them open onto terraces that overlook the station forecourt. Limited room-service is usually available, such as bed tea and soft drinks; sometimes tea, soft drinks and a newspaper are included in the room rate.

There are twin-bedded rooms (known as 'doubles'), single bed rooms and dormitories. Dormitories will have their own shower and toilets attached, with a locker for each occupant to store his belongings in. If you are travelling alone and are wary about sharing a room, or dorm, with strangers, doubles can be let for single occupancy but you must pay the double rate.

Many rooms are air-conditioned with huge boxes containing alternators chugging away during the night to pump in cold air. I prefer a fan at night but I discovered that at some stations the AC rooms are much larger and, since they are regarded as prestige accommodation, they are cleaner and better serviced too.

I've only once found bed bugs under my mattress in a retiring room, in the same room where the attendant locked me in and wouldn't let me out, after waking me at 0300 hours to catch my train, until I'd given her a tip. I was pleased to notice on my second visit, after I'd complained to the DRM, that both bed bugs and attendant had gone.

Retiring rooms are charged per 24 hours. No matter what time of day or night you arrive, the room is yours for 24 hours from time of check in. Payment is made on arrival to the attendant in charge, or to the SS. Some stations increase the room rate by 25 or 50 per cent for the second 24 hours. Occupancy is only permitted to rail travellers with tickets, or to Indrail Pass holders.

Apart from the cost advantage, railway retiring rooms are ideal for those with pre-dawn departures. Their proximity to station facilities such as restaurants and, at New Delhi station, to the ITB, also adds to their appeal. A disadvantage can be the noise of the CCTV and of diesel engines hooting in the night, although waking up to the whistle of a steam engine shunting past the window could thrill the nostalgic.

A major snag is that, while foreign rail travellers may not know about railway retiring rooms, Indians certainly do. So they are very popular. At busy stations, you need to arrive early in the morning to secure one. Only one room per station can be reserved in advance, otherwise rooms are allocated on a first come first served basis.

To reserve a room write as far in advance as possible to the SS of the station, enclosing a rupee money order in favour of the SS for the cost of the room, giving details of date and time of arrival.

Rendell A. Davis agreed that retiring rooms are great value and wrote: 'When I talked with officials at New Delhi station about the problems I had in getting a retiring room, they advised me to (in the future) go to the Station Superintendent, wave my Indrail Pass, and insist on being treated like a VIP. I tried that technique and it worked.'

Since Indian railway travellers are well versed in using influence of their own to secure a room, do not be reluctant to take advantage of the privilege the IRP brings, but its importance is only likely to be recognized by the SS, not by the retiring room caretaker.

Ian Scrimgeour of Thunder Bay, Canada, recalled his stay at the retiring room, Renigunta. 'I was stationed there in 1945–6 and life in the area was so dreary that it was not unknown to have parties in the refreshment room at Renigunta with some of the more overcome by Parry's gin ending up upstairs!'

Even though alcohol is no longer available in the refreshment rooms, the retiring rooms are still there. The rates are to be found in the zonal timetables. They range from Rs10 for a dormitory bed to Rs150 or Rs200 (except for the Rs300 charged at New Delhi) for a twin-bedded AC room.

Railway hotels

Not strictly hotels, but neither are they retiring rooms, are two of the best places to stay for convenience, comfort, security and price in Delhi and Calcutta, called Rail Yatri Niwas (rail travellers' inn).

The one at New Delhi station is three minutes walk from the Ajmeri Gate (not the main) exit. Dive through the scrum of taxi drivers and touts and head for the puce, granite building of some eight stories you can see on your left. It is best to make a reservation in advance since there is a big demand for rooms there. Reservations can be done through the ITB or direct by mail to Rail Yatri Niwas, New Delhi Railway Station, Gate Number 2, New Delhi 110002, tel: 3315445, enclosing a money order for the full amount with details of your arrival and departure days and times, plus ticket (PNR) or IRP number. Only in transit rail passengers can stay there, maximum three nights.

If you don't have a reservation, you'll stand a better chance of a bed at weekends, and if you arrive around 1000 hours, the hour of check in or check out. (If you check in between 0400 and 1000 an extra 20 percent is payable.) The charm of the place may escape you during the chaos of registering (full fee is demanded in advance plus Rs100 key deposit) but this can be a fun place once you've established rapport with the staff.

There are 71 rooms, 244 beds; fans, no AC. The best are the 36 rooms (at Rs175) with twin beds and en suite showers/toilets and morning tea service. Dormitory beds were Rs50 in 1992 but a price rise was planned. Not many foreigners stay there and I don't know why not since it is clean and convenient with Connaught Place only minutes away by cutting through the station. There is a restaurant where you have to pay the cashier before getting your meal; it's a bit gloomy but the food is much better than the usual railway catering.

I made the mistake on my last visit of trying to get my laundry done officially which took three days. A Brit who was staying there was smarter. He gave the dormitory attendant 12 items including his precious jeans and got them back washed and ironed in four hours.

The Rail Yatri Niwas at Howrah station is built on a grander scale as part of the extension housing platforms 18 to 21. Even if you don't stay there the Yatrik restaurant is worth a visit. The architects have joyfully

Oberoi Hotels International.
Where everything has to be just right.

*Gracious hospitality. Five Star
international standards. Impeccable
service. Exclusive facilities for businessmen,
around the clock. Oberoi Hotels
International. The finest hotels worldwide.
Because you deserve the best the
world has to offer.*

Oberoi Hotels International

AUSTRALIA, EGYPT, INDIA, INDONESIA, NEPAL, SAUDI ARABIA, SRI LANKA followed old traditions with a high ceiling, a vast room and sophisticated decor of murals and pastel panels. The menu includes standard veg meals at Rs20, and specials at Rs30. The special non-veg meal at Rs35 consists of soup, chicken masala, vegetables, pulao, rumali roti or paratha, dal fried, salad, pickle, papad, fruit salad and icecream. Real, not bag, tea is served.

There are 115 beds on two floors. Eight rooms have AC (at Rs300 for two), 14 are non-AC (at Rs200) and six are non-AC triples at Rs225. There are 53 dormitory beds in five and seven bedded dorms at Rs50 each. No advance reservations are accepted but you can arrive in the morning and pay the full room rate to secure a room later the same day. Rooms are let on a day to day basis from 1000 to 1000. The stay can be extended from 0800 each morning up to three nights. The room rate is payable on check in together with a refundable deposit of Rs50. Bed tea and a newspaper is included; there is a left luggage storage facility at Rs3 per item. You must hold an IRP or a current inward or outward ticket for a journey of at least 200 km.

Many of the rooms have balconies and are superb for watching the sun rise over the Hooghly River and seeing the city of Calcutta from a safe distance. Not so safe are the metal arms at eye level at both ends of the beds, designed for draping mosquito nets over, but more dangerous to your eyes and head than a mosquito would be.

Two splendid old style hotels are operated by South Eastern Railway (SER). There is one at Ranchi, established in 1915, and another at Puri, built in 1925. Both are worth a visit for the pleasure of staying in them.

At Ranchi, the hotel is a sprawling bungalow type with 22 rooms and shuffling waiters wearing the livery of the former Bengal and Nagpur Railway. The waiters at the Puri hotel, which is in a garden setting near the beach, dress and serve in the same old world manner.

Economy rates. Reservations can be made through the Deputy Chief Commercial Superintendent (Catering), 14 Strand Road, Calcutta, 700001; tel: 232936, or direct with the hotel managers (address in accommodation list).

City hotels

When I want to stay away from railwayland in a town I've not visited before, the only option I consider viable is a good 5 star hotel. There are practical reasons for this. After several nights on a train, there is nothing better than to check into the best hotel and be pampered. You'll feel you deserve a comfortable hotel in which to sleep properly, have the laundry done, luxuriate in a hot bath, watch TV, indulge in a wide choice of good food, and drink a cold beer. (A 5 star hotel is about the only place where you'll get a drink on a 'dry' day.)

With rates reaching US$200 a night, and even more, 5 star hotels are not for every traveller nor for every night, but the best are worth the extravagance, especially when set against the savings being made through travelling by rail.

For older train travellers who are suffering from lack of their usual comforts, a good 5 star hotel is the best antidote. Even one night tended by caring, alert staff who know their job can be a restorative and fortify for the journey ahead.

For younger rail travellers, some 5 star hotels are an experience not to be missed, as much as for the beauty and grandeur of their buildings as for the luxury of their service. It all costs less than comparable hotels at home. Being able to pay with a credit card, including Visa and Access, is useful, too, since it preserves rupees for train expenses.

Sometimes an Indian 5 star hotel is not from the same constellation as international 5 star properties but those of the major chains like Oberoi, Taj and the Welcomgroup usually are. Oberoi Hotels have a pleasing mix of modern amenities and old world charm and tradition. (The modern New Delhi and Bombay Oberoi hotels actually have a team of butlers attending every room around the clock.) Oberoi was the first Indian hotel company to hire educated people for such run-of-the-mill jobs as waiters and bellboys, and to employ women in house-keeping and as receptionists and guest relations staff.

Welcomgroup run the remarkable Umaid Bhawan Palace Hotel which any visitor to Jodhpur should try to stay at for a taste of the Maharaja life style. They also operate the custom built colonial delight, the Windsor Manor Sheraton in Bangalore where the Oberoi group have also opened a splendid property.

One of the most recognizable hotels in India belongs to another luxury hotel chain, the Taj group. Photos of the Lake Palace Hotel at Udaipur, as it seems to float on the blue waters of Lake Pichola are one of the enticements to visit India. It's not far from Udaipur railway station.

The luxury hotels and the ordinary retiring rooms (always the best bet for the low-budget passenger) where I've stayed are mentioned in detail under the destination headings. Low and medium budget hotels exist in every town and city and information on them can be found in the general guides to India (such as Lonely Planet's) and from state tourist offices.

Below is a list of some recommended Oberoi, Taj, Welcomgroup and other special hotels easily reached from railway stations. An asterisk (*) by a hotel indicates that I enjoyed staying there and think it's worth the train ride. Since hotel rates rise every year, I'm not quoting the prices but have given an indication of whether the rates (but not necessarily the hotel) are in the Luxury, Standard or Economy bracket.

A selection of recommended hotels

Establishment/Address	Telephone	Telex	Rate
Bangalore *Welcomgroup Windsor Manor Sheraton 25 Sankey Road Bangalore 560052	79431	8458209	LUXURY
Bhubaneswar *The Oberoi Nayapalli, Bhubaneswar 751013	56116	67348 HOBIN	STANDARD
Bombay *The Oberoi & Oberoi Towers Nariman Point, Bombay 400021	2025757	4153 OBBYIN	LUXURY
Taj Mahal Hotel & Taj Mahal Intercontinental, Apollo Bunder Bombay 400039	2023366	112442 TAJBIN	LUXURY
Calcutta *The Oberoi Grand 15 Jawaharlal Nehru Marg, Calcutta 700013	292323	7248 OBCLIN	LUXURY
*Rail Yatri Niwas, Howrah Railway Station Calcutta			ECONOMY
Cannanore *Choice Sea Side Hotel Cantonment Cannanore 670001	63352		ECONOMY
Cochin (Kochi) *Casino Hotel Willingdon Island Cochin 682003	048468	08856314	STANDARD
Coonoor *Taj Garden Retreat (formerly Hampton Manor) Church Road, Coonoor, TN 643 101	04264 20021	0853 234	STANDARD
Delhi *Rail Yatri Niwas, New Delhi Railway Station New Delhi, 110002	3315445		ECONOMY
*Oberoi Maidens 7 Sham Nath Marg. Delhi 110054	2525464	66303 OMDLIN	STANDARD

Establishent/Address	Telephone	Telex	Rate
*The Oberoi Dr Zakir Hussain Marg, New Delhi 110003	363030	63222 OBDLIN	LUXURY
Taj Mahal 1 Mansingh Road, New Delhi 110011	3016162	314758 TAJDIN	LUXURY
Welcomgroup Maurya Sheraton Diplomatic Enclave, New Delhi 110021	3010101	61447	LUXURY
Goa Oberoi Bogmalo Beach Bogmalo, Dabolim Airport, Goa 403806	2191	297 OBGAIN	STANDARD
Hyderabad *The Krishna Oberoi Banjara Hills, Hyderabad 500034	222121	6931 OBHIN	STANDARD
Jaipur Rambagh Palace Bhawani Singh Road, Jaipur 302005	75141	365254 RBAGIN	LUXURY
Jaisalmer *Hotel Jaisal Castle 168 Fort, Jaisalmer, Rajasthan 345001	62	Cable: JAISAL	ECONOMY
Jhansi Jhansi Hotel Shastri Marg, Jhansi, U.P.	1360		ECONOMY
Jodhpur *Welcomgroup Umaid Bhawan Palace Jodhpur 352006 Rajasthan Kottayam	22516	552202	LUXURY
Kottayam *Anjali Hotel Kottayam Kerala	3661	888212	ECONOMY
Lonavla Farivas Holiday Resort PO Box 8 Frichley Hill Lonavla 410401	2701	0113272 ABAN	STANDARD

Establishment/Address	Telephone	Telex	Rate
Madras			
*Taj Connemara Hotel	860123	418197	STANDARD
Binny Road		CHIN	
Madras 600002			
Taj Coromandel	474849	417194	STANDARD
17 Nungambakkam High Road,		TAJMIN	
Madras 6000034			
*Trident	434747	4126055	STANDARD
1/24 G.S.T. Road,			
Madras 600027			
Welcomgroup Chola Sheraton	473347	417200	LUXURY
10 Cathedral Road			
Madras 600018			
Welcomgroup Park Sheraton	452525	416868	STANDARD
132 TTK Road,			
Madras 600018			
Matheran			
*Lord's Central Hotel	28		ECONOMY
Matheran 410102			
Ooty (See Udagmandalam)			
Puri			
SE Railway Hotel	2063	Cable:	ECONOMY
Chakratirtha Road,		SURF	
Puri			
Ranchi			
*SE Railway Hotel	21945	Cable:	ECONOMY
Station Road		RESTFUL	
Ranchi, Bihar			
Shimla			
*Oberoi Clarkes	6091	206	STANDARD
The Mall,		OBCLIN	
Shimla 171001			
Tiruchchirappalli			
*Jenney's Residency	41301	455279	ECONOMY
(formerly Rajali Hotel)			
3/14 McDonald's Road,			
Tiruchchirappali,			
Tamil Nadu 620001			
Udagmandalam (Ooty)			
*Fernhill Palace	3097	853246	STANDARD
Udagmandalam 643004			

Establishment/Address	Telephone	Telex	Rate
Udaipur			
*Lake Palace	23241	33203	LUXURY
Pichola Lake,		PALIN	
Udaipur 313001			
Rajasthan			
Shivniwas Palace	28239	33226	LUXURY
Udaipur, Rajasthan		PALIN	

Railway retiring rooms

Rates in these retiring rooms range from Rs10 for a bed in a dormitory to Rs200 for a twin-bedded AC room. Some stations have only one retiring room and others (where indicated) have only a dormitory. Facilities are sometimes only basic.

Station

Abohar	Asand
Abu Road	Asansol
Adra	Aurangabad
Adoni	Ayodhya
Agra Cantt	
Agra Fort	Badarpur Jn
Ahmadabad	Badaun
Ahmednagar	Badnera
Ajmer	Bagaha
Akola	Bagalkot
Aligarth Jn	Baheri
Alipurduar Jn	Bahraich
Allahabad	Baidyanathdam
Allahabad City	Baijnath Paprola
Alleppey	Balasore
Alwaye	Ballia
Alwar	Balotra (Dorm)
Ambala Cantt (Dorm)	Balrampur
Amethi	Balugaon
Amlai	Banda
Amritsar	Bangalore City
Anand	Bankur (Dorm)
Anandnagar	Barajamda (Dorm)
Anantapur	Barauni
Ankleshwar	Barddhaman
Annavarum	Barmer (Dorm)
Ara	Bareilly
Arakkonam	Barpeta Road
Araku (Dorm)	Basti
Aravanakadu	Bathinda (Dorm)
Arsikere	Begusarai

Station

Belgaum
Bellampalli
Bellary
Berhampur Court (Dorm)
Berhampur (Ganjam)
Bhadohi
Bhadrachalam Road
Bhadrak (Dorm)
Bhaga
Bhagalpur
Bharatpur
Bharuch
Bhatni
Bhavnagar
Bhilwara
Bhimavaram
Bhiwani (Dorm)
Bhopal
Bhubaneswar
Bhuj
Bhusaval
Bijapur
Bikaner
Bilaspur
Bina
Bishnupur (Dorm)
Bokoro Steel City
Bolpur
Bombay Cent
Bombay VT
Bongaigaon
Burnpur (Dorm)
Buxar (Dorm)
Bettiah
Betul (Dorm)

Calicut
Cannanore
Chakradharpur
Champa (Dorm)
Chandigarh
Chandrapur
Chaparmukh
Chenganur
Chenganacheri
Chhapra Jn
Chidambaram
Chinnaganjam

Chirala
Chitrakutdham
Chittaranjam
Chittaurgarh
Chittoor
Coimbatore
Coonoor
Cuddapah
Cuttack

Darbhanga
Davangere
Daund
Dauram Medhepura
Dehra Dun
Dehri-on-Sone
Delhi
Deoria Sadar
Dhanbad
Dharmanagar
Dharmavaram
Diamond Harbour
Dibrugarh Town
Dimapur
Diphu
Dongargarh
Durg
Durgapur
Dwarka

Eluru
Ernakulam Jn
Erode Jn

Faizabad
Fakiragram Jn
Falna
Farukhabad
Fatehpur
Firozabad
Firozpur
Forbesganj

Gadag (Dorm)
Gandhidham
Gandhigram
Gaya
Ghazipur City

Station

Godhra
Golagokarannath
Gomoh
Gonda
Gondal
Gondia
Gopalganj
Gooty
Gorakhpur
Gudur
Guna
Guntakal
Guntur
Guwahati
Gwalior

Hajipur
Haldwani
Hanumangarh (Dorm)
Harpalpur
Hardoi
Haridwar
Harmuti
Hassan
Hazaribagh Road
Hojai
Hospet
Howbagh
Howrah
Hubli
Hazrat Nizamuddin

Indore
Itarsi
Izatnagar

Jabalpur
Jagi Road
Jaipur
Jaisalmer
Jaipur-Keonjhar Rd (Dorm)
Jalandhar City
Jalgaon
Jamalpur
Jammu Tawi
Jamnagar
Jasidih

Jaynagar
Jhanjharpur
Jhansi
Jharsuguda
Jiribam
Jodbani
Jodhpur
Jolarpettai
Junagadh

Kadur
Kakinada Town
Kalka
Kamakhya
Kanniya Kumari
Kanpur Anwarganj
Kanpur Central
Karaikkudi Jn
Karimganj
Karwi (Dorm)
Kathgodam
Katihar
Katni
Katpadi
Kazipet
Khagaria
Khalilabad
Khandwa
Kharagpur
Khurda Road
Kishanganj
Kiul Jn
Kodaikanal Road
Kolhapur
Kota
Kotdwara
Kottayam
Krishnanagar City (Dorm)
Kumarghat
Kumbakonam
Kurnool Town

Laheria Sarai
Lakhimpur
Lar Road
Lovedale
Lucknow (NR)
Lucknow Jn (NER)

Station

Ludhiana
Lumding Jn

Madgaon
Madhubani
Madhupur
Madras Central
Madras Egmore
Madurai
Mahesana
Maihar
Makrana (Dorm)
Malda Town
Mangalore
Mankapur
Manmad
Mantralayam Road
Mariani Jn
Mathura
Mathura Cantt.
Mau Jn
Mayiladuturai
Meerut City (Dorm)
Merena
Mettupalaiyam
Midnapur
Miraj
Mirzapur
Moradabad
Morbi
Motihari
Mughal Sarai
Muri
Murshidabad
Muzaffarpur
Mysore

Nagappattinam
Nagda
Nagercoil
Nagore
Nagpur
Nainpur (Dorm)
Najibadad (Dorm)
Nanded
Narkatiaganj
Nasik Road
Naugarh

Nautanwa
New Alipurduar
New Bongaigaon
New Coochbehar
New Delhi
New Jalpaiguri
Nidadavolu
Nidubrolu
Nirmali
Nizamabad
North Lakhimpur

Ongole

Pakur
Palakollu
Palani
Palanpur
Palasa
Palghat
Palimarwar (Dorm)
Parbhani
Parlivaijnath
Pathankot
Patna Jn
Patna Sahib
Pendra Road (Dorm)
Pilibhit
Pipariya
Pollachi (Dorm)
Pondicherry
Porbandar
Pune
Puri
Purnea Jn
Purulia

Quilon

Rae Bareli
Raichur
Raigarh
Raipur (Dorm)
Rajahmundry
Rajgir
Rajkot
Rajnandgaon
Ramagundam

Station

Rameswaram	Surendranagar
Rampur	Suri
Rampurhat	
Ranchi	Tarakeswar
Raurkela	Tatanagar
Renigunta	Tenali
Ratlam	Tenkasi
Raxaul	Thanabihpur
Rayagada (Dorm)	Thanjavur
Renigunta	Thiruvarur
Rewari (Dorm)	Tinsukia Jn
Roorkee	Tiruchchirappalli
	Tiruchendur
Sagarjambagaru	Tirunelvelli
Saharanpur (Dorm)	Tirupati
Saharsa Jn	Tirur
Sakri	Tiruppur
Salem Jn	Titlagarh
Samastipur	Trichur
Sambalpur	Trivandrum Central
Sanchi	Tulsipur
Sasaram	Tundla
Satna	Tuticorin
Sawai Madhopur	
Sealdah	Udagamandalam
Secunderabad	Udaipur City
Shahganj	Ujjain
Shahpur Patoree	
Shahjahanpur	
Shantipur	Vadodara
Shimla	Valsad
Sidhawalia	Varanasi Jn
Silchar	Vasco da Gama
Siliguri Jn	Veraval
Simaluguri Jn	Vijayawada
Sitamarhi	Villupuram
Siuri	Vindhyachal
Sivakasi	Viramgam
Siwan	Virudhunagar
Sitapur	Visakhaptnam
Solapur	Vizianagaram
Sonagir	Vriddachalam
Sonpur	
Sriganga Nagar	
Srikakulum Road	Wadi
Srirangam	Warangal
Supaul	Wardha (Dorm)
Surat	Wellington (Dorm

Chapter 8

The Journey Begins

Since most visitors to India arrive by air at the airports of Delhi, Bombay, Calcutta or Madras, their rail journey is likely to begin from a station in one of those cities. This chapter looks at the facilities in those cities, and in two other cities with airports served by flights from abroad: Trivandrum and Tiruchchirappalli. Goa is covered in Chapter 10.

DELHI

For many readers of this book, their first experience of Indian railways will be at New Delhi or Delhi stations. That is unfortunate because both stations give a dreadful first impression with which to begin your journey. They are quite unlike Delhi itself which is pleasant and enjoyable.

Much of the negative reaction inspired by Delhi's two main stations is due to a traveller's own frame of mind. If you go to the station straight off the plane after a long-haul flight, you're bound to be appalled by the heat and squalor. Allow yourself a chance to adjust to the time change, jet lag and culture shock before attempting to buy a ticket. At least the ITB (see Chapter 3) relieves most of the hassle, but you'll need to be in top form for the station itself.

There is a desk operated by Northern Railway at Delhi's Indira Gandhi International airport where reservations can be made by arriving passengers. It is open from 0000 to 0800 hours, the period during which many long-haul flights arrive.

Delhi is the headquarters of Northern Railway (NR), the biggest zonal railway in the country. Its 10,977 route kilometres serve a population of nearly 200 million in Punjab, Haryana, Uttar Pradesh, Rajasthan, Himachal Pradesh, Jammu and Kashmir, and parts of Gujarat as well as Delhi and Chandigarh. Stretching 1168 km from Amritsar to Varanasi, NR also connects with the Pakistan rail network at Atari and Munnabao. NR runs 270 mail/express and 650 passenger trains daily, carrying about 1,200,000 people a day.

The NR zone abounds in pilgrim places: Amritsar, famous for the Golden Temple; Haridwar, the holiest Hindu centre; Allahabad, the site of the Triveni sangam, the confluence of the Ganga, Yamuna and

KEY

① INTER-STATE BUS TERMINUS
② Y.M.C.A. TOURIST HOTEL
③ ASHOK NATRI NIWAS HOTEL
④ TAJ MAHAL HOTEL
⑤ THE OBEROI HOTEL
⑥ MAURYA SHERATON HOTEL
⑦ OBEROI MAIDENS HOTEL
⑧ INDIRA GANDHI AIRPORT
⑨ JAWAHARLAL NEHRU STADIUM
⑩ RAIL TRANSPORT MUSEUM
⑪ DELHI AIRPORT

DELHI

the invisible Saraswati rivers; Varanasi, the oldest pilgrim centre. The Himalayan resorts of Shimla and, via Jammu Tawi, of Kashmir, are accessible by NR.

Trains from Delhi give access to colourful historical centres: Agra, the capital of the Mughal empire, famous for the Taj Mahal; Fatehpur Sikri with its magnificent monuments of Mughal glory; Lucknow, the cradle of Muslim culture; Bikaner, a city renowned for Rajput chivalry; Jodhpur, famous for its massive fort; and even the unique desert outpost of Jaisalmer.

Since you'll have to pass through one of Delhi's stations to get to those exotic places by train, it's as well to be prepared for a low-key beginning.

New Delhi Station

It's not a major terminus in the grand style (like Bombay VT for instance) but a depressing transit station with overstretched facilities. The catering outlets are poor. At platform level, there is a snack counter staffed by people who make it obvious they have no interest in being helpful. The restaurant upstairs, opposite the ITB, is like the canteen of a small, rundown factory. The whole station has an unwelcoming atmosphere and it's a relief to jump on a train and get out.

There are waiting rooms for upper and 2nd Class passengers, with a separate one for ladies, and there are toilets with showers. The general public have a waiting area with fans above their seats. There are cloakrooms, a telegraph office, phone booths for local and trunk calls and a post office.

There is a current reservations booking office for same day departures as well as ticket counters for non reserved travel. On the left as you enter the station building is a lobby from where stairs (or a lift) lead to the first floor where the ITB is located. It's a haven from the chaos below.

On the second and third floors are the retiring rooms. The point in their favour is their proximity to the ITB. Rs 300 per night for the AC room seems a lot, even if it does have an old fridge, a TV and free soft drinks; it's just not very nice. There is a view from the terrace of the small forecourt below, bright with colour from yellow-topped taxis and red-shirted porters.

Reservations for the retiring rooms are made on the ground floor where there is a desk behind the current reservations counter. The six AC and four non-AC rooms are usually fully booked which shows my own feelings about the station are not shared by everyone.

Actually, out of the station building and along the platforms, the atmosphere does change. It becomes almost rural. At the end of platform 1 there are plants in pots and hibiscus bushes in bloom. A gate leads to railway offices and housing, and there are intriguing coaches parked in an adjoining siding. You might spot the royal blue

Ultra Sonic Rail Testing Car URT100 Matix System here. At the other end of the platforms, there are nine in all, is a temple, serenity amidst the shunting trains.

Near platform 9 is the base kitchen where 25 cooks prepare over 3,000 meals a day to put on trains. Also near the platform, through the Ajmeri Gate exit and across a compound, is the Rail Yatri Niwas, a hostelry for transit passengers opened in March 1988 (see Chapter 7).

Information on other places to stay can be gouged out of the staff at the Delhi Tourist office tucked away in a corner close by the lift to the retiring rooms. The staff are so fed-up with being asked the times of trains, their response to questions is almost automatically negative. But they have booklets to sell.

It is possible to walk from New Delhi station to Connaught Place, the hub of the city, and to the computerized reservation complex 10 minutes walk from the station. Tourists, however, would fare better by using the facilities of the ITB for their ticket purchase and reservations.

Some of the major trains originating at this station are the 2180 Taj and the three Shatabdi Expresses, including the early-morning departing 2002 which, like the Taj, calls at Agra, and the 2302 and 2962 Rajdhani Expresses to Howrah and Bombay Central respectively. To Madras there are daily departures by 2616 Grand Trunk and 2622 Tamil Nadu Expresses. Over two dozen other major expresses link the capital with Lucknow, Puri, Guwahati, Patna, Indore, Allahabad, Bangalore, Secunderabad, Trivandrum or Mangalore, Kalka, Amritsar, Jammu Tawi and Varanasi.

Delhi Station

Delhi station (sometimes called Delhi Main) is to the north of New Delhi station and can be reached by train from there, either on suburban or main line services. It has a friendlier atmosphere than New Delhi but is bereft of more than essential amenities. Kiosks and snack counters are grouped along the length of the main platform where there is a charmless self-service restaurant.

There are 18 platforms, three of which are for metre gauge trains. There is a counter where reservations can be made for the retiring rooms which can be reached by lift. The retiring rooms – at least the one I had in 1992 – gave me the feeling that I would rather be elsewhere, and the attendants seemed to wish that too. There is a barber shop.

Reservations for departures from this station by foreign tourists can be made at the ITB. There is a computerized reservation booking office at the station. An occasional steam train can be seen puffing through the station which redeems its dismal atmosphere.

A dozen metre gauge trains originate at Delhi including the 2901 Pink City Express to Jaipur and the 9615 Chetak Express to Udaipur

City and other trains to Bikaner, Jodhpur, Rewari and Ahmadabad. Some major trains on the broad gauge line are the 4647 Flying Mail to Amritsar, the 4041 Mussoorie Express to Dehra Dun and trains to Sealdah and Howrah, Guwahati, Jammu Tawi and Muzaffarpur.

Do not get confused with your departure station since they are not close together. If you go to the wrong one, it will take at least 30 minutes by taxi to switch from one to the other.

Hazrat Nizamuddin Station

To take the pressure off New Delhi this station, located in the southeast of the city, close to the luxury hotel area, has been expanded to serve as a terminal for trains to/from the south. It is also the major station on the ring railway. A computerized reservations complex is 500 m from the station. Current reservations can be made in the booking hall which is a contrast to the scrum of New Delhi station. There is a left luggage cloakroom. Two retiring rooms and a dormitory are off platform 1, which also has refreshment and waiting rooms; more facilities are planned. Platforms 4 and 5 are the main ones, at present receiving nine pairs of trains a day plus eight EMUs.

Trains originating here include the 1450 Mahakosai Express to Jabalpur, 2702 Goa Express to Miraj, 7022 Dakshin Express to Hyderabad, 8478 Kalinga Utkal Express to Puri and 8544 Samta Express to Visakhapatnam.

Ring Railway

Delhi's ring railway gives a marvellous view of the backside of suburban city life, often literally as people use the line as a toilet. It was opened in 1982 and girdles the city, covering a distance of 35 km.

The trains make four circles clockwise and four anti-clockwise a day, from Hazrat Nizamuddin to 20 stations. There are two morning runs, and two evening ones. In the morning, one train provides a link from New Delhi (departing at 0740) to Delhi (arriving at 0753).

This is an EMU service, which means an Electrical Multiple Unit is used to pull it. It is supposed to stop for only 30 seconds at stations so passengers have to move sharply. It is very popular with commuters; if you want to try it, the best time is at a weekend when it is not so busy.

The seats are wooden and there are lots of handles for standing passengers, as well as plenty of fans. The doors are kept open all the time and no smoking is allowed. One of its stations, Safdarjang, is near the Rail Museum.

Rail museum

The rail museum, set up in New Delhi in 1977, was the first of its kind in India. Engines and carriages, all refurbished and painted in their original colours, are exhibited on tracks of different gauges laid out in a 10 acre 'railway yard'. Six display galleries and a padlocked, glass walled building housing the museum's star exhibit (the Fairy Queen), a toy train and a restaurant, are included in the museum grounds.

For those fascinated by the sight of old locomotives, the museum is delightful. When I was there off-season (in July) it looked a bit neglected with bored attendants and overgrown gardens but nothing could detract from the majesty of the engines on view.

The Fairy Queen is claimed to be 'the oldest surviving locomotive in perfect working order anywhere in the world.' It was purchased by the East Indian Railway in 1855, two years after the inauguration of the first rail line in India. It was built by Kittson, Thompson & Hewitson of Leeds, UK, and looks eager to keep on running. However, the claim to be the oldest is disputed. In a letter to *The Guardian* in April 1989, George Shuttleworth of Leighton Buzzard says there are older locos in working order in Austria ('Liacon' built in 1851) and in England ('Lion' built in 1838). Close to her is half an engine, a locomotive built in 1891 in Glasgow for the Nizam's Guaranteed State Railway, and sliced lengthways to show its workings.

On tracks among the grass, where you can wander at will, are more than two dozen vintage locos and a score of carriages, including an armoured train. Such trains, with 'Maxim Guns' were extensively used up to the 1920s by the British Army. The MG train in the museum was built in India prior to the First World War on wagon stock of the 1880s. Each carriage is provided with an armoured plate ½ inch thick, with felt lining 3 inches thick and another armoured plate of ¾ inch thick to protect the occupants against normal gun fire.

Other spectacular carriages are the white painted Vice Regal Dining Coach (1889) with its entrance platforms at both ends and the saloon coach of the special train of the Maharaja of Mysore. This coach could be run on broad gauge as well as metre gauge with a change of bogies without disturbing the royal family during their journey from Mysore to Madras. The other two carriages which made up the Maharaja's train are in the rail museum in Mysore (see Chapter 10).

The Prince of Wales saloon coach has its original fittings and furnishings. It was built for the visit to India of the Prince of Wales (later Edward VII) in 1876, and is provided with sunshades on both sides. A fourwheeler sheep van (built in 1929) is divided into four compartments with two tiers to accommodate 176 sheep. It also has sunshades.

The wooden Nilagiri passenger coach (built 1914) used on the rack and pinion railway up the steep gradients of the Nilagiris has canvas curtains as protection against the sun, wind and rain, its only difference from the wooden coaches in use today.

A new addition to the museum is an X-Class metre gauge loco of the types still used on the Nilagiri Mountain Railway. The Shimla Railcar (built 1931) fitted with a 4-cylinder petrol engine and painted in white and light blue, is a small version of the rail cars used on the Kalka/ Shimla line.

Other delightful oddities include Ramgotty, with wooden brakes, built in France and converted from 4 ft gauge to 5 ft 6 in in 1896, and the steam monorail engine which ran on a single rail with an outrigger wheel running on the road alongside the track Originally monorail trains were pulled by mules of the Patiala State Monorail Trainways on a 50 mile track.

A behemoth hulking over pygmy locos is the Garratt, built by Beyer, Peacock of Manchester in 1930 for the Bengal Nagpur Railway. This engine could easily haul 2,400 tons of trailing load on a 1 in 100 up gradient. Not all the engines are steam. Sir Roger Lumley built in 1930 for the Great Indian Peninsula Railway is electric powered. One of the first EMU coaches introduced on the Bombay suburban section of the Bombay, Baroda and Central India Railway (BBCIR) in 1928 is also on display.

The galleries have a variety of mementoes and models of early as well as current Indian railway equipment. There is some of the Burmese teak furniture from the BBCI Railway; the Miraj station clock (1926), engine plates, special coach fittings and displays showing the development of signalling and telecommunications.

An astounding sight in the middle of the technology is the skull of an elephant whose firm refusal to budge from the track caused the derailment of the entire seven carriage Calcutta to Nagpur mail in September 1894.

Souvenirs on sale in 1992 included original builder's plates and motor plates from scrapped steam locos at Rs300 to Rs400 each, and some rail history books as well as a pack of 10 colourful postcards of the exhibits, and a bottle opener/ice-breaker (Rs12). There is a good, if out of date, guide to the museum available. The exhibits are well labelled with description, year built, builder and area of service.

Admission is Rs 2 for an adult, Rs 1 for a child, with a charge of Rs 5 for every camera taken in. On Tuesdays, entry is free for children below 12 years old. The museum is open from 1000 to 1730 but the ticket office closes at 1700 hours. It is closed on Monday and on Republic Day, Holi, Idn'l Fitr, Independence Day, Mahatma Gandhi's birthday, Dussehra and Diwali.

The most appropriate way to get to the rail museum is by train. It is five minutes walk from the ring railway station of Safdarjang, in the southwest of New Delhi. It is close to the Chanakyapuri Diplomatic Enclave, an easy ride by taxi or auto-rickshaw from the Welcomgroup Maurya Sheraton or Taj Palace hotels.

Rail Transport Museum, Shantipath, Chanakyapuri, New Delhi, 110021 .Tel: 601816. Curator, Rail Transport Museum, Room 536D, Rail Bhavan, New Delhi, 11001. Tel: 383624.

Delhi Cantt
This MG station could almost be part of the museum. It has the period look of the 1930s, heightened by seeing the Palace on Wheels train which departs from here; the setting is perfect for its antique-style carriages. The station is off the road to the international airport on the western outskirts of the city, beyond the Dhaula Kuan roundabout.

The 4893 Jodhpur, 4791 Bikaner and 9901 Ahmadabad Mail trains stop here for a few minutes on their way out of Delhi, as do the 4789 Bikaner, 9903 Ahmadabad, 9615 Chetak (to Udaipur City), 9931 Aravali (to Ahmadabad) and 9733 Shekhawati Expresses and several steam-hauled passenger trains.

There are several stations with the word Delhi in their name, but they are halts on the main or suburban passenger lines: Delhi Azadapur, Delhi Kishanganj, Delhi Safdarjang, Delhi Sara Rohilla and Delhi Shahdara Jn.

Delhi reservation offices
Indira Gandhi International Airport
ITB, New Delhi Station
IRCA Complex (adjacent to New Delhi station)
Delhi Junction
Hazrat Nizamuddin (near railway station)
Sarojini Nagar (near railway station)
Kirti Nagar (near railway station)
Delhi Shahdara (near railway booking office)

Railway Enquiries:
Delhi/New Delhi/Nizamuddin stations. Tel: 3317575 or 3313535.
Reservations. Tel: 344877.

Where to stay
The nearest top hotel to New Delhi station is also the newest, the 500 room Holiday Inn Crowne Plaza (Tel: 3320101) which opened in October 1988 and is about five minutes away.

The Taj Mahal Hotel (1 Mansingh Road, ND. Tel: 3016162) is popular with New Delhi regulars. It has a lively bar off the lobby and a roof top restaurant, where Italian/Indian buffet lunches are served. The rooms have twin beds and small bathrooms; there are 308 units including some magnificent suites. The practice of serving a tea bag in a plastic flask in my room for breakfast reminded me too much of railway retiring rooms, but a good feature is the illuminated 'Do Not Disturb' sign outside each room.

The Oberoi Maidens Hotel (7 Sham Nath Marg, Delhi. Tel: 2525464) is convenient for Delhi main station and is a firm favourite with British travellers, perhaps because of its colonial style as well as its superb value for money with even standard rooms having a separate sitting room. It is one of the oldest hotels in India, and was the centre

of Delhi's social life during the days of the British raj. It was *the* place
to stay then, and there is a story about two young ladies who were
guests there when their funds ran out. They telegraphed their father in
England: 'Please Send Money Fast Or Can No Longer Stay Maidens.'

The Oberoi (Dr Zakir Hussain Marg, Delhi; tel: 363030) was India's
first modern luxury hotel when it was opened in 1965. It is given
warmth and soul by the butlers who attend guests in every room, an
innovation that confused me at first as I wondered what a butler did.
Mine organized my photocopying and shopping as well as polished my
shoes. When I mentioned this book he gave me tips on which trains to
try.

BOMBAY

For the rail traveller, Bombay is an exciting introduction to India: the
city's stations have all the rail glamour you could want, as well as trains
that go to most major destinations. The booking and information
system works well, if you're patient, for it isn't that simple. There is
the added attraction of Bombay itself – an exciting and bustling
metropolis.

If you arrive by air, there is a railway enquiry desk and reservations
centre at Bombay's international airport, open from 2300 to 0700, to
coincide with flight arrivals. If your itinerary is complicated, though,
wait until you get to the Foreign Tourist desk at Bombay VT station.
As with New Delhi, I recommend a day to settle in before trying to
sort out your onward rail travel.

Your first problem will be to find out whether your train leaves from
Bombay VT or Bombay Central or even from Dadar, an important
subsidiary station. The confusion is compounded by there being two
railways in Bombay: Central and Western.

Central Railway (CR) does not operate trains from Central station
but from Bombay Victoria Terminus, known as Bombay VT. Trains
from Bombay Central station are operated by Western Railway (WR).
It takes time to unscramble, especially if you try to make a reservation
on a WR train which should be done at a third station, Churchgate,
which is not a main line station but a suburban one.

Bombay VT

At first sight it seems unbelievable that the Victorian Gothic pile with
its stained glass windows, cathedral arches and stone animals leaping
from its walls like gargoyles, is a railway station. It is regarded as one
of the finest station buildings in the world, from the architectural point
of view. In May 1988 it was 100 years old.

Entry to the station is not actually through the portals of this
glorious façade but around the back to the side of it. What you see
when you stand and stare in amazement at the front of it is the

RACE COURSE to Dadar

Chowpatty Beach

BACK BAY

Malabar Point

GATEWAY OF INDIA

KEY

1. BOMBAY CENTRAL RAILWAY STATION
2. KAMALA NEHRU PARK
3. VICTORIA TERMINUS RLY. STN.
4. G.P.O.
5. CHURCHGATE RAILWAY STATION
6. OBEROI HOTEL
7. TOURIST OFFICE
8. AMERICAN EXPRESS & THOMAS COOK
9. AIR INDIA & INDIAN AIRLINES
10. TOWN HALL
11. TAJ MAHAL HOTEL
t. TEMPLE

BOMBAY

0   1
km

N

administration building; for VT is the HQ of CR. The entrance gate is guarded by two massive stone animals, a lion and tiger, representing the United Kingdom and India.

Originally the Great Indian Peninsula Railway Company, CR has grown into one of the country's major railway systems. With 6,486 route kilometres, it traverses six states: Maharashtra, Madhya Pradesh, Uttar Pradesh, Haryana, Karnataka and Rajasthan. Within its jurisdiction are some famous tourists spots, including the Taj Mahal at Agra, Ajanta near Jalgaon and Khajuraho (which has no rail station) near Satna (which has).

The VT complex has reached saturation point having expanded as much as possible during its century of existence. As well as its suburban services, it handles 55 trains a day from platform 8 to 13. The suburban platforms 1 to 7 are across the road from the station and handle 1,003 EMUs – the local suburban commuter trains – a day. A new terminal is planned at Kurla, north of Dadar, its other overflow station.

In the station, there is a non-veg restaurant (open 0630–2130) on the second floor which serves the usual range of railway food. Its attraction is the Victorian furniture: umbrella stands, dressers, and a wooden and mottled glass screen concealing the kitchen. Also on the second floor is an attractive fast food self-service snack bar (1100–1900, closed Sundays), and a veg restaurant at the other end of the corridor.

The retiring rooms are located upstairs in the main station building, with tall, polished wooden doors and huge brass bolts, and there are two dormitories with six beds in each. Waiting rooms here are large and peaceful.

In the station concourse there are electronic indicators, coach guidance systems and train time indicators. It has all the amenities and ambience of a major station with plenty of thrills, tearful farewells and the last minute panic associated with train departures.

Adjoining the station is the new (1987) CRS building, built to fit in with the Gothic grandeur of the station. It houses a computer reservations system like the one in New Delhi, with a telex room linking it with other stations. There are counters (numbers 21 and 22) for foreign tourists on the ground floor. Start with the tourist guide at counter 22; he will check your reservation requisition chit, your date of entry into India in your passport, and your IRP. If you intend to buy a single journey ticket, you can only do so here with UK pounds or US dollars or with rupees accompanied by a photocopy (which he will keep) of your foreign currency encashment certificate. The guide will stamp authorization on the reservation chit and pass it to his colleague who will issue the computer reservations coupon. Reservations from the foreign tourist quota are available only one day in advance, except for IRP holders. The IRP can be bought here.

Because of lack of space, you'll have to stand in a queue although there are some chairs beside the guide's desk on which you might be invited to sit. The counter is open 0800 to 1630 (lunch 1330 to 1400), closed Sundays; the computer is manned daily until 2000 hours, including Sundays.

Services from this station go east and south and some northwards, serving among others: Bangalore, Bhusaval, Chhapra, Cochin, Delhi, Faizabad, Firozpur, Gorakhpur, Guwahati, Howrah, Hyderabad, Itarsi, Jabalpur, Jhansi, Kanniya Kumari (via Trivandrum), Kolhapur, Lucknow, Madras, Mangalore, Miraj (for Goa), Nagpur, Pune, Secunderabad, Sholapur and Varanasi.

The suburban services almost overwhelm VT station. The suburban booking office is on the right of the main concourse; gaze up at the ceiling and you'll feel you're in church. Suburban trains are operated from here, carrying passengers in chaotic, crowded conditions which have become notorious. The trains are fast and frequent and during offpeak hours are a pleasant way to traverse the city; they have 1st Class and Ladies Only carriages.

Tickets can be bought at any counter in the booking hall. There are no waiting rooms on the platforms served by EMU trains and the free toilets are busy because the EMU trains don't have any. Electronic displays indicate train departures, platform and destination.

CR publish a small booklet containing details of all the suburban services from Bombay VT, heading northwards to Dadar and beyond.

Dadar Station

A small terminal was provided at Dadar in 1968 to cope with the increasing demand by passengers. It is the only Bombay station served by trains of both Central and Western Railways. It is used as a transfer station by passengers on Bombay VT bound trains who want to change to a train bound for Bombay Central or Churchgate, and vice versa.

WR's main line trains both outward and inward stop here and it is a main stop on WR's suburban service. Dadar is 8.85 km from Bombay VT, 4.48 km from Bombay Central, and 10.17 km from Churchgate.

Some main line expresses which originate and terminate at Dadar, are the 1057 to Amritsar, the 1027 to Gorakhpur, the 6511 to Madras and the 6657 to Cochin and Mangalore. The 2161 Lashkar Superfast goes to Agra Cantt, the 1147 Shram Shakti to Muzaffarpur, the 7399 Sevagram to Nagpur, the 7311 Sahyadri to Kolhapur and the 6063 Chennai to Madras.

Churchgate Station

This station, under the control of Western Railway, was built for suburban services. The station is in Bombay's central business area and is of interest to foreign tourists because of its proximity (across the road from its eastern exit) to WR's reservation office and a Government of India Tourist Office.

The tourist office is open from 0830–1800 Monday to Friday; 0830–1400, Saturday and holidays; closed on Sundays. It is staffed by charming ladies who hope you're not going to ask about train times since the rail office is next door. They will supply information or pamphlets on most places in India.

The Western Railway's reservation office is open 0800–1400, 1415–2000 and on Sundays 0800–1400. The place for foreign tourists is the desk at the far end of the office (which is on the mezzanine floor). The guide I met there in 1992, Kamal Singh, is a remarkable character with train information in his head and an abiding concern for the welfare and travel arrangements of foreign travellers. He is at his desk from 0930 to 1630 and, on Saturdays, 0930 to 1430. He explains all the reservation details and directs tourists to counter 28 for actual ticket purchase. The Indrail Pass is also sold there. Don't go to Churchgate for reservations to Goa, that's done at VT station but Churchgate does have computer ability for making reservations on the Delhi and Madras terminals.

When I asked why, in the age of computers, a tourist can't make a reservation from the foreign tourist quota at Central station, instead of having to come to Churchgate, I was told that any problems can be resolved immediately at Churchgate since it is the HQ of Western Railway. As with the other foreign tourist bureaux, remember a photocopy of a rupee encashment certificate if you plan to purchase a ticket with rupees.

Kamal Singh explained to an anxious tourist that berth numbers are not entered on the reservation coupon since the allocation of berths is only done on the day of departure of the train. However, if a lower berth, or a coupé, is requested at the time of booking, that information is entered on the computer and, while it cannot be guaranteed, foreigners get preference over everyone except government VIPs, so requests are usually granted.

As the suburban terminal for WR, Churchgate station has 91 trains arriving during the three-hour peak period in the morning, with each EMU train discharging nearly 3,500 commuters.

The traffic is unidirectional which makes it a concentrated flow from north into Bombay in the morning and from south to north in the evening, like a human assembly line. Bombay's suburban services are the most intensively utilized in the country, carrying 70 to 75 per cent of India's commuter traffic.

There are 28 stations in the WR suburban network, extending 59.82 km from Churchgate to Virar. In 1993, electrified suburban services to Bombay completed 65 years. While WR is proud of its 95 per cent punctuality rate, delays are often caused when pedestrians use the tracks as a passage between built-up areas.

Tourists find the suburban system an excellent way to travel across the city, but not in rush hours. One family told me: 'It's clean, fast, safe, cheap and well sign-posted. The only problem is when you arrive at a station there are no signs to show which end of the platform has the exit you want. One is the main exit and the other leads to the back, but how do you know which one?' You don't.

Bombay Central Station

This station can be reached by the suburban line from Churchgate on one of the EMUs. The journey takes 10 minutes. There is no direct suburban line link from Bombay VT to Bombay Central. So if you arrive at one station to leave from another, the best method is by taxi which is unlikely to take less than 30 minutes.

The entrance to Central station is surprisingly rural, a small building with a driveway. It has been landscaped with place of honour in a park given to an NG loco (563K) of the old BB & CI Railway, formerly on the Bilimora and Waghai section. There is a tiled lobby with local and long distance platforms and the usual station facilities including a pharmacy.

There are 10 retiring rooms on the top floor with wooden doors and western movie style swing shutters. The waiting rooms are on the first floor overlooking the passenger hall and a notice advises passengers to leave luggage in the 'clock' room where, in fact, a list of the times it is open is on display.

The computer reservations office has no facilities for foreign tourists who should go to Churchgate.

The Non-Veg restaurant is somewhat lavatorial, the Veg one with blue tiles is larger and brighter with a self-service counter and payment at the end according to what you take, a good way of trying some of the exotic snacks on display when you don't know what to ask for.

The Western Railway zone reaches up to Agra Fort and New Delhi, embracing Rajasthan (Jaipur and Ajmer) as well as the whole of Gujarat. It also has services branching eastwards across country to Jalgaon and Bhopal, destinations it shares with Central Railway.

The most important train from Bombay Central is the Rajdhani Express which speeds for New Delhi on Mondays, Tuesdays, Thursdays, Fridays and Sundays, taking 16 hrs 55 mins for the journey.

Among the score of other expresses are trains to Ahmadabad, Amritsar, Dehra Dun, Hapa, Porbander, Surat and Vadodara.

Enquiries

Central Railway: Tel: 2623535; Western Railway: Tel: 4937575/49333535.

Where to stay

The nostalgic head like homing pigeons for the Taj Majal Hotel with its Intercontinental Hotel appendage in Apollo Bunder (Tel: 2023366). There is a new hotel, the Bombay Oberoi, which is also part of a pair as it is joined to the Oberoi Towers, a short taxi ride from Bombay VT station (Nariman Point. Tel: 2025757, room price includes butler.) The management are proud of this hotel and it shows in everything, even down to the brightly polished buttons on the liftboys' spotless white uniforms. It's quite a wrench to get back on a train.

CALCUTTA

Calcutta is fun; a sophisticated city despite the teeming millions, but it is not the best city in which to begin a rail journey. If you do arrive at Dum Dum airport wanting to catch a train, there is a good rail booking office there with quotas for a same-day travel on some main trains but your best bet would be to wait until you get to the Fairlie Place reservations office.

Calcutta is served by two main line stations, Howrah and Sealdah, and two railways: Eastern (ER) and South Eastern (SER). Both railways have their headquarters in Calcutta although SER doesn't actually have a station to itself; it rents platforms at Howrah and Sealdah from Eastern Railway. There is also a circular railway run by ER and India's first underground railway, the Calcutta Metro.

The Eastern Railway network fans out westwards with Bangladesh to its east and the mouths of the Ganga to its south. It serves the states of West Bengal, Bihar, eastern Madhya Pradesh and part of Uttar Pradesh. It covers 4,290 route kilometres and 730 stations of which about 30 are on narrow gauge lines.

It handles 1,550,000 originating passengers daily who travel on 1,300 trains of which roughly two thirds are suburban trains. ER has approximately 1,118 locomotives, 3,000 passenger coaches, 1,000 EMU coaches and over 96,000 wagons.

It needs so many wagons as it is mainly a freight carrying railway, serving the major coalfields at Asansol, Jharia, Karanpura and Singrauli. Many of the tourist sites within the ER zone are religious, such as the footprint of Lord Vishnu at Gaya and the Buddhist temples at Bodhgaya and Sarnath.

South Eastern Railway celebrated its centenary in 1987 as the direct descendent of the BNR. It serves stations in six states: West Bengal, Orissa, Andhra Pradesh, Bihar, Madhya Pradesh and Maharashtra. It deals with two lakhs of passengers a day at Howrah alone.

Despite carrying nearly 195 million passengers in a year, it is primarily a freight carrying railway serving an area rich in basic materials such as coal, iron and manganese ore, limestone and bauxite. The raw materials of seven major steel plants are carried by SER which also serves three major coalfields and two aluminium complexes.

With the coalfields in its area, it is not surprising that SER has lots of steam locos: in 1988 these amounted to approximately 341 BG and 56

CALCUTTA

(Showing Metro Stations)

NG engines. It also had 351 BG electric engines and 355 diesel, with 59 NG diesel. The railway had 2,760 BG and 472 NG passenger carriages with 51,700 BG and 1,803 NG wagons. But here, as in other zones, steam is on the way out.

Another side of this industrial railway is seen in SER's afforestation programme. In five years from 1981 to 1986, 74.60 lakhs of saplings were planted by SER; with a survival rate of 80 per cent, that's a lot of trees. In its zone are the picturesque wilds of Saranda, the greens of Chhotanagpur and the foliaged heart of Madhya Pradesh.

Reservations

Eastern Railways is proud of its computerized reservation system (CRS) which enables 'an intending passenger to obtain a reservation for any train (ER or SER) in any class on any date within the advanced reservation period from any of the computerized reservation counters in Calcutta.'

Yet for the foreigner there is only one place where reservations can be obtained from the foreign tourist quota, that is Fairlie Place, which is not even near a mainline station. It is close to the BBD Bagh station which is on ER's circular railway but it is easier to get there from Howrah Station by ferry. The terminal for the Chandal Ghat Ferry is at the end of the road that splits Howrah station in two. The ferry operates at 15 min intervals from 0815 to 2000 daily, except Sundays. The fare is 70 paise for the ride across the river to the BBD Bhag ferry terminal. Once there, you walk across the railway line and Strand Road, then into the thoroughfare opposite, where the Fairlie Place building is on the right, at number 6.

This ancient building used to belong to the army. A sign saying Computerized Railway Reservation Office hangs over the doorway, with working hours given as 0900–2100 on weekdays, 0900–1400 on Sundays and the three national holidays (January 26, August 15 and October 12). Another sign says Computerized Foreign Tourist Bureau. Outside on the pavement are shoe cleaners and wayside kitchens, inside on the ground floor is all the chaos of general reservations: any counter for any train to any destination.

Upstairs on the right of the entrance is the foreign tourist bureau (working hours 0900–1600, lunch 1300–1330; 0900–1400 on Sundays). The atmosphere is pleasant and friendly. The office is air-conditioned and box-like with chairs for waiting passengers, a counter with chairs in front of it and, when I visited in 1992, only two computer monitors. There is a railway guide to help plot itineraries and a very helpful staff although their ability to deal with lots of tourists is limited by having only two computers. In the season, there can be as many as 100 tourists a day trying to make bookings, so start early in the day.

Applications for reservations are made on the usual requisition slips and can be made here for all mainline trains. Payment for tickets must be in foreign currency; if you only have rupees, you'll have to buy your ticket downstairs.

Indrail Passes can also be purchased at Fairlie Place and, when possible, the staff try to accommodate passengers who want to begin travelling that very day. Reservations can be made for Darjeeling if the line is open.

Howrah Station

The distinctive brick coloured station on the opposite bank of the river to the Fairlie Place office, was built in 1905. A few years ago there was an attempt to paint it lemon yellow but public protest kept it brick red. A road (vehicles, except taxis, allowed for a toll of Rs 20) divides the station into north and south sections, and provides access to platforms 8 and 9.

The north side opens onto the non-ticket area running alongside the entrance to platform 1. It also links up with a subway entrance with shopping kiosks on both sides. The 2nd Class booking office is here and also lots of fresh fruit stalls.

The north section has a first-aid post with a doctor available for a few hours every day from 1000 and there is a medical hall (chemist) in the centre of the concourse. Bridging the road is a large mural over the platforms. The main entrance is flanked by ornamental wood panelling which used to front the old booking office. At this side of the station are three restaurants: a coffee corner serving non-veg meals (I had a very good western style lunch there) and, from 1400 to 2100 hours, Chinese meals. Adjoining this is a veg self-service restaurant, with waiters in attendance at meal times, and next door a non-veg restaurant with lurid green tables. Both are open 0600 to 2200.

In the main concourse is Wheelers book kiosk and a delight is the Globe Nursery, a florist. Behind this is the entrance to the retiring rooms which, in 1992, had been reduced to four. A grand staircase, close to the computerized train enquiries office, leads to the various classes of waiting rooms which are rather airless although there is a view of the river and the traffic-clogged Howrah Bridge from the terrace.

Beside the staircase is a new feature, the Railway Art Gallery. Next to it is a war memorial with a brass crest of the old East Indian Railway. Other features of this station include a 'public grievance redressal booth' in MCC stripes of red and yellow, a West Bengal State Tourist Office and, on the right of the wood panelled entrance, a barber shop which probably hasn't changed much since the station opened. Another relic of the past are the hand-pulled rickshaws which can be hired outside the station. Turn right at the exit to walk the 200 m to Howrah South Station.

Opened in 1992, this building is a paler version (pink instead of rust) of the formidable main station, a graceful reproduction with towers, arches and balconies like its neighbour, senior by 85 years. There is no platform to platform link so for platforms 18 to 21 served by the new station complex, you have to come out of the main station and walk around to your right, passing the open air barbers on your right, and the main entrance to the Rail Yatri Niwas.

The station entrance is narrow with an alcove on its right with an emergency desk and booking hall for that day's departures. The 2nd Class sleeper waiting room is upstairs. Also upstairs, on the first floor, is the computer reservations complex, open 0900–2100, Sundays 0900–1400, where there is no special counter (yet) for foreign tourists. There were 10 terminals when the complex opened, but space for 24.

When I visited in 1992 the station forecourt with its direct access to its four platforms had not gained much character. Its cleanliness was due to the banning of fruit stalls although there were snack bars. A cafeteria is on the mezzanine floor with a gallery where passengers can sit and watch trains arriving. Electronic indicators show departures and arrivals. Up another floor are the waiting rooms for upper class passengers, the gents room glorying in planters chairs with reclining backs and long arms.

The platforms can accommodate trains 22 coaches in length and the station is easing the pressure on Howrah which handles 540 million passengers a year. It cost over 10 crores to build. If you are travelling on any of these expresses, Howrah South is your station of arrival or departure: 8033 Ahmadabad, 8029 Bombay, 2611 Bangalore, 2841 Coromandel, 2859 Gitanjali, 8015 Hatia, 8045 Hyderabad East Coast, 8007 Puri, 8409 Sri Jagnath, 8005 Sambalpur, 8079 Tirupati, 8001 Bombay Mail via Nagpur, 6003 Madrail Mail and 201 Puri passenger.

Trains from Howrah's main station are led by the 2301 Rajdhani Express which departs at 1600 for the 17 hours 50 minute run to New Delhi (1445 km) but not on Wednesdays and Saturdays. Also for New Delhi are the 2381 and 2303 AC Expresses and there are major trains for Bombay, Kalka, Amritsar, Gorakhpur, Lucknow, Agra, Secunderabad and Dehra Dun.

Sealdah Station

The first thing to learn about this station is how to pronounce it. The locals say Sheldah. It deals mainly with suburban and local trains and is used by about a million passengers a day. The main station building, the north block, was built in the 1970s and has ten platforms. The computerized reservation counters on the first floor are open 0900–2100 and 0900–1400 on Sundays and holidays. In special cases, foreign tourists can make reservations here though there is no special counter, or even signs, for them. Better to head for Fairlie Place.

Sealdah station is in the heart of the city of Calcutta, on the eastern bank. Mainly serving commuter traffic, most main line trains leave from platform 8 which is on the right as you wander into the station.

Vehicles have access to this platform. Electronic signs indicate from which platform the trains leave, but you'll have to decipher the code of abbreviations. The computerized reservations complex on the first floor is usually very crowded. Also on the first floor is the V and NV restaurant, a haven – but a dull one – from the chaos in the booking hall below.

The retiring rooms are on the second floor. All four of them are non AC and rooms 2 and 3 are bright, with windows that open onto a view of the forecourt below. The dormitory is very basic. The waiting rooms are spartan with stone benches. The SS here has two offices, one on the first floor and the other off the booking hall where he can be found during important train arrivals and departures.

Platform 8 is for VIP trains and has a VIP waiting room. There is a Passenger Guide on duty with his own desk and a 'May I Help You' booth open for important trains. There is a bookstall and a first-aid post as well as kiosks selling soft drinks.

Departures from Sealdah include the 3111 Delhi, 3151 Jammu Tawi and 5185 Chhapra Expresses, the 3143 Darjeeling Mail going to New Jalpaiguri, the 3153 Gour Express to Malda Town, the 2557 Kanchenjunga Express to Guwahati and the 3103 Bhagirathi Express to Lalgoda.

Shalimar Station

Under construction and expected to open sometime in the 1990s, Shalimar station will be run by South Eastern Railways. The goods terminal there is being shifted to Sankrail. Completion is linked with that of the second Hooghly Bridge. It will handle main line and suburban trains.

Suburban services

The SER has had EMU suburban trains in operation since 1968 and runs 140 EMU local trains daily, carrying about 200,000 passengers. Services are Howrah to Kharagpur/Midnapore, Panskura/Haldia, Santragachi/Bargachia.

A circular railway system is run by ER operating a stretch of 10.5 km between Prinsep Ghat and Ultadanga Road stations with work under way on the final 3.5 km section to Dum Dum Jn. You can try this line from BBD Bagh station (the initials stand for Benoy Badal Dinesh) to Prinsep Ghat.

Trams

Leave Howrah Station by the subway off to the left, close to platform 1, and you come to the bus station and, a real treat for rail buffs, the tram station. Trams from Howrah serve 10 routes, including the journey across the river that takes you to the public relations office of Eastern Railway. It is a journey backwards in time, making you wonder how the trams have managed to survive in such crazy traffic. Ride the trams on a holiday and you can buy a ticket for unlimited travel for Rs3. Fares, according to stages, are between .70p and .90p for 1st Class and between .60p and .80p for 2nd Class. There are two carriages, both with special seats for ladies.

The Metro Railway

The idea for building an underground railway in Calcutta was conceived in 1949 but it was 20 years before the project was studied and a plan for a Mass Rapid Transit system prepared. The foundation stone was laid in 1972. That it was able to open at all amazed observers but in 1984 the first part was inaugurated. Now 10 km out of 16.43 km and 11 stations out of 17 are under commercial operation, from Tollygunge to Esplanade and Belgachhia to Dum Dum.

When completed it will carry more than 60,000 commuters per hour each way on trains following each other at intervals of two minutes. Every day about 1.7 million transit trippers are expected to use the Metro. From Dum Dum to Tollygunge will take 33 minutes. There are eight coaches per train, each one able to carry 278 passengers standing and 48 sitting.

A ride begins by buying a printed ticket, issued by a machine, from the ticket counter, at a cost of Rs 1 or Rs 1.50 depending on destination. Tickets can be bought in carnets of ten for the cost of nine. Entrance is through turnstiles where ticket checkers are on duty. Passengers should keep their tickets while travelling in case of onboard checks, but there is no checking at the exit.

The timetable says 'Do not squat, vend, eat, smoke or drink in Metro train or premises' and the cleanliness of the station owes much to the pride with which its users regard it. Potted plants grow undisturbed on platforms and the station walls are free of graffiti. Each station has a wide island platform with trains entering on either side. Murals adorn the entrances and walls of some stations and the customary CCTV plays full blast.

Replicas from the Calcutta Museum are on display in showcases at some stations. A cute idea at Esplanade Station is a noticeboard for personal advertisements. It adds a bit of charm to the strictly functional lines of the station. Off peak, many lights are dimmed to save electricity, but no one turns down the CCTV.

Users are so proud of the Metro, they reprimand those who don't show proper respect for it. I queried the reason for the sign that says 'Photography Prohibited' and was told the reason was 'security'. And when the Metro's own staff photographer took a picture of Esplanade Station he was curtly told off by a passenger for not obeying regulations.

As soon as a train has pulled in, its doors open automatically. There is no time to dawdle as they snap shut within seconds, but only after a

KEY

① Beach Railway Sta.
② Zoo
③ Central Railway Sta. and Advance Reservations Centre
④ Egmore Railway Sta.
⑤ Govt. India Tourist Office

MADRAS

recorded announcement in Hindi, Bengali and English, and a bell, has warned that they are about to close.

The seats are metal benches running the length of the coaches, which have the familiar appearance of mainline carriages having been built at the same factory in Madras. They are fully vestibuled with no doors dividing them. Some of the carriages are very noisy because of the air-blowers which keep them cool. These drown out the recorded announcements, in three languages, made on the approach to each station, giving the station's name, and whether the platform is on the left or right.

Where to stay

There are several hotels of character in Calcutta, as befits the former capital of British India with its ornate Victorian architecture. The old tradition of gracious living is preserved at the Oberoi Grand which dates back to the 1870s. The style of the hotel is grand but not snooty. It is in Chowringhee which is practically equidistant from Howrah and Sealdah stations, in case you need an excuse to justify the enjoyable extravagance of staying there.

At Howrah Station is the Rail Yatri Niwas (see Chapter 7.)

Rail data

ER Booking and Information, 6 Fairlie Place. Tel: 204025
ER Enquiries. Tel: 230138
SER Booking and Information, Esplanade Mansions (opposite Raj
   Bhavan). Tel: 289530
SER Enquiries. Tel: 239124.

MADRAS

Madras may not at first seem an obvious place from which to begin your rail journey but it has a lot of advantages. The atmosphere is right: hustling isn't brazen, people are polite and there seems to be a feeling that rushing around isn't really worthwhile. Madras is a gentle introduction to India.

There are now direct flights to Madras from Europe and there is a rail booking-cum-reservation counter at the International airport. This is open 1000 to 1700 hours daily, and there is a rail facility at the domestic air terminal too.

The major advantage of starting a rail journey in Madras is that it is the HQ of the best railway in India: Southern Railway (SR). It's not my view alone, ask Indians themselves. The trains are cleaner, the service friendlier, the food better and the entire journey on an SR train seems more enjoyable.

The reason is probably because SR is a passenger oriented railway. SR's passenger earnings are almost 45 per cent of its total earnings against an all Indian railway figure of 27 per cent. SR carries a million passengers a day on 900 different passenger trains. (There are about 400 goods trains.)

The railway was founded in 1951 by the integration of the erstwhile Madras and Southern Maharatta Railway, South Indian Railway and Mysore State Railway. It traverses 6,729 route kilometres serving over a thousand stations. It covers about 10 per cent of India's land area with a passenger catchment of 14 per cent of the country's population.

It links the southern states of Tamil Nadu, Kerala, the major portion of Karnataka, a small part of Andhra Pradesh and the Union Territory of Pondicherry with the rest of India. It is an area of great variety for the tourist with beaches, hill resorts, forests and animal parks, monuments, temples and ancient traditions, with a welcoming people.

'It's the people that make Southern Railway better than the others,' a passenger told me. 'Better staff and better passengers.' There are better public relations, too, with 'May I Help You' booths located at important stations to attend to passengers' problems.

A train conductor suggested that SR is better because the competition from road transport is greater in the south than in the north so, to keep business, Southern Railway must offer a better service. Another theory is that the nature of people in the south is placid so they do not misuse the railway.

Reservations

At one side of Madras Central station is a new building looking like a modern hotel; this is the advance reservations centre and is part of the suburban station complex. The office is open 0700–1300 and 1330–1930 daily, and 0700–1300 on Sundays. The best time to make reservations is early morning, 0700 to 1000. Bed rolls can be reserved from the same counter where reservations are made. There is a separate counter for ladies.

Foreign tourists should go to the first floor where there is a special office and computer just for them, so the process of booking and getting confirmation is streamlined. Even if there is no foreign tourist quota on the train you want to go on, the staff make a special effort to find space.

There are three main stations in Madras: Central, Egmore and Beach, dealing with broad gauge, metre gauge and suburban services respectively. A rail minibus service links Central with Egmore station, meeting important trains.

Madras Central Station

This is a distinctive rust pink building with white trimmed arches but inside it is less romantic, overwhelmed by passengers and with a patina of grime. At night, when energy-saving yellow sodium lights are switched on, it looks Dickensian.

At this station the SS has his name in lights. His office is on the right of the entrance to the booking hall which leads from the forecourt. Opposite his office are counters for platform tickets and current reservations.

Before the barrier leading to the platform, on the right, there is a Tamil Nadu Tourist Office (open 0715–1900 every day). Twin flights of stairs lead up to the first floor where there are upper class waiting rooms and a restaurant (open 0600–1430 and 1530–2130). Both have wide balconies overlooking the station forecourt.

The waiting rooms (one is for ladies) have bathrooms with showers and toilets and mirrors. A table on the balcony of the restaurant is good for a meal with a view of the city; the staff will sometimes cook something special if you ask.

Activity on the passenger concourse can be watched from the landing in front of the restaurant. Down a passage to the left is a corridor leading to the retiring rooms. These are airless and depressing with king size rats and reverberate with the noise of CCTV. (At this station, children who are separated from their travelling companions and found by station staff are shown on the CCTV screen for them to be claimed.)

Downstairs, the entrance to the concourse is on the left of the lobby with a large Higginbothams bookstall (open 0630–2130) just inside on the left. There is also an India Tourism Development Corp counter for tour bookings and a kiosk selling airpillows with hand woven pillow cases.

The cloakroom for left luggage is down a passage on the left with separate counters for deposit and collection. Boards with the reservation lists for 2nd Class are in the central waiting area; upper class reservation lists are in the main entrance hall.

The veg refreshment room is a grubby, standing-only outlet with a self-service counter containing bins from which various snack items can be removed with tongs. Paper plates are charged extra; a public cup is chained to the water cooler. A medical shop is next door (open 0600–2200). There is also a cafeteria with various kinds of fried cakes and a coffee counter before the ticket barrier.

At the other side of the concourse, beyond the mass of people sprawled on the ground and in plastic chairs in the fan-cooled general waiting area, are more refreshment kiosks.

A glass-fronted cabinet containing uncollected mail addressed to passengers hangs outside the platform inspector's office, and self-help trolleys, wheelchairs and bed rolls are kept here under the inspector's watchful eye.

For passengers wanting to send letters, a post office is at the corner, on the right of the station, near the suburban booking hall. It is closed on Sundays and holidays. A telegram and STD call office is near the public telephone booths on the other side of the entrance.

Outside is a taxi park with auto-rickshaws parked on the right and children asleep on the pavement. Taxi drivers have an agreeable approach and even the begging is restrained. One man asked me politely for the train fare home, saying he'd lost his ticket. I steered him towards the office of the SS, just in case he was genuine.

There are two crack trains a day taking about 34 hours to New Delhi, the 2615 Grand Trunk and the 2621 Tamil Nadu Expresses. To Bombay VT is a daily departure by the 7010 Bombay Mail which takes just over 30 hours while to Dadar there is a daily morning departure by the Dadar Express, arriving 27 hours later. The daily 2842 Coromandel Express takes 27 hours to reach Calcutta/Howrah and the 6004 Howrah Mail also makes the trip daily but takes two nights to do it. Expresses pass through Madras from Trivandrum, Cochin and Bangalore on their way to Calcutta and/or Guwahati on different days of the week. Nearly 30 express, mail and passenger trains a day leave Central station, with a further 20 trains providing a less than daily service.

Madras Egmore Station

If the minibus isn't available from Madras Central to Egmore station, a taxi takes about five minutes. Egmore Station is exclusively metre gauge, serving the southern part of India. The station is a sedate, Victorian (1880s) style, brick red building with a canopy covered entrance off its courtyard. The station now has a splendidly ornate (red walls and cement scroll work) new annexe in keeping with the flourish of the original station, with a computer reservations complex. Any train anywhere in India, not just MG from Madras, can now be booked here, but there is no special provision for foreign tourists.

There are three main line platforms at Egmore and two suburban ones. The 15 retiring rooms are on the first floor with a view from the gallery of the lively action in the street. Waiting rooms are also on this floor.

One of the special trains that departs from Egmore nightly is the 6117 Pandyan Express to Madurai with its 1st Class AC sleeper carriage and other comfortable accommodation (see Chapter 11). The fast day time 2nd & AC Chair Car 2635 Vaigai Express also goes to Madurai. The 2nd and AC Chair Car 2605 Pallavan Express provides a daytime link to/from Trichy, with the 6153 Cholan Express taking the longer, partly coastal route; the 6177 Rock Fort Express goes to Trichy overnight.

Trains to Rameswaram from Egmore include the 6113 Sethu Express overnight and the 6101 Rameswaram Express. The 6119 Nellai Express goes to Tirunelveli while the prettily named 6103 Pearl City Express leaves for Tuticorin every night. The 6105 Quilon Mail meanders through the south, taking 19 hours overnight to reach the west coast town of Quilon.

Madras Beach Station

This is the main suburban line station located behind Burma Market, a street of kiosks selling luxury imported (smuggled?) goods that runs parallel to the platforms. There are six platforms in the station, and a veg restaurant. It is the terminating station for MG trains. There is an EMU MG service to Tambaram/Chengalpattu and there are BG suburban services.

Rail data

Central station enquiries. Tel: 20048.

Where to stay

Madras has some very good budget hotels, especially around Egmore station. A hotel re-opened in late 1989 directly opposite Egmore station is the Hotel Impala Continental (12, Gandhi Irwin Road, Madras 60008) with low-budget prices for suite-style rooms. Only Indian cash accepted. The hotel also operates the grandly named Impala Vegetarian Heart Queen Cleopatra Pleasure Palace – a snack bar. At the airport, there is an orange courtesy coach which meets all flights to take passengers to the nearby Trident Hotel. A useful feature of this garden hotel, opened in 1988, is its special 12 hour rate. This is not the same as a day rate since it applies for any 12 hours, even overnight such as 0200 to 1400. It works out at 40 per cent less than the rack rate. Ideal if you just want to recover from a flight before taking an overnight train.

TRIVANDRUM

One of the pleasantest places to arrive to begin a rail journey is Trivandrum, capital of Kerala, in India's deep south. The airport is small and leisurely with none of the frenzy of India's major airports; it is only 6 km from Trivandrum central station and served by seasonal charter flights from Europe as well as by scheduled flights from Colombo, the Maldives and the Gulf States, and by domestic flights.

The station building is Victorian, extending the length of its main platform. 1st and AC Class tickets for current trains are sold from a counter on the left of the main entrance where timetables and platform tickets are also sold. The entrance lobby itself is small; steps lead from it upstairs to the SS's office and a porticoed gallery where the nine excellent retiring rooms are located. There is also a dormitory with eight beds.

The computerized reservations office is in a building adjoining the station. Downstairs are the counters selling 2nd Class tickets for same day trains. Up the stairs at the side is the long room where advance reservations are made at counters marked by destination. The office is open 0700–1930, lunch 1300 to 1330; only current reservations, enquiries and cancellations on Sundays.

Indrail Passes can be bought here. The Chief Reservation Supervisor (CRS) has his office at the head of the stairs and foreign tourists should go in and see him. 'They can stand in a queue at one of the counters if they like,' he told me, 'but we don't insist.' In fact, foreigners who do join a queue are quickly directed to his office or counter 8.

Trivandrum Central has all the atmosphere of a major station with none of the hassles. There are three platforms, number 1 having the usual offices, restaurants and waiting rooms. The Deputy Station Superintendent's office is near the entrance and that's where to apply for a retiring room by filling in a requisition slip.

The lobby of kiosks includes a milk counter, a fruit stall, a nut vendor (cashews are locally grown), a bookstall and an apple-juice bar. A notice at the station entrance warns 'Beware of pickpockets, jewel snatchers and baggage lifters'.

Although it is so far south, Trivandrum Central is a gateway to all parts of India with daily direct trains for New Delhi (3054 km), the 2625 Kerala Express; Bombay (2061 km), the 1081 Kanniya Kumari Express; Madras (907 km), the 6320 Madras Mail; Mangalore (635 km), the 6349 Parasuram and 6029 Malabar Expresses; and Bangalore (851 km), the 6525 Bangalore Express.

There are also trains daily to Shoranur (302 Venad Express), Erna-kulam Jn (6304 Vanchinad Express) and Cannanore (6347 Cannanore Express) and Kanniya Kumari (express and passenger). Weekly, or bi-weekly, there are direct trains to Guwahati (3625 km) by the 2601 Guwahati Express and to Rajkot via Ahmadabad (2734 km) by the 2604 Rajkot Express.

Popular destinations from Trivandrum are Quilon (65 km) which can be reached by northbound expresses or slower passenger trains, and Coimbatore (for Ooty) on the main line to Madras. To go to Cochin from Trivandrum, take a northbound train to Ernakulam Jn.

The beach resort of Kovalam is 16 km away. Its somewhat lack-lustre Kovalam Ashok Beach Resort is the foremost hotel in the area.

The Rockholm at Vizhinjam, Kovalam, is close to the lively beach, built on a sandy cove, looks good and is recommended by many; economy.

Trivandrum central enquiries. Tel: 62966/63066.

TIRUCHCHIRAPPALLI

Tiruchchirappalli, mercifully shortened by everyone to Trichy, has an international airport 15 minutes from the main station, Tiruch-chirappalli Junction. The airport, served by international flights (from Colombo) is a frustrating experience due to the slow processing of passengers. Trichy Jn station, however, is well run and good for starting a journey, especially by metre gauge train through the south Indian countryside.

Trichy is a town of nearly 400,000 inhabitants, dozens of exotic temple towers and no less than six railway stations. It is situated on the banks of the Cauvery River and is a blend of history and tradition as well as a pilgrim centre and a thriving commercial city.

The main station serves broad and metre gauge. All the express trains are diesel hauled, while about 25 pairs of passenger trains are pulled by steam locos. Built in 1935, the station has been selected for transformation into a model one.

To the left of the spacious forecourt a new building houses the computerized reservations centre. It has the atmosphere and facilities of an efficient system, with a bright waiting area, CCTV, fans, a refreshment stall, a pay toilet, and a suggestion box. My suggestion was that there should be a sign indicating which counter attends to foreign tourists. Counter number 2 deals with enquiries and foreign tourists should start there.

Reservations can be made here for trains leaving from Madras as the system is linked to Madras. A sign says 'Any Class, Any Train, Any Counter, Anywhere.' Another reads 'Please buy tickets 0800–1000 to avoid rush.' Surprisingly since Trichy is an international gateway into India, the IRP is not on sale here, but holders can begin their journey here.

The station has a good Tamil Nadu tourist information office on the right of its entrance. Steps lead up to refurbished retiring rooms (14 doubles, two with AC) and dormitories for 24. Room service is available. There is now a non-veg refreshment room and a reception desk for the retiring rooms, presided over by a matron. Passengers staying in the rooms are lulled to sleep, or jerked awake, by the sound of steam trains (MG) shunting throughout the night. The rooms are fronted by a wide veranda with a view over the station forecourt where local buses wait for major trains.

The platforms are linked by a tunnel and five of them are for MG trains. Platform facilities include veg and non-veg restaurants, a book-shop and book trolleys that meet all important trains. One of these is the fast 2605 Pallavan Express running daily between Trichy and Madras Egmore. It is all chair car with a pantry car, and is painted an eye-catching silver grey and white.

Some MG trains also stop at Tiruchchirappalli Town, a new (1988) temple-like station at the end of a pot-holed village street. The reservation and booking counter there is open 0700–1130, 1430–1730, and there are pleasant waiting rooms with toilets and showers. The station handles mainly commuters although it is an ideal halt to see the nearby Rock Fort.

Srirangam Station (10 km from Trichy Jn) is another new building designed to fit in with its surroundings. It is popular with pilgrims who come to visit the Vaishnavite temple with its 21 towers built in the 13th century AD. The upstairs of the station has two twin bed retiring rooms with writing desks and dorm beds. Trichy's other MG station is Golden Rock. Two other BG stations are Palakkarai and Trichy Fort.

Where to stay

Possibly the best value accommodation in Trichy is Room 8 at Trichy Jn station. This AC twin bedded room is as big as a hotel suite with wallpaper, wall to wall carpet, dressing table, settee and armchairs, lots of lights, fans and a dining-cum-work table. A dressing room leads to a large bathroom with western style toilet, and loo paper, and a hot water shower. There is even a private balcony with a view over the platform roof of the sunrise.

Jenney's Residency (formerly the Rajali Hotel) is a luxury hotel with economy rates per 24 hrs – any period of 24 hrs, not just from check-in to noon) only minutes walk from the station, It has 78 bedrooms and suites and a renowned restaurant. There's a friendly atmosphere, especially in the Soaring High bar by the swimming pool (the only one in Trichy and open to non-residents). A teleprinter in the lobby chatters out the UNI news. Address: 3/14 McDonalds Rd, Trichy. Tel: 41301.

प्रथम दिवस आवरण FIRST DAY COVER

1887-1987

दक्षिण पूर्व रेल शताब्दी
CENTENARY OF SOUTH EASTERN RAILWAY

Chapter 9

Around India by Rail

DESTINATIONS

A list of the most popular destinations for foreign rail travellers, after the cities of Delhi (the top favourite), Bombay, Calcutta and Madras, has been compiled by studying the travel patterns of foreign tourists from bookings made at the ITB (see Chapter 2). Rail tourists tend to follow itineraries of their own devising, to the chagrin of the planners at ITB who have prepared itineraries which rail travellers ignore.

For many rail travellers, part of the fun is poring over timetables to draw up one's own itinerary. The *Trains At A Glance* timetable is the best for that. Zonal timetables are useful for local passenger trains and for discovering through-carriages attached to different trains so you can reach your destination without changing.

Some places popular with visitors do not have a dedicated railway station, so a bus or taxi will be necessary to get there from the nearest railhead. Stations (and the distance from the place) are listed here.

Srinagar – Jammu Tawi
Mount Abu – Abu Road
Khajuaraho – Jhansi (172 km) is best; also Harpalpur (94 km); Mahoba (65 km); Satna (117 km)
Pushkar – Ajmer
Kodaikanal – Kodaikanal Road (or Madurai)
Yercaud – Salem

Buddhist Tour

Bodhgaya – Gaya, via Varanasi
Sarnath – Varanasi (10 km)
Kushinagar – Gorakhpur (54 km)
Sravasti – Balrampur via Gorakhpur
Lumbini – Naugarh via Gorakhpur
Kapilavastu – Naugarh

National Parks

Dachigam – Jammu (200 km)
Keibul Lamjao (Manipur) – Dimapur
Corbett – Ramnagar (51 km)
Sultanpur Sanctuary – Gurgaon (15 km)
Keoladeo Ghana (Rajasthan) – Bharatpur (2 km)
Sariska Tiger Reserve (Rajasthan) – Alwar (36 km)
Desert (Rajasthan) – Jaisalmer (32 km)
Gir (Gujarat) – Sasan (1 km)
Tarboa – Chandrapur (45 km)
Bandhavgarh – Umaria (35 km) Satna (112 km)
Chilika Sanctuary – Balugaon
Kaziranga – Jorhat (95 km)
Manas Tiger Reserve – Barpeta Road (41 km)
Sunderbans Tiger Reserve – Canning (105 km)
Nagarjunasagar Srisailam Sanctuary – Machesla (13 km)
Nagarhole Sanctuary – Mysore (96 km)
Bandipur – Nanjungud (20 km)
Mudumalai Sanctuary – Udagamandalam (Ooty) (64 km)
Periyar – Kottayam (114 km)

Indian Railways has a directorate of rail tourist guides who are professional itinerary planners. The directorate can be contacted in advance if help is required. (Directorate of Tourism, Railway Board, Government of India, Rail Bhavan, New Delhi. 110001.) Another source of help would be the Chief Public Relations Officer (CPRO) of each zonal railway.

Popular destinations are listed below with gateway stations although not all linking trains run daily, and not all intermediate stations are mentioned.

Agra Cantt from Ahmadabad (to Agra Fort via Ajmer and Jaipur), Amritsar, Bangalore, Barmer, Bhopal, Bilaspur, Bombay, Calcutta, New Delhi, H. Nizamuddin (Delhi), Firozpur, Gwalior, Hyderabad/Secunderabad, Indore, Jabalpur, Jaipur (to Agra Fort), Jammu Tawi, Kanniya Kumari, Kathgodam (to Agra Fort), Lucknow (to Agra Fort), Madras, Pune, Puri, Ratlam, Trivandrum, Varanasi, Vasco da Gamma.

Aurangabad from Bombay, Kacheguda (via Secunderabad), Manmad, Nanded, Nizamabad.

Bangalore City from Ahmadabad, Bombay, Calcutta, New Delhi, Guwahati, Hyderabad, Madras, Mangalore, Miraj, Mysore, Nagercoil, Simoga Town, Solapur, Talguppa, Tiruchchirappalli, Trivandrum, Vasco da Gama.

Bhubaneswar from Bangalore, Calcutta, Cochin, H. Nizamuddin, New Delhi, Guwahati, Hyderabad, Madras, Puri, Secunderabad, Trivandrum.

Gorakhpur from Ahmadabad, Allahabad City, Barauni, Bombay, Calcutta, Chhapra, Cochin, New Delhi, Guwahati, Gwalior, Hatia, Hyderabad, Kanpur, Jammu Tawi, Lucknow, Muzaffarpur; also daily passenger trains from Nautanwa or Naugarh (from Nepal).

Jaipur from Agra Fort, Ahmadabad, Ajmer, Barmer, Bikaner, Delhi, Jodhpur, Lucknow, Sawai Madhopur, Udaipur.

Jaisalmer from Jodhpur.

Jalgaon from Ahmadabad, Amritsar, Bangalore, Bombay, Calcutta, Cochin, Firozpur, Gorakhpur, Itarsi, Jammu Tawi, Kolkapur, Madras, Nagpur, Pune, Varanasi, Vasco da Gama.

Jammu Tawi from Ahmadabad, Bombay, Calcutta, Delhi, Kanniya Kumari, Madras, Pune, Vasco da Gama, Trivandrum

Jhansi from Ahmadabad, Allahabad, Bangalore, Bilaspur, Bhopal, Bombay, Chhapra, Cochin, Delhi, Firozpur, Gorakhpur, Gwalior, Hyderabad, Indore, Jabalpur, Jammu, Kanniya Kumari, Lucknow, Madras, Pune, Puri, Secunderabad, Trivandrum, Ujain, Varanasi.

Madurai from Coimbatore, Madras, Rameswaram, Quilon, Tiruchchirappalli, Tirunelveli, Tirupati, Tuticorin.

New Jalpaiguri (for Darjeeling) from Bangalore, Bombay, Calcutta, Cochin, Delhi, Guwahati, Trivandrum.

Puri from Bhubaneswar, Calcutta, Delhi.

Quilon from Bangalore, Bombay, Cannanore, Delhi, Ernakulam, Guwahati, Jammu, Kanniya Kumari, Madras, Mangalore, Shoranur, Tiruchchirappalli, Trivandrum.

Rameswaram from Coimbatore, Madras. (The ferry service from Rameswaram to Sri Lanka is suspended.)

Shimla from Bhiwani (to Kalka), Calcutta (to Kalka), Delhi (to Kalka); Kalka, and other connections via Ambala to Kalka.

Udagamandalam (Ooty) from Coimbatore and from Madras to Mettupalaiyam; Coonoor, Mettupalaiyam, and trains from Trivandrum, Bombay, Madras and Delhi to Coimbatore.

Varanasi from Agra, Ahmadabad, Allahabad, Amritsar, Bombay, Calcutta, Dehra Dun, Delhi, Dhanbad, Gorakhpur, Gwalior, Jammu, Ludhiana, Lucknow, Madras, Puri, Sonpur.

Vasco da Gama from Bangalore, Bombay and Delhi (change at Miraj);
Miraj, Mysore, and from Agra via Miraj.

ITINERARIES
New Delhi/Agra/New Delhi
If you only have time for one rail trip in India, it will probably be this:
to Agra to see the Taj Mahal. There are two good trains from New
Delhi which allow enough time to see the sights and return in the
evening, but it means an early start.

2002 Shatabdi Express ↓	New Delhi:	leave 0615 arrive 2220 ↑
	Agra Cantt:	arrive 0810 leave 2021
2180 Taj Express ↓	New Delhi:	leave 0705 arrive 2200 ↑
	Agra Cantt:	arrive 0950 leave 1845

Delhi/Jaipur/Delhi
The Pink City Express is another popular train which allows a few
hours for sight seeing on a day trip, in this case to Jaipur.

2901 Pink City Express ↓	Delhi:	leave 0600 arrive 2210 ↑
	Jaipur:	arrive 1105 leave 1700

Delhi/Jaipur/Agra/New Delhi
This itinerary, combining two popular places, is possible over two or
three days:

Delhi Jaipur	2901 Pink City Exp.	lv: 0600
Jaipur		ar: 1105
(Overnight in Jaipur)		
Jaipur	2922 Agra Exp.	lv: 0610
Agra Fort		ar: 1100
Agra Cantt	2001 Shatabdi Exp.	lv: 2021
New Delhi		ar: 2220

Indian Railways has several set itineraries for Indrail Pass holders for
which reserved train accommodation can be guaranteed as long as
arrangements are made at least 90 days in advance. A selection of the
itineraries is included here although I don't think the trains they
recommend are very practical.

For instance, there are many timings like this:

Day 3.   Arr: Varanasi 0200
             Dep: Varanasi 2350.

That makes a long day without sleep. So I am not quoting the suggested trains, only the stations as a guide to the best sequence of travelling.

7 day tours

Buddhist tour: New Delhi / Gaya / Varanasi / Gorakhpur / Naugarh (for Lumbini in Nepal by road) / Lucknow / New Delhi.

Rajasthan tour: Delhi / Jodhpur / Jaisalmer / Udaipur / Jaipur / Agra / New Delhi.

Temple tour: New Delhi / Agra / Jhansi (for Khajuraho by road) / Varanasi / New Delhi.

To Goa: Delhi / Jaipur / Agra / Jalgaon / Bombay / Vasco da Gama.

City & Cave: New Delhi / Jalgaon (by road to) Aurangabad / Secunderabad (by road to) Hyderabad / Madras / Bombay.

City & Cave: Bombay (Dadar) / Madras / Bangalore / Lonavla / Bombay.

Temple & Hill: Calcutta (Howrah) / Varanasi (by bus to) Mughalsarai / New Jalpaiguri / Darjeeling / New Jalpaiguri / Calcutta (Sealdah).

Temple Tour: Calcutta (Howrah) / Nalanda / Rajgir / Gaya / Varanasi / Gorakhpur / Agra / New Delhi.

15 day tours

Temple & Beach: Bombay / Jalgaon (by road to) Aurangabad / Secunderabad / Madras (change at Khurda Road) Puri (for Konark). Varanasi / Agra / Jaipur / Delhi.

Desert & Caves: Dehli / Jaipur / Jodhpur / Jaisalmer / Udaipur / Khandwa / Jalgaon (by road to) Aurangabad / Secunderabad / Agra / New Delhi.

North to South: New Delhi / Madras / Madurai / Kanniya Kumari / Trivandrum / Cochin / Ooty (by road to) Mysore / Bangalore / Hyderabad / Bombay.

Religion & Wild Life: Delhi / Jaipur / Bharatpur / Agra / Jhansi / (for Khajuraho by road) / Varanasi / Haridwar / Dehra Dun / Delhi.

City Tour: New Delhi / Bombay / Madras / Bangalore / Bhubaneswar / Calcutta / Varanasi / Amritsar / Delhi.

South Tour: Madras / Bangalore / Mysore (by road to) Ooty / Cochin / Trivandrum / Kanniya Kumari / Madurai / Trichy / Thanjavur / Villupuram / Pondicherry / Villupuram / Madras.

21 day tours

Miscellany: New Delhi / Sawai Madhopur (wild life) / Jaipur / Agra / Varanasi / Calcutta / Puri / Madras / Bangalore / Vasco da Gama / Lonavla / Bombay.

New Delhi / Jammu Tawi (by road to Srinagar and back) / Varanasi / Gaya / Calcutta / Madras / Bangalore / Secunderabad / Agra / New Delhi.

Calcutta / Puri / Madras / Bangalore / Secunderabad / Bombay / Aurangabad (by road to) Jalgaon / Agra / New Delhi / Varanasi / Calcutta.

30 day tours

Madras / Puri / Calcutta / Darjeeling / Varanasi / Haridwar / Delhi / Agra / Jaipur / Udaipur / Chittaurgarh / Indore (by road to) Mhow / Jalgaon / Bombay / Miraj / Vasco da Gama / Miraj / Bangalore / Trichy / Madras.

Circular tours

The zonal railways have devised their own circular tours for which a circular journey ticket (CJT) can be purchased at the station of origin, with reservations made at the same time. Details appear in the zonal timetables.

Tour group itineraries

There are few travel agencies which specialize exclusively in organized tours by rail in India, although many tour operators do feature some rail travel in their package holidays to India.

All India Rail Tours are run by J.A. Butterfield, Burton Fleming, Driffield, Yorkshire YO24 0PQ. Tel: 0262 87230. (See Chapter 11, *Great Trips*).

The Palace On Wheels tour can be booked through Dr Dandapani (see page 40), major travel agencies, or in India through Central Reservations, Rajasthan Tourism Development Corporation, Chandralok Building, 36 Janpath, New Delhi 110 001. Tel: 3321820; telex: 03163142. The itinerary is: Delhi Cantt / Jaipur / Chattaugarh / Udaipur / Jaisalmer / Jodhpur / Bharatpur /Agra / Delhi Cantt. 7 days. (See Chapter 11, *Great Trips*.) Prices, inclusive of meals and tours, start at US $200 per person per day.

TRAVEL TIMES

The time it takes to travel by the fastest trains between Delhi, Bombay, Calcutta and Madras, and some popular destinations is listed

Itinerant musicians by the Parlakamidi Light Railway, Andhra Pradesh.
(Anthony J. Lambert)

Sunrise on the Taj Mahal, as seen from across the Yammuna River, Agra.
(Hugh Ballantyne)

One of India's most extraordinary hotels, the Lake Palace, seems to float on the
waters of Lake Pichola, a five-minute drive from Udaipur City station.
(Gemunu Amarasinghe)

here in hours and minutes. Where there is no time given, there is no direct service from that city, so a change of train will be necessary.

	Delhi	Bombay	Calcutta	Madras
Agra	1.55	25.10	29.20	33.06
Bhubaneswar	29.35		7.05	19.50
Bombay	16.30	–	33.10	26.45
Calcutta	18.15	33.00	–	27.40
Delhi	–	16.55	17.50	33.45
Jammu Tawi	10.45	33.00	37.30	62.45
Jhansi	4.24	20.00	24.20	27.40
Madras	33.20	26.10	27.05	–
Secunderabad	26.15	14.20	31.20	14.20
Trivandrum	53.20	44.35	48.10	18.15
Varanasi	13.15	27.10	14.40	39.00
Vasco da Gama	41.30*	20.20*		

(*Includes wait of 30 minutes for change of train from BG to MG at Miraj.)

(A blank space indicates no direct service.)

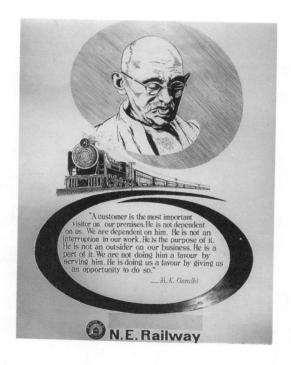

"A customer is the most important visitor on our premises. He is not dependent on us. We are dependent on him. He is not an interruption in our work. He is the purpose of it. He is not an outsider on our business. He is a part of it. We are not doing him a favour by serving him. He is doing us a favour by giving us an opportunity to do so."

— M. K. Gandhi

N.E. Railway

Madras Egmore station.

Profiles of Some Popular Rail Destinations

AGRA

Agra has seven stations but only two of them, Agra Fort and Agra Cantt, are frequented by tourists. **Agra Fort** station was built in 1891 as a halt for colonials on picnic expeditions to the Red Fort and Taj Mahal. It is a Western Railway station with MG trains to Rajasthan and Gujarat. There are also BG trains to Lucknow, and it is a stop for the Toofan Express linking Delhi with Howrah. There is one BG platform and three MG ones, which actually have a separate entrance at the city side of the station.

Walls of the Red Fort tower over the station and the Taj Mahal is a short auto-rickshaw ride away. There is a fine view of the Red Fort from the terrace in front of the six-bed dormitory and the retiring rooms. The railway offices and waiting rooms are off platform 1 (BG) but the cloakroom is on platform 4 (MG). In the main lobby, the reservation office is on the left and the BG booking office on the right. First class reservations on all trains can be made at the counter by the enquiry office.

This enquiry office is a separate kiosk where foreign tourists can obtain help. A useful feature of Agra Fort station (which could be copied by other stations with lots of foreign passengers) is a sign which states: 'In case of difficulty, the Indrail Pass holders should approach CRS.' Although it doesn't explain what CRS means, it's nice to know foreigners are being thought of.

The auto-rickshaw drivers and their touts lurking to prey on tourists in the small forecourt are rapacious. Be firm, though, and they will soon lower their prices. The fare to Agra Cantt station drops after stern bargaining and it is an exotic ride through bazaars and pot-holed roads.

At **Agra Cantt** station, the taxis and rickshaws are organized by their own unions and have printed tariff cards which they show to passengers as they come off the train. Taxis and tour buses park on the right of the forecourt with auto-rickshaws gathered around the circular

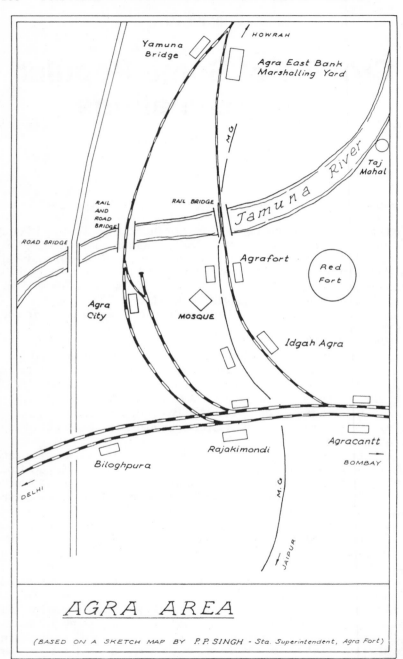

AGRA AREA

(BASED ON A SKETCH MAP BY P.P. SINGH - Sta. Superintendent, Agra Fort) gardens and cycle rickshaws and tongas on the left. The tour buses are run by the Uttar Pradesh Tourism Dept and the UP Transport Dept and link with the arrival/departure of the Taj Express. Tour tickets (taking in the major sights) are sold on board the trains, and from a booth on platform 1. There is a very helpful Uttar Pradesh tourist bureau (0800 to 1500) in the station lobby. If you are wait listed for the return journey to New Delhi, check at the counters on the right of the booking hall; number 3 is for upper class reservations, number 6 for the Taj Express and number 7 for the Shatabdi Express. They all function at different hours with 'bookings for counter number 7 between 1400–1700 being done on counter number 6.' There is no counter dedicated to foreign tourists which is puzzling since so many foreigners use the station and the Indrail Pass can be bought there (at the upper class counter, but there's no sign saying so). There is a 2nd Class booking hall for local trains in an annexe to the station.

The present station was constructed in 1960 and has retiring rooms: six non AC double rooms and two AC and a large dorm with 10 beds. Bottled mineral water can be bought at this station and a variety of nasty plastic models of the Taj Mahal. There is a post office at the end of platform 1.

Agra Cantt: Tel. 649776.

AHMADABAD

The delights of Ahmadabad station are many which is fortunate since, as the junction for trains to and from Rajasthan, Gujarat and Bombay, it handles 174 trains and serves over 105,000 passengers a day, many of them being tourists stuck there while they await a connection. But if you want to phone home you can since there is a streamlined, modern telephone complex on the right of the lobby where faxes and telexes can be sent, and a 'Home Country Service' where collect calls (to USA, Japan, UK, Spain, Netherlands, Italy and Singapore) can be made at the press of a button.

The station has 12 platforms of which 1 to 4 are BG, 5 and 6 both BG and MG according to demand (thanks to a unique dual track which has three rails) and 7 to 12 for MG. There is another exit from the station by platform 12 but don't use it since all the action, and efficiency, is at the BG side, the main exit to the town.

The waiting rooms are large and some have wooden beds. The retiring rooms are on the first floor, with three dormitories offering 32 beds and other rooms for singles, doubles and triples. The best, number 23, has a fridge as well as a TV and four AC units and an Indian-style toilet. The floor overlooks the booking hall and on the opposite side there is a V and Non-V restaurant but vegetarian food is practically obligatory in Gujarat and the variety is much greater from the platform mobile food vendors. There is also a 'Medicell' (medical shop) and some bookstalls with counters both on the lobby and platform sides. The tourist office in the lobby is only open occasionally.

At the left luggage office a sign advises passengers not to keep 'eatable items in luggage to avoid damage of your articles by rats.' Worth remembering in the retiring rooms of most stations too. The office closes for 30 minutes three times in 24 hours. Current bookings can be done in the lobby where there is also a helpful enquiry office.

For advance reservations, Ahmadabad has a computerized reservations building to the left of the station. This is better than many in other major cities being clean (no food vendors inside) and air-conditioned for passengers not just for the computers. It is open 0800–2000, Sundays 0800–1400 and handles about 12,000 reservations a day. Foreign tourists should head for the supervisor's counter, number 12, where physically handicapped, senior citizens, grievances and freedom fighters are also dealt with 'on personal appearance'.

Gujarat being India's only dry state need not deter you. Ask a taxi to take you the six km drive to the Cama Hotel where a very trendy looking liquor shop provides a permit 'to possess and use foreign liquor for personal consumption' and permission to buy one unit (equivalent to one bottle of spirits or 10 bottles of beer) a week. The chit is Rs35.

ALLAHABAD

There are two sides to Allahabad station: the residential side and the city side. A bridge links all nine platforms whereas previously passengers had to use two. The bridge is a boon for passengers since reservations are done on one side and tickets purchased on the other. Close by there is another station, Allahabad City, for MG trains.

The main booking counter for 2nd Class reservation and tickets is in the lobby. None of the counter signs are in English but there is an enquiry office (with its sign in English) where directions can be obtained. At the side of this complex is a counter for buying upper class tickets, but not for making reservations which has to be done across the bridge.

The retiring rooms at Allahabad are on the second floor, city side, with access by steps from the 2nd Class waiting hall. There are 13 rooms and two dormitories. The upper class and ladies waiting rooms are on the first floor. There is a restaurant (open 0730 to 2300) off platform 1 with ancient, grouchy waiters. It has a separate section specializing in 'South Indian dishes'. There are lots of snack bars and book stalls: Allahabad is the HQ of the A.H. Wheeler's chain of station bookstalls.

Notices on the platform say 'Alight here for Sangam Pilgrimage'. Located at the confluence of the Ganga, Yamuna and the invisible

Saraswati rivers, Allahabad, the City of God, is one of the important ancient cities of India. As a sacred centre, it attracts thousands of rail passengers every day.

It is on the main line from Calcutta to New Delhi. Among the major expresses stopping are the Tinsukia and Kalka Mails, the Rajdhani Express and the Delhi/Howrah, Neelachal, North East, Amritsar and Toofan Expresses; Delhi is 627 km distant, Howrah 814 km. There are lots of trains from Allahabad to Satna where there is a road link to Kharjuraho.

ALLEPPEY

This station, opened in 1989 as the temporary terminus of the new BG line from Ernakulam Jn, is destined to become popular on the tourist circuit as it gives access to the inland waterways from Cochin. When construction is completed on the through-line down the Kerala coast from Ernakulam, it will be a stop on the way to Trivandrum. It has a Veg snack counter, two spacious retiring rooms and a small dorm. The sole platform can take 34 carriages at one time, and land is available for station expansion.

There are booking counters at one side of the bright lobby with counter 1 handling advance reservations. The quotas have been inherited from the Alleppey out agency which used to be near the boat jetty and is now closed. A huge, locally made coir mat hangs like a tapestry above the booking office with a vivid design of the Kerala boat races.

With the opening of Alleppey station, it has become the ideal railhead for a backwaters boat trip. The jetty is 3 km from the station with occasional buses available. The boat journey to Quilon is overnight so pointless if you want to see the scenery; better is the shorter (2½ hours) trip to Kottayam (qv). Boats leave Alleppey throughout the day with a seat costing a few rupees, tickets available on board. In 1990 with some friends I chartered a 'pilot' (read pirate) boat to Kottayam for Rs250. It was a memorable trip by canals and lakes alongside waterlogged paddy fields and coconut groves. Well worth it.

Few trains serve Alleppey as yet. One that does is the 8689/90 express which leaves the station every morning at 0530 for the 2,428 km journey across India to Bokaro Steel City via Madras, Visakhapatnam and Ranchi. There is also an overnight express (6041/42) between Alleppey and Madras.

AMBALA CANTT

Ambala is a major transit station in the Northern Railway network where passengers from Shimla connect with Lucknow and Jammu Tawi trains. It can be a pleasant place to wait. Just outside the station are some open air restaurants with comfortable seating and brick ovens for cooking chapatis. There is also an English wine shop open all day selling Indian spirits and chilled beer. The NV restaurant at the station has some magnificent pieces of antique furniture, almirahs, dressers, a hat stand and screens, in daily use. There is no special counter for foreign tourists but there is a helpful reservations counter open 0930 to 1630 daily.

AMRITSAR

If Amritsar is on your itinerary, there are several trains to get you there, including the 1057 express from Dadar, the superfast 2925 Paschim Express, and the 2903 Frontier Mail from Bombay; the 2459 superfast from New Delhi and the 4647 Flying Mail from Delhi. Rob Dobson reports that people at the station are geared up to taking you to the Golden Temple by bicycle rickshaw and then putting you back on a train again.

Access to/from Pakistan is via Atari with the 4607 I.P. Express listed as leaving Amritsar at 0930, arriving at Atari at 1010, returning at 1420, arriving Amritsar at 1500. From Atari you take a minibus to Pakistan.

AURANGABAD

Aurangabad, a popular place to stay while exploring the caves at Ellora (30 km distant) and Ajanta (106 km) is now linked by BG line to Manmad with a direct Bombay–Aurangabad express. Recently remodelled the station has five platforms, receiving and despatching MG trains from/to Secunderabad as well as the BG link to Manmad.

Some travellers prefer to go to Jalgaon instead for access to the Ajanta Caves (59 km distant), since many trains stop at Jalgaon as it is on a broad gauge line linking it with Bombay and other main stations (see Chapter 9 for connections).

Aurangabad Station enquiries: Tel. 4815.

BANGALORE

Bangalore is expanding so fast as an industrial and business centre, its beauty as a garden city has been obscured. Infrastructure is struggling to keep up but the railways recognized the boom and, in 1981, made it a fully fledged division of Southern Railway. Bangalore is about to become the fourth major metropolis of India, overtaking the position held by Madras. In 1988 a new railway administration building was opened, next to the City station, and it has been crowned with the nose of a metre gauge steam engine as an authentic replica of the Indian Railways emblem.

At **Bangalore City** station, the high-ceilinged lobby has a booth for the Karnataka State Tourism Development Corporation promoting its tours. The bus station is opposite the railway forecourt and tourist agencies line the road to the right. Also in the entrance-lobby is a police information kiosk where a notice warns passengers about unauthorized 'ticket nippers'. The chemist (open 0600–2200) sells bottled mineral water and the bookshop (0900–1300, 1400–1700) has lots of locally produced guides about India.

Tickets for same-day departures can be bought in an annex to the lobby. For advance reservations go to the new building on the right of the station forecourt where there is a special Indrail Pass counter where foreign tourists can buy tickets and make reservations. This counter (number 1) can be busy as it is for foreign tourists, freedom fighters, concession holders and handicapped and senior citizens so allow plenty of time. The station has 12 platforms, six BG and six MG, with self-help trollies, wheel-chair assistance and 270 licensed porters.

There is a vegetarian restaurant off platform 1 with mechanized food mixers and fast-food boilers. A non-veg restaurant is on the upper floor, beside the gallery overlooking the booking lobby. Waiting rooms are also there. The 23 retiring rooms are much in demand, double rooms all have twin beds, fans, settee and armchairs, a writing desk, dressing room and bathroom with hot water and towel. There are dorm beds in a ward-like atmosphere.

In keeping with its new image as the city of the future, Bangalore has an extensive system of direct rail links with the rest of India. There is a nightly departure by the superfast Karnataka Express to New Delhi, a journey of just over 40 hours. The Udyan Express takes 24 hours to Bombay while an MG mail passenger train gives a daily service to Vasco da Gama (Goa). To Madras, there are morning, afternoon and evening departures taking between six and seven hours for the 362 km journey.

Bangalore Cantonment station is more rural with light blue tiles lining the platform walls and an odd cluster of arches opposite platform 1. No trains originate here; it is a halt for those going to and from Bangalore City station. It has a bank to facilitate customers clearing freight from the goods yard that adjoins it. Bangalore is an inland port linked with Madras for imports and exports. In one shed in the yard I saw hundreds of drums of aspirin being loaded into a rail container for direct shipment to the UK.

Not far from both stations is the Welcomgroup's Windsor Manor Sheraton hotel (25 Sankey Road, Bangalore. Tel: 79431), an Indian architect's interpretation of an English stately home. Although constructed in 1983, it blends in perfectly with Bangalore's genuine historic buildings. The hotel is popular with local and foreign tourists and business visitors both to visit (the Royal Derby bar reeks of British nostalgia) and to stay. The city's newest hotel is the opulent Oberoi, (tel: 585858).

Bangalore City station enquiries: Tel. 77918.

BERHAMPUR

A small station with fantastic connections. You can get here any day from Howrah or Bhubanswar by superfast trains, and also from Madras (on the Coromandel Express or Howrah Mail) or from Hyderabad by the East Coast Express, and from Tirupati too. Once a week, expresses stop from Trivandrum, Guwahati and Cochin.

You go to Berhampur to get to Gopalpur On Sea, a beach resort on the Bay of Bengal. It is also the station closest to the huge (70 km by 15 km) freshwater Chilka Lake, which the railway runs beside. There are dorm beds at the station and doubles. Buses and taxis go to Gopalpur On Sea, 18 km distant.

BHUBANESWAR

There are plans to make Bhubaneswar into a model railway station with a new building opposite the existing station to house a computer reservations facility and other offices. The station built in 1965, is on the Calcutta–Madras main line with the railway tracks separating the new town from the old. Bhubaneswar is famed as the temple city of India and taxi drivers pester passengers with offers of city temple tours as soon as they arrive.

A staircase off the booking hall leads to the retiring rooms of which the best are the AC rooms at a rate which includes tea and newspaper. I didn't fancy the dormitory nor the gloomy waiting rooms. On the same floor are doors marked Veg and Non-Veg which open into the same restaurant. The 2nd Class waiting hall is downstairs at platform level. As well as the Wheelers bookstall there is a Sarvodaya stall with locally produced guide books among the religious tracts. I was astonished to find a telex bureau off the booking lobby.

Bhubaneswar's attractions are historical as it is part of ancient India although its proximity to the coast resort of Puri (reached by train) and to the Sun Temple at Konark (reached by bus) draws visitors. Rob Dobson recommends a modest but comfortable, central hotel near the station with good views of the city gardens: Hotel Keshari, 113, Station Square – economy rate. There is a hotel (the Oberoi) at Bhubaneswar built in 1985 that has become an attraction in itself because it has been conceived along temple lines with an outer sanctum leading to another and on to the inner heart of the hotel, in this case a pool and garden surrounded by rooms. At this hotel, before serving my beer, the barman asked 'Are you German or English, sir?' When I said English he tilted the glass and poured the beer frothless and to perfection. The hotel is 4 km from the station, at Nayapalli. Tel: 56116.

Bhubaneswar station enquiries: Tel. 402042.

CANNANORE

Not many foreign tourists find their way to Cannanore but it has a vast beach (no beach life or hotels though) and is a friendly, middle class town. The pleasure begins at the station where the five retiring rooms (above the police post) are well managed, each one with a comments book on which the SM takes action. Room number 5 overlooks the tiny station garden. Both the VRR and the NVRR serve good food, the NVRR in a charming small restaurant, the VRR in a dining room. A station door marked 'Hindi Class' does not refer to a class of passenger but to lessons for railway staff. There is an info counter off the large entrance lobby where the advance reservations desk deals very effectively with foreigners, open 0900–1300; 1400–1700.

There is a forlorn, colonial style hotel, the Savoy, one km from the station. On a cliff overlooking the sea, the economy rate Choice Seaside Hotel, once a tea planters' retreat, is an amazing find which guests like to keep secret, so only go there if you're good company.

CHANDIGARH

A modern looking station with very clean waiting rooms, on the line from Delhi to Kalka (for Shimla). There are two retiring rooms, both at the end of the office block on the sole platform. The reservation office says it's open 24 hours but is actually closed between 0130–0200, 0630–0900 and 1800–1830. Chandigarh is the capital of Punjab and Haryana States and the station is 8 km from the centre of the city planned by Le Corbusier. The 0600 hours departure of the 4095 Himalayan Queen express from New Delhi gets to Chandigarh (244 km distant) at 1012 and the station is on the run of the 2311 Howrah to Kalka mail which arrives at 0355 daily after leaving Delhi at 2245.

Chandigarh station enquiries: Tel. 22105.

CHITTAURGARH

Set in the plains of Rajasthan, Chittaurgarh station is on the MG line. It has a long tree-lined platform which doubles as 1 and 2 with retiring rooms, refreshment room and separate Ladies and Gents upper class waiting rooms beside it. The station is basic in appearance with a lobby that leads to a combined enquiry and reservation kiosk (open 1000–1700) with signs in English. A booking office for general tickets is on the left and a waiting hall on the right. The station is 6 km from the impressive fort ruin which is what visitors come to see.

A portion of the 2901 Pink City Express takes nearly 12 hours for the 622 km day-time journey from Delhi. Overnight there is the 1300 departure from Delhi by the 9615 Chetak Express via Jaipur which gets in at 0452. The same trains link Chittaurgarh with Udaipur 117 km away. You can get here from Secunderabad (a distance of 1129 km) on the daily 1635 departure of the 582 fast MG passenger train to Ajmer which arrives at 1255 after two nights, or on the faster 1940 departure of the 7570 Express to Jaipur, arriving at 0440, two nights later. From Jaipur, there is the 7569 Express and two other trains a day come from Ajmer.

COCHIN (KOCHI)

The full name for this station on India's south-western coast in Cochin Harbour Terminus and it is built on Willingdon Island in a natural harbour famous for its maritime history. Access to Cochin is also via Ernakulam Jn (qv). It's recently been renamed Kochi. The station is simple and small (one island platform) compared with its importance with direct services to Ahmadabad, Bangalore, Bilaspur, Bombay, Coimbatore, Gorakhpur, Guwahati, Howrah, Hyderabad, Indore, Madras, Patna, Trichy and Varanasi. A reminder of the train called the Tea Garden Express exists in the old 1st and 2nd Class sleeper coach and the general unreserved coach attached to the nightly Cochin to Trichy Express (6366) for Ooty-bound passengers. At Coimbatore (qv) the two coaches are shunted into a siding for four hours then attached to the Nilagiri Express (6105) for the ride to Mettupalaiyam (change for Ooty). On the return journey the coaches enable through-the-night travel to Cochin without changing at Coimbatore.

To cater for passengers a restaurant was opened opposite the station in the 1950s to which were added three bedrooms to qualify for a liquor licence. It was given a flashy name, Casino, to attract customers. Now it has grown to a hotel of five-star luxury. Several readers share my opinion that Cochin's Casino hotel rivals India's top hostelries for comfort, service and good food, and all within low, standard rates. Arrangements (including permit) are handled here for a fascinating side trip, a flying visit to the only island in the **Lakshadweep** group open to foreigners. The Casino Hotel runs the Bangaram Island Resort; it's in the luxury rate category but a wonderful way to relax after too much rail. (Casino Hotel, Willingdon Island, Cochin 682003; tel: 04846281.)

Cochin H.T. station enquiries: Tel. 6050.

COIMBATORE

This station, perhaps because it's new (1987), is one of the cleanest on Indian Railways. It isn't particularly pretty – they call Coimbatore the Manchester of South India because of its industry – but it is neat, tiled, bright and well-run. You can judge a station's efficiency by the number and appearance of the mobile vendors on its platforms. Coimbatore excels: they are many and they are smart, even the profit/loss accounts are displayed on the wall of its NV restaurant. You change trains here on the way to Mettupalaiyam for Ooty (see *Udagamandalam* in this chapter), unless you are coming from Madras on the 6105 Nilagiri Express which stops in transit for 30 minutes. The station is served by a dozen major trains daily, and by a score more on a weekly or bi-weekly basis.

The spacious lobby has an expanse of granite floor tiles and natural light from its many windows. On the left on entering from the forecourt is the cloakroom and a Tourist Information Centre (0700–1900, except holidays: 1000–1730). A tunnel leads to each of the station's six platforms, numbers 5 and 6 being MG.

Unreserved tickets are sold at the counters to the right of the lobby. Computerized reservations are made in a separate hall upstairs. There are no foreign tourist quota berths available but an enquiry to the CRS or SS (his office is on the ground floor) will bring instant and friendly help. On the first floor, on the other side of the gallery overlooking the lobby, are the retiring rooms with non AC doubles and an AC apartment.

The Hotel Sri Thevvar, 500 m from the station near the flyover (153 Avanashi Road, Coimbatore, Tamil Nadu 641018. Tel: 24135) has rates even less than the station retiring rooms. There is a day-time room service, a restaurant and a cellar bar (1100–2300) where drinks are sold at close to retail prices.

Coimbatore station enquiries: Tel. 37716

DEHRA DUN

This station is the rail gateway for Mussoorie, 22 km distant by bus or taxi. Mussoorie is a picturesque hill resort commanding views of Himalayan snow ranges to the northeast and of the Doon Valley, and Haridwar to the south. There are retiring rooms at the station, with the usual rates for a double room being increased during the May to October peak season. The station is served by the daily Dehra Dun Express direct from Bombay via Delhi, a 1701 km journey covered in 42 hours. From Delhi (320 km away) the trip takes 10 hours overnight by the Mussoorie Express or nine hours during the day by the Dehra Dun Express. The Doon Express terminates in Dehra Dun at the end of its 36 hour (1524 km) run from Howrah via Lucknow. There is also an Express from Varanasi. By train to Shimla or Jammu Tawi is via Laksar and Ambala Cantt.

ERNAKULAM JN

This is Cochin, although trains bound for Cochin terminate at the Harbour Station on Willingdon Island. If yours doesn't go there, alight here for the 8 km ride by bus or taxi, unless you are staying on the mainland. There are no special facilities for foreign tourists at Ernakulam Junction although the station does have an information counter. There is a computerized reservations office. Stairs from the lobby lead to the three double retiring rooms and a new dormitory. The station is served by direct expresses from Bangalore, Bombay, Delhi, Madras and Trivandrum while other trains stop at Ernakulum Town. A rail link to Alleppey (qv) was opened in 1989.

Ernakulam Jn Enquiries: Tel. 353100.

ERNAKULAM TOWN

This is a halt station for incoming trains that bypass Cochin HT and could be the station you go to by mistake when you should be catching your train from Ernakulam Jn. If you alight here, buses go to Junction station, Cochin or the ferry jetty. There are no retiring rooms but several tourist hotels opposite the station.

Ernakulam Town Enquiries: Tel. 353920.

ERODE

More people pass through this station than join trains here, which is not surprising since the station entrance with booking hall is 100 m down a tunnel (under the goods yard) from the platform. Five retiring rooms overlook the goods yard and are reached by dual staircases with 1920s iron bannisters. Food vendors patrol the platform throughout the night when nearly 30 BG trains stop for a breather. 120 locos are based at Erode.

Erode station enquiries: Tel. 74444.

GAYA

This Eastern Railway station teems with begging children, shoe cleaners and vendors of *gram* which people spit into your face as they talk with mouths full. Yet this is the station from which to travel (15 km by bus or taxi) to the great pilgrim centre for Buddhists, Bodhgaya. Gaya itself is a centre for Hindu pilgrims. The station has four retiring rooms with two beds in each and two with AC. It is well served by main line trains and can be reached by direct expresses from Delhi (984 km in 18 hours, approximately), Howrah (458 km/8 hrs), Bombay (1715 km/30½ hrs), Jammu Tawi, via Lucknow and Varanasi (1509 km/36 hrs), Puri via Bhubaneswar (589 km/17–18 hrs), Patna (92 km/2 hrs) and Ranchi (337 km/8½ hrs).

GORAKHPUR

Gorakhpur is the HQ of the North Eastern Railway served by broad and metre gauge trains (see Chapter 9). Its attraction to foreigners is as a transit station to Nepal or for a visit to Kushinagar where Lord Buddha died. It is a spacious station with its upper class facilities centred around the main entrance, under a clock tower. Reservations are computerized. Train timetables are in Hindi although there is an illuminated sign in English giving current departures and platform numbers. A left luggage office is on the right, with the sign in Hindi.

The lobby leads to the platforms where there is a book stall (open 0430–0130 daily) and a combined veg and non-veg restaurant (0630–2130) with an all-night refreshment stall outside it. Waiting and retiring rooms, some with AC, are upstairs. The one I stayed in actually had toilet paper to go with its western toilet. There is a deluxe double with TV, fridge and two cold drinks. There are 25 beds in three dormitories; plans are in hand to construct a 35 bedroom railway hotel at the station.

An Uttar Pradesh Tourist Bureau is on platform 1 where an excellent set of leaflets is available, including one about Buddhist pilgrimages in the area. There are also police assistance, tourist help and grievance redressal booths on the platform. People in a hurry who have a complaint can collect a stamped lettergram to complete at their leisure and mail back to the station. Buses meet the main trains and from the nearby bus station buses leave on the hour for the 54 km ride to Kushinagar. Kushinagar can also be reached by bus (35 km) from Deoria Sadar station, 45 minutes by train from Gorakhpur.

There are several ways of reaching **Nepal**. Nautanwa (close to the border) is served by daily MG fast passenger trains, the best one departs from Gorakhpur at 0615 and arrives at Nautanwa two hours later. The train leaves Nautanwa at 0910 and arrives back at Gorakhpur at 1130. The closest station in India for Lumbini (Buddha's birthplace in Nepal) is Naugarh. This can be reached via the MG loop line from Gorakhpur with the passenger train taking 60 minutes to Anandnaga which is a junction from where trains go to Naugarh (a further 52 minutes). Another way to Naugarh is by bus from Basti, a station on the main line to Gorakhpur from Delhi and Bombay which has the cleanest dormitory bathroom of any I've seen in India. The journey via Raxaul station involves too many changes to be practical. The final leg over the border is by bus or taxi.

Visas for Nepal are necessary. You'll need a re-entry visa to return to India but this has to be applied for at the time you apply for the original visa to enter India (ask for a double or triple entry then). When you arrive at Gorakhpur from Nautanwa by train, you could be subjected to a casual customs search on the bridge from the MG platform to the station exit. If you are coming from Kathmandu or Pokhara in Nepal, beware of travel agents there who offer tickets on Indian Railways. A Chief Travelling Ticket Inspector (CTTI) on NE Railway told me he has discovered at least 20 cases of foreigners being overcharged. He proved it when we met a young German who had been charged Rs 200 more than the correct fare for his ticket to Cochin.

'The foreigner is an innocent, we must help him', the CTTI said. He advises foreigners travelling from Nepal to leave purchasing their Indian Railway tickets for onward journeys from Gorakhpur until they are actually in Gorakhpur. The Indrail Pass is sold there and single journey tickets are available. If reservations are difficult, the CRS or SS could be asked for help; it's better than being ripped off.

HARIDWAR

Situated at the foot of the Shivalik Hills and on the banks of the Ganga River where it enters the plains from the mountains, Haridwar is one of the holiest of Hindu religious places. It is on the line to Dehra Dun (qv) and is served by the same trains. The holy town of Rishikesh with its hanging bridge over the Ganga is 24 km and about an hour away by passenger train. There are several wild life sanctuaries within a few kilometres drive from Haridwar.

HYDERABAD

Look for Hyderabad – 'the City of Love' – in *Trains At A Glance* and it says 'Please see Secunderabad' but this station is the terminus (and starting point) for several important trains and is the one foreign visitors are likely to use when coming to see the city's best known landmark, the Charminar, four minarets, built in 1591 (5 km distant). The station has a large courtyard and six platforms and a reservation office in the main building. It is more relaxed than its twin, Secunderabad, and handles about half the number of passengers. There are no retiring rooms.

It is served daily by the 7053 Madras and 6059 Charminar Expresses from Madras (793 km/16½ hrs) and twice a week by the 7029 Cochin Express which also terminates here. It is the final destination for the daily 7022 Express from H. Nizamuddin (Delhi) station, via Agra, 1675 km in 35 hours. The 7031 Bombay Express via Pune also terminates here, taking 18 hours for the overnight 790 km journey from Bombay VT. The 8045 East Coast Express comes daily from Howrah via Bhubaneswar and Berhampur, and the 7007 Godavari Express provides a daily link with Visakhapatnam. It is 10 km from Secunderabad station and through trains generally stop at both.

There is only one five star hotel in Hyderabad, the Krishna Oberoi

The Darjeeling Himalayan 'toy train'. (Anthony J. Lambert)

One of the 2ft gauge 0-6-0 tank engines that once worked the Matheran Hill Railway is preserved outside Bombay Central station. (Anthony J. Lambert)

Passengers riding on the roof at Bamourgaon station near Gwalior. . .

. . .despite official discouragement. (Photos by Anthony J. Lambert)

ಪ್ಯಾಸಿಂಜರ ಪ್ರಯಾಣಿಕರಿಗೆ ನಿರೋಧಿಸು ವದೇನೆಂದರೆ
ಗಾಡಿಯ ಡಬ್ಬಿಯ ಮೇಲೆ ಪ್ರಯಾಣ ಮಾಡ ಬಾರದು

यात्रियों से अनुरोध है व डिब्बों की
छत पर यात्रा न करें।

PASSENGERS ARE REQUESTED NOT TO
TRAVEL ON ROOF OF TRAINS

(Banjara Hills, Hyderabad. Tel: 222121) and it is so new that taxi and auto-rickshaw drivers don't know it, so you'll have to ask for 'Five star hotel' to get there. It is 7 km from Hyderabad station, 5 km from the airport. The hotel is an extravagant fantasy of white marble in a created garden setting; even the lifts have marble floors. There are 286 rooms (luxury rate) and a smart Indian restaurant with an electrically operated punkah.

JAIPUR

Jaipur station has been built (in 1956) in imitation of the flamboyant buildings which abound in this laid-back city of pink proscenium arches and turreted palaces.

Camels loping through the city's traffic are just one of Jaipur's extraordinary sights. The city has gone over the top with its fondness for pink. Horse-drawn buggies, and some buses, are painted pink and even carrots sold by sidewalk vendors are crimson. You'll see pink-bottomed monkeys gambolling on the rooftop terraces of the one-storied pink walled shops that add to Jaipur's fascination.

At the station, the coolies (porters) wear red Rajasthan turbans. The city's street people congregate at night to view the 24-hour CCTV in the booking hall and you'll have to pick your way over them to get to the enquiry desk in the lobby.

If you want to make an advance reservation, go to the new computerized reservation building on the right of the station as you leave it. In the centre of the forecourt is a park with an MG steam loco on a plinth. The reservations complex has its entrance at the side furthest from the station. The 'any counter, any train, anywhere' rule applies here, with queues at all counters instead of a single queue for all the counters. Foreigners have their own window, 769, but since it's also for 'Handicapped persons, freedom fighters and senior citizens' it is usually as crowded as the other windows. It's open 0800–1400, 1415–2000, Sundays 0800–1400.

There is a real rogues gallery at Jaipur Station with framed photographs of what the SS calls 'mischief makers' on several of its walls. Off platform 1 is the tourist office with well presented literature about Rajasthan including an elaborate map which may cost you Rs 5 or may be free. The soft drinks counter is not open in winter; there is a restaurant with tables reserved for vegetarians marked with cards.

The retiring rooms are upstairs with a bright reception office (CCTV also here). There are 17 double rooms, three AC doubles, nine singles and two dormitories, one for women (four beds) and one for men (12 beds).

Dinner tip: while waiting for a train, I discovered the Handi Restaurant with superb lamb and chicken barbecued at its entrance; you eat in a thatch covered courtyard. It's near something called the

Copper Chimney, about a mile's auto rickshaw ride from the station. For a drink, try the rundown palace style villa called the Tourist Hotel operated by the Rajasthan Tourism Development Corporation; great fun in its first floor bar. The Handi Restaurant in its courtyard is not the one I recommend above.

Jaipur, known as the Pink City and the Gateway, and Jewel, of Rajasthan, is one of the most popular destinations for foreigners and has been extensively covered in guide books and colour supplements. It is easy to reach from Delhi, by MG trains, and is a convenient day trip. If you do want to stay, and fancy a night in a former Maharaja's palace, the Rambagh Palace (Bhawani Singh Rd, Jaipur. Tel: 75141), run by the Taj group, is Jaipur's finest hotel with superb lawns and palatial atmosphere.

Jaipur Railway station, enquiries: Tel. 72121.

JAISALMER

After a day or night run through the desert from Jodhpur (the only way to get there by train) the sight of Jaisalmer station, small though it is, is welcome. Its sand-coloured buildings date from 1967 when the line to Jaisalmer was laid.

Opened in late 1991 was a Northern Railway sponsored office for foreign tourists offering comfortable seats, occasional folkloric shows and quota tickets on a strict waiting list basis. It is run by the same amiable character responsible for the Jodhpur office. There is a reservations office open 0800–1100 and 1400–1600 for the two trains (at 0900 and 2115) to Jodhpur. Trains leave Jodhpur for Jaisalmer at 2230 (arrives at 0735) and at 0820 (arrives at 1820). The trip of 295 km is dusty, hot (no AC) and slow (it's MG) but worth it. Take your own bottled water.

Jaisalmer is about 120 km from the Pakistan border, which is perhaps why there are signs at the station, in English, proclaiming: '(1) Be Indian. Buy Indian. (2) Kashmir to Kanniya Kumari, India is one. (3) Many religions, one nation. Let us be proud of it. (4) India is our country, let us help make it strong and prosperous.' Jaisalmer was left undisturbed by tourists until 1974 when a tourist bungalow was built; now there are over 30,000 tourists a year.

The attraction is the fort settlement, emerging out of a hillock in the desert like a phenomenon of nature until you are inside and see the intricate designs of balconies and doors wrought by skilled craftsmen over centuries. There are jeeps and auto-rickshaws to take rail passengers to the gates of the fort and then it is a fascinating ramble through alleyways and alongside temples watched by hospitable and curious people. Actually many of the traders, street musicians and hangers-on are there for the pickings and don't come from Jaisalmer at all.

Chilled bottled mineral water is to be had at a reasonable price in the town square but for a beer wend your way through the alleys (or ask for directions) to the Hotel Jaisal Castle. (Fort Jaisalmer, Rajasthan. Tel: 2362, cable: JAISAL). It has no sign outside and is fashioned out of the walls of the fort, above the scrub and new buildings of the outer town. A narrow balcony with space for two hangs out over the fort wall and is a heady place on which to drink that ice cold beer. The hotel is the perfect desert guest house; cool, whitewashed walls, low-ceilinged rooms with ornate hangings and rustic furniture, and clean, attached bathrooms with showers and western toilets with loo paper too. Although there is a tiny restaurant, dinner can be served on the roof under the stars. Economy bracket.

Jaisalmer ITB, Tel: 2354.

JAMMU TAWI

This busy station is the best railhead for Kashmir, abounding in touts to help or confuse the traveller heading for the bus stand for transport to Srinagar. Since the station is on the 'new town' side of the Tawi River, you'll have to take a mini-bus to the bus stand on the other side. There are retiring rooms at the station; doubles and dorm beds.

It can take between 10 and 15 hours to travel the 585 km to Jammu from Delhi, depending on which train you choose; all trains are overnight. The superfast originating at Bombay Central twice a week goes via New Delhi from where it takes 11 hours to Jammu. There is also a direct train from Madras via all three mainline Delhi stations three times a week, and from Pune the daily Jhelum Express via Agra and New Delhi. The journey from Pune to Jammu takes 41 hours for 2180 km and provides a link with Goa since trains between Vasco da Gama/Bombay VT stop at Pune. There are also direct trains from Calcutta (1967 km) via Lucknow and these bypass Delhi; the journey is about 45 hours.

The real train nut may want to try the longest haul of all, from the Cape to Kashmir, the 6017/18 Himsagar Express. This runs the length of India between Kanniya Kumari and Jammu Tawi a distance of 3,726 km, via Trivandrum, Madras, Agra and New Delhi. The departure days of this once a week trip change according to the season, so I dare not quote them, but it means four nights on the train.

However you travel by train, advance reservations are essential, especially in the season (summer) and are best done through your Indrail Pass GSA before going to India, or at the ITB in New Delhi station. For return reservations, make them at Jammu Tawi on your way to Kashmir or contact the Railway Booking Office at Srinagar to avoid having to hang around Jammu while waiting for a berth on the way back.

JAMNAGAR

Jamnagar in Gujarat is not on the usual tourist route. There are two platforms, a modern entrance lobby and an old fashioned advance reservations system (brain and ledger, no computer) in the station, built in 1987 far from the town and isolated amidst salt pans that pong a bit. There are two retiring rooms and a six-bed dorm on the first floor, pleasant enough and ideal for watching the BG steam locos hauling local trains with their picturesque passengers, especially the oddly-garbed milkmen with their churns hanging from the windows. The old station, a splendid rococo affair with a clocktower, stands abandoned downtown.

Catering and other services are limited. You'll get a meat fix at a place popular with the military stationed in Jamnagar, at Hotel Daavat, Bagga Mansion, opposite Amber Talkies, Jamnagar.

JHANSI

You would only want to get out at this station if you're going to see the erotic temples at Khajuraho, and that's 172 km (five hours) away by bus. The list of trains that stop at Jhansi is long because of its location at the centre of lines running north, east, south and west. Not many people stay, though, and there is only one, rather nasty, retiring room and a dormitory for six adjoining platform 1. Both are controlled by formidable ladies who lock you in on arrival and only let you out on demand. The restaurant (open 0600–1900) is small and gloomy; behind it is a major, modernized base kitchen with capacity for 3,000 meals a day. The dinner that is served (included in the fare) on the evening run of the Shatabdi Express from Bhopal to Gwalior, Agra and New Delhi is prepared here. The Shatabdi Express is the best train to take to get to Jhansi, leaving New Delhi at 0615 and arriving at Jhansi, 414 km distant, at 1039, averaging 92 kph (see Chapter 11).

The station has two tourist bureaux; the one for Madhya Pradesh is very helpful with lots of leaflets; the one for Uttar Pradesh was closed whenever I visited. There is a rash of electronics here: digital clocks in the retiring and waiting rooms, and a display board that flashes when a train comes in. The gents upperclass waiting room has taped music. If you have to stay at Jhansi, escape from the station and try what is called 'the oldest western style hotel of Bundelkhand', the Jhansi Hotel (Shastri Marg, Jhansi, UP. Tel: 1360) a short auto-rickshaw ride away, where tea is served in silver pots left over from British days and there are some remarkable oil paintings of colonial gents above the bar and in the TV room. There is a full range of accommodation at Khajuraho which is actually closer (65 km) to Mahoba station than to Jhansi but the train links are impossible for same-day onward travel.

JODHPUR

When I saw the booking counter at Jodhpur station had a notice saying 'Foreign' in English above it, I was pleased this small station had a counter dedicated to foreign tourists. I was wrong. On this notice, 'foreign' means the counter sells tickets to 'foreign' stations, those outside the Northern Railway zone, not to foreigners. However, the station does have more signs in English than most. It also has a rail tourist bureau, an offshoot of the ITB in New Delhi and a sister bureau of the one newly opened in Jaisalmer. This is run by a personable gentleman called M.M. Purohit, whose enthusiasm for tourists knows no bounds. He has become famous among rail travellers for the help he dispenses. The office is now in new quarters, alongside the retiring rooms. It is open 0500–2300 daily especially to help foreign tourists with reservations, ticket purchase and information, and it also serves as a waiting room, a temporary left luggage office and it even has a toilet. Run by Northern Railway, it is a facility that other stations frequented by foreigners could copy. Jodhpur has been computerized for making advance reservations.

The station is on the MG line and is the junction for trains to Jaisalmer (qv). There are two overnight trains to Jodhpur from Delhi; the fastest being the 2461 Mandore Express which leaves Delhi (626 km distant) at 1810 and arrives at 0605. From Jaipur, which is where most visitors stop before coming to Jodhpur, there is one day-time train, the 5315 Marudhar Express (leaves Jaipur at 1400, arrives Jodhpur at 2205) and two overnight trains. You can get to Jodhpur from Bombay by changing trains at Ahmadabad. The 5314 Marudhar Express (MG) leaves Jodhpur at 0620 daily for Jaipur, Agra Fort and Lucknow.

The city isn't just a transit stop on the way to Jaisalmer but worth a longer visit for its grand palaces, 15th century fort and the bazaar atmosphere of the old town. Another reason for staying is to check into the fabulous Umaid Bhawan Palace (Jodhpur 342006. Tel: 22316), six km from the station, which is a museum and a maharaja's home as well as an unusual and very stately hotel, actually built 1929–42. If its hallowed marble halls, filled with western classical music, are too intimidating, dive down to the basement for a swim in its subterranean pool reminiscent of the pool on the old *Queen Mary* liner and open to non-residents. Room rates are in the luxury bracket. Rob Dobson discovered modest but comfortable accommodation opposite the station at Shanti Bhawan Lodge, economy bracket.

A treat for rail buffs is the sighting of the private railway carriages of the Maharaja of Jodhpur. These can be chartered for the ride through the desert to Jaisalmer, a unique experience which the new Palace On Wheels train can't match. Contact the Umaid Bhawan Palace Hotel. Jodhpur ITB, Tel: 25052.

KANNIYA KUMARI

You go to Kanniya Kumari (KK), Cape Cormorin, because it's there – at the tip of India where the Indian Ocean and the Arabian Sea meet the Bay of Bengal – and to see the sun rise. It is the Land's End of India and has probably the only station in the world with a specially-built sunrise observation roof and sunset and sunrise times posted in an information booth. The SS wears green epaulettes with gold stripes on his smart white uniform and proudly shows visitors around the station. There are two single retiring rooms, two doubles and one dormitory with eight beds; all are basic but convenient for the early-morning stint at the viewing platform. Since that faces east, for sunset and simultaneous moon rise on full moon days, head for the sea shore, within walking distance. September to January is the best time; March 15 to July 15 is the period of summer vacation so KK, which is really rather seedy, is packed then.

Separate counters cater for ladies and gents bookings in the station lobby. The reservation counter is open 0800–1200 and 1400–1600 but it is advisable to fix up your reservations before coming here because of limitations, or check with the SS. Not many trains come to KK because it is the absolute terminus, but every afternoon the 1081 KK express completes the 2149 km journey from Bombay. It leaves for the return trip before sunrise and takes almost 48 hours to reach Bombay VT. There are three other daily arrivals/departures, all passenger trains, from/to Nagercoil Jn, or Tirunelveli Jn.

Once a week the 6017/18 Himsagar Express comes from Kashmir and returns 13 hours later (see Jammu Tawi).

KARJAT

Mainline trains heading south from Bombay stop at Karjat, 100 km from Bombay VT station, to have one or two extra locos attached to the rear of the train to push it 28 km up through the ghat section to Lonavla where the extra locos are detached and sent back to Karjat to start again. There are suburban EMU trains to Karjat from Bombay VT but none up to Lonavla (qv) because of the steepness of the ghat section. There are 1st Class waiting rooms/toilets on both main platforms. Tourists heading south after a visit to Matheran use this station to connect with main line trains after taking the suburban service from Neral to Karjat.

KOTTAYAM

On the main line between Trivandrum and Ernakulam, Kottayam station seethes with pilgrim traffic from November to January. 34 trains a day stop there for a few minutes. There are good V and NV restaurants as well as fruit stalls, apple juice and milk counters. The exit is up a flight of stairs, where the waiting and five retiring rooms are also located. An information bureau is in the centre of the entrance lobby with advance reservation and current booking offices at the sides.

Auto-rickshaws are available in the forecourt for the 2 km ride to the Kottayam boat jetty. Boats leave throughout the day for the 2½ hour cruise through the backwaters to Alleppey (qv). The Anjali Hotel (4 km from the station) is highly praised and has a smart ground floor restaurant, a rooftop bar and a Chinese restaurant. Run by the same people who own the Casino Hotel in Cochin, modest standard rate. In Kottayam, don't miss a ride through the coconut grove countryside and a taste of toddy, the liquor extracted from the coconut flower.

LONAVLA

Situated 127 km out of Bombay on the line to Pune and beyond (to Madras or Goa), Lonavla is a small station you may not notice except when the train stops for the locos that pushed the train from Karjat to be detached. At 625 m above sea level, it is a hill resort popular as an escape from Bombay's heat; it gets chilly in winter. You alight here for the 2,000 year-old Buddhist caves at Karla (10 km). The station forecourt is small and the station building barely seems to be a station at all. There is a booking office inside but the main platform is the centre island platform, number 2. There are no retiring rooms and few facilities. The 1st Class waiting room has a fine dressing table from the British period which looks out of place in its drab surroundings. Foreigners are rare at this station and should seek out the SS (his office is on platform 2) for any special requirements.

Trains from Bombay VT and Dadar stop here and so does the 2123 Deccan Queen every evening from VT station, taking just over two hours for the journey. As well as being well-served by commuter trains, there are direct trains from Bangalore City (130 Udyan Express), Hyderabad (number 7032), Secunderabad (2102 Minar Express), Kanniya Kumari (1082 KK Express) and from Madras and Miraj (with connections from Vasco da Gama). An EMU service at peak times connects Lonavla with Pune, a journey of 90 minutes.

Lonavla has some lively eateries, and is famous for its sweet confection, *chikki*. A tourist information bureau is near the station, and there are several places to stay at economy rates within its vicinity.

Lonavla station enquiries: Tel: 2215.

LUCKNOW

There are two stations at Lucknow (at Charbagh, three km from down town), both in the same compound but otherwise quite different in facilities and atmosphere. The main one is the stone building with dozens of turrets that symbolizes Lucknow for the visitor. A stone set into the wall of the station proclaims: 'Within this turret wall was laid on the first day of August, 1925, by G.I. Colvin, Esq. CB, CMG, DSO, agent of the East Indian Railway, a casket containing current coin with newspapers of the day to commemorate the successful completion of the foundations of the building'.

That is one of the few signs in English. The lobby of the station is hung with signs in Hindi, including one saying enquiry office, so you'll have to ask for it unless you can read Hindi.

On the left of the lobby are counters for upper class same day reservations. There is an Uttar Pradesh tourist bureau (open 0800–2000) with a leaflet on Lucknow which puts Charbagh Railway Station (this station's real name) as the first on its long list of 'What To See'. It says the station was built in typical Rajasthani style and stands in place of the gardens of the nawabs from where it derives its name – Charbagh means four gardens.

A story told to illustrate the sophistication of Lucknow residents is of the two nawabs who kept on requesting each other to board their train first, until the train puffed out of the station leaving both of them behind.

Lucknow station which, in 1988 won my award for the filthiest platforms, has cleaned up its act. Step out of the booking hall and you see a spacious square where taxis and rickshaws are prevented from blocking the access road. On the right is the new (1991) reservations complex built in the flamboyant style of the old station. Computerized reservations to any station (by BG or MG) can be made here. There are two counters (601/602) for foreign tourists and various other categories, so they are usually busy. Better to dedicate one counter exclusively for foreigners. The office is open 0800–2000, Sundays until 1400. No luggage is permitted inside the complex, but there is a free luggage room opposite the entrance.

In the station there is an assistance booth on platform 1 and an enquiry office (with a large sign in English). The Tarana self-service restaurant (open 0600–2200) has a wall of 1930s mirrors; it also has a private dining room furnished like an Indian stereotype with couches, hukka water-pipe and fringed lamp shades.

Upstairs (there's a lift) on the first floor are various waiting rooms which have retained their original ornate green wall tiles. There are seven retiring rooms, two with AC and one deluxe which has three beds and is reached through the dormitory where there are 16 beds. The booking office for these rooms is on platform 1.

Lucknow's other station, run by North Eastern Railway, is called **Lucknow Jn** and used to be exclusively MG, now three platforms are BG. It is situated on the left of the forecourt of the main station and has had a face-lift and false turrets added to make it a scaled-down version of its neighbour. It is compact and neat, and is being upgraded to a model station.

There are two AC and four non AC rooms plus two dormitories (on the noisy side of the station) with nine beds in each. Downstairs, on the left of the station concourse, is the V and NV restaurant, called Apoorna which could have a bright view of the MG platform but for the curtains. There is a fast food counter in front of it. Potted plants have been placed on the platforms and in the forecourt to give the station a pleasing appearance.

The station superintendent here is proud of his 'pictogram' signs. By no means easy to understand, the one that seems to depict a dustbin with an open lid is actually a book and pen and indicates where complaints can be made.

There is also a station called **Lucknow City**, about six km away. No trains originate there and only some halt there on the way to and from the main Lucknow stations. Since it is served by trains of Northern and North Eastern Railways, Lucknow has many direct connections with northern India. It is on the line from New Delhi (507 km) and trains stop here on the way to/from Gorakhpur (276 km), New Jalpaiguri (1118 km) and Guwahati (1541 km). The fastest from New Delhi is the Shatabdi Express which leaves ND at 0620 and arrives at 1255. From Bombay VT there is a superfast express which takes 26 hours for the 1414 km trip via Bhopal and Jhansi.

Several trains a day link Lucknow with Varanasi (302 km). There is a nightly MG service between Agra Fort and Lucknow (486 km/13 hrs) by the 5313/14 Marudhar Express.

Lucknow station, NR enquiries: Tel. 51234. NER enquiries: Tel. 51433.

MADGAON (GOA)

Madgaon is the official name for this station but people refer to it as Margao. It used to be recommended as the railhead for Goa's capital, Panaji, but now its bus station has been moved 5 km from the station, it is best to stay on the train to Vasco da Gama (qv) and get a bus there. You're near the tourist area at Madgaon station, obvious from its signs warning passengers 'not to entertain touts'.

MADURAI

The sigh of steam is often heard at Madurai station as 24 of its 42 trains a day are steam hauled. They are the local passenger trains; all the 18 expresses are diesel. Madurai is an MG station but buildings are being put up for the day when it will be served by BG trains. The present station, remodelled in 1979, was re-remodelled at the end of 1988. A later addition was the opening of the computerised reservations complex in 1991.

The facelift to Madurai station included improvements to the retiring rooms which are reached by a flight of stairs from platform 1. (There are four platforms.) Ten double rooms, AC room, two family rooms and two dormitories are here. The rooms open onto a long gallery overlooking the station forecourt, with the bathrooms (western style) backing onto the station roof.

Station facilities include a large 2nd Class waiting hall, a vegetarian restaurant with a 'Tiffin and Coffee Section' (open 0430–1000, 1700–2130) and a 'Meals Section' (open 1830–2130). The booking hall has drawings of trains above the reservation charts so that passengers can identify their carriages. There is also a diagram of the station showing its facilities. Madurai itself, for all its bustle, has a certain raffish charm. It is dominated by the Meenakshi Temple complex with its orange and black vertical striped walls around which traffic swirls. It is a determined shopper's haven, as well as a focal point for pilgrims.

The hill resort of **Kodaikanal** is 120 km by road from Madurai station and a tourist leaflet advises visitors to wear 'tweed and flannel' during the day. The closest rail access is Kodaikanal Road, but that's actually 80 km from it. There is a rail booking office at Kodaikanal run by a licensee. Important trains serving Madurai are listed in Chapter 9.

Madurai station: Tel. 37595.

MAHE

Mahe station is not actually in the Mahe part of the Union State of Pondicherry but in Kerala. Not surprising since Mahe is only 3 sq km in area, embracing the River Mahe and containing 30 bars and 32 wholesale liquor shops (it's cheaper here than in Kerala) and countless coconut trees. There are about 30,000 inhabitants too.

The station is delightfully rural, a short rickshaw ride from Government House or the liquor shops that constitute downtown. Nowhere much to stay unless you try the upstairs Green Tourist guest house opposite the R.C. Church. Hotel Coolland on the Mahe side of the river is an inexpensive eatery. There is a fruit and tea stall at the station and the 1st Class waiting room has a beautiful umbrella stand and antique chairs and a table embossed with SIR (South Indian Railway). 16 trains a day stop at Mahe at convenient times in the morning to give you a chance to stock up with booze and leave in the afternoon.

MALDA TOWN

Clinging to the edge of West Bengal, above Bangladesh, Malda Town is the last major station in the Eastern Railway zone before the

Northeast Frontier zone station of New Jaipalguri. Its attraction is that it is small and friendly with ticket collectors who wear ties and uniform jackets and smile, and a passenger information centre that actually helps instead of staff merely repeating train times by rote.

My regard for Malda Town began when, having sent a message ahead for soda water, I was met at the carriage door by the SS and his traffic inspector who both apologized for there being none available. At another station, my message would probably have been ignored. Since I was feeling pretty rotten, I decided to stay.

The station was built in the 1960s and is in the process of being modernized. On the first floor there are two non AC retiring rooms with two beds and one AC room and two dormitories of four beds in each. The roof of the station at the end of the corridor has been converted to a terraced garden with a forest of plants in pots. Access to the rooms is by stairs alongside the passenger information counter and the reservations office. Since my stay at Malda Town was unscheduled, unannounced and on impulse, and it was a Sunday night, I was very impressed by the help I received.

The reservation office opens 0900–1330 and 1600–1930 and is on the right of the small entrance lobby. The 2nd Class waiting hall, not very comfortable, is on the left; the 1st Class waiting room shows its need for modernization. There are signs in English as well as Hindi and Bengali for the various facilities. The station is two km from downtown where there is the West Bengal Tourist Development Corporation operated Malda Tourist Lodge (Malda, West Bengal. Tel: 2213). A sign in reception says 'Lunch/dinner compulsory'.

The town is also called English Bazaar, a name derived from Englezabad; it dates from 1680. The station is on the line between Calcutta and New Jalpaiguri, and between Delhi and Guwahati as well as Howrah and Guwahati. On a gruesome note, look down out of the window as the train approaches the next station of New Farakka and you'll see the bloated bodies of the dead bobbing against the sluice gates where the railway bridge spans the holy Ganga river.

MANGALORE

There are three retiring rooms at Mangalore, on the first floor gallery overlooking the booking hall. The rooms are compact and clean with twin beds, a western style bathroom and hot shower. There are also eight beds in a large, well ventilated room. The station has lots of reading matter on its noticeboards with one advising on 'Guidelines for passenger grievances'. The booking office is open 0200–2200, with separate queues for ladies and gents, and the advance reservations office opens 0900–1300, 1400–1700. It is being computerized. There is no special desk for foreigners but instructions are that they should

have priority; if no berths are available efforts are made to accommodate them through the emergency quota.

The station is the terminus for both broad gauge and metre gauge.
The BG line follows the Malabar coast northwards from Shoranur (see
Chapter 11) and is linked with Madras by the daily 6027/28 West Coast
Express and the 6001/02 Madras Mail. The MG line, sometimes closed
through landslides, provides a spectacular ride through the western
ghats to Hassan. Access to the town at Mangalore station is easier
from the end of platform 2 or 3 than from the main entrance/exit.

MATHERAN

There is a garden refreshment room attached to this fairytale station,
run by a Matheran personality, J.Y. 'Baba' Diwadkar, who also
operates the Divadkar Hotel opposite the station (it has a full bar and
economy rate rooms). Tickets for the downhill journey are sold 45
minutes before a train's departure; reservations for onward journeys
can be made up to three days in advance, with the booking office open
0930–1300; 1400–1800. The free baggage allowance is 7.5 kg in 1st
Clas and 5 kg in 2nd, with penalties for excess, but don't worry.

Across the line from the station, on a plinth, is a gaily painted engine
with the inscription: 'Here rests the steam locomotive which moved up
and down in the service of the people of Matheran for over 77 years,
manufactured in 1902, rendered service since 1905, year of opening of
section.' Photos of the two pioneers whose efforts brought about the
opening of the railway, Sir Adamjee Peerbhoy and Abdul Hussein
Adamjee Peerbhoy, known as Matheran Railwaywala, hang above the
booking counters.

Within walking distance from the station along a red carpet (of mud)
is Lord's Central Hotel, an amalgamation of buildings that were
previously a Christian bakery, a Jewish photographers and a Muslim
bungalow. This hotel is unique in the 'hill station' tradition with
country house hospitality from its owners, Mr & Mrs 'Jimmy' Lord.
Upper economy bracket.

MIRAJ

The signs at Miraj station give an idea of the place: 'This way to the
Railway Police Station', 'Do not exhibit your valuables and ornaments
while sleeping or sitting near the window', and 'To be safe from
pickpockets, take care of your luggage'. There is a disturbing atmosphere about the place and the 30 minute wait here while changing
trains to/from Vasco da Gama and Bombay or Delhi will be ample for
most travellers. If you want something else to look at, there are some
attractive ceramic tiles fronting the counter selling soft drinks. The
metre gauge and broad gauge tracks serve different sides of the same

platform. There are retiring rooms here but the less said about them the better.

MUGHAL SARAI

You'll probably stop at this north Indian version of Crewe without knowing it. A major junction for trains running between Calcutta, Bombay and Delhi, 80 trains a day pause here, mostly in the dead of night. You'll not miss much although the cafeteria on platform 2 (standing room only, no seats) has a menu which offers Chilly Chicken and Egg Chowmein takeaways.

The station entrance is modern and if you come here by road to catch a train (which is what you'll have to do if connections from Varanasi aren't convenient), be warned you'll have a long walk from the booking hall up steps and over a bridge to the platforms.

The enquiries booth (where you should ask for your train's departure platform before trekking in search of it) is on the left of the booking hall, as is the left luggage cloakroom. Up the steps on the left with its entrance marked by a mosaic mural are the functional retiring rooms, six non AC, two AC and a dorm.

In a desperate effort to add some charm, potted plants have been suspended from the ceiling of the bridge. There is lots to read, with signs in Hindi and English, such as 'Remember all the garbage which you do not like to touch and you are disposing of on the platform has to be cleared by another human being just like you.' And 'Spitting at open places is injurious to health.'

MYSORE

From the outside it is difficult to know that Mysore station really is a station. Built during the days of maharajas it is on palatial lines with a domed clock tower and wide verandas on its first floor. A road used to run onto the main platform to allow the maharaja to drive right up to his private carriage. The main lobby has the booking office (open 0400–2300) and a pay toilet. A separate lobby leads to the advance reservations counters (0730–1330, 1400–2000) with an enquiry desk where the needs of foreign travellers are attended to promptly. A display cabinet shows photos of the stunning Western Ghat rail journey – the Emerald Route – from Hassan to Mangalore.

The main platform is wide and clean with Victorian cast iron pillars (down the inside of which the rain runs) supporting the roof and adding to its period appearance. Zinc-topped tea counters do a brisk business alongside the V and NV restaurants which are only open during train departures. A wheelchair and self-help trolleys are available, and there is a bathing cubicle on the island platform. A dormitory of 10 beds, each with its own locker (bring your own padlock) is at platform level.

The retiring rooms are on the first floor and are rated the best in the Southern Railway zone. They have high ceilings and a walk-around veranda with a view of the pretty station forecourt on one side and trains shunting on the other. Number 1 has been air-conditioned yet it was built with high arched doors and windows that, pre-AC, could be opened to catch the breeze from different directions.

Mysore is renowned as a leisurely city, famous for its jasmine, maharaja's palace, zoo, and government sandalwood oil and silk factories. The Brindavian Gardens and Krishnarajasagar Dam are 19 km distant by road. The main way to get to Mysore by rail is via Bangalore (139 km) from where there are daily expresses taking about 3½ hours. Other routes are from Mangalore (qv) via Hassan or from Arsikere (also via Hassan). You can get to Mysore from Goa via Arsikere instead of via Bangalore. The station is also linked by MG passenger train to Chamarajanagar (61 km/2 hrs 20 mins). There is only a road link with Ooty (Udagamandalam).

Mysore station enquiries: Tel. 37300.

Rail museum

Walk to the end of the platform at Mysore station, cross the track to the Krishnarajasagar Road and follow the curve of the road northwards for about 100 metres and you will find the entrance on your right to the Regional Rail Museum. Admission tickets are sold from a guard's brake van that came from an old goods train; camera permits cost Rs 5, and Rs 15 for a movie camera. The museum was set up in 1980 as the first (so far there are no others) regional display of India's railway heritage. It is small and seems somewhat neglected although its gardens are well maintained and it is a fascinating place to visit. A guide booklet is available.

The Chamundi Gallery houses a series of paintings and photographs about the history of the railways. The adjacent Sriranga Pavilion is home to two coaches which formed part of the royal train of the Maharaja of Mysore; the Maharani's saloon, built in 1899, and the kitchen/dining car, built in 1914. (The Maharaja's saloon is at the Rail Museum in Delhi.) These coaches are adjustable to BG or MG track. The saloon is complete with platform and brass railings, bedroom, bath and lavatory, luggage room and servants quarters. Rail bygones in the gallery include a Theobold's Block instrument used before 1929 between Dodjala and Devanahalli stations on the NG line, and a Mysore State Railway clock, made in New York in 1889. Wooden pillars, doors and balustrades from the old Srirangapatna railway station were used in the construction of the gallery itself.

In the grounds are various MG and NG steam engines and a coach, built in 1927, from the Bangalore to Bangarapet NG line with bench type seating facing the sides, not forwards, and its special dog box. The oddity is an Austin motor car, adapted to run on rails as an inspection vehicle. A battery operated electric mini-train, built at the Mysore Railway Workshop mostly out of scrap metal, runs on a small circular track to provide a joy ride for children.

The Mysore Rail Museum, K.R.S. Road, Mysore, 570001.

NAGPUR

If you have to waste time waiting for a connection, there can be few pleasanter stations to linger at than Nagpur. Trains between Calcutta and Bombay, or Delhi and Madras, pause here about 20 minutes while meals are put on from the (very clean) base kitchen and the train is watered. In the season you can buy oranges here as it is the orange city of India and few travellers can resist a few, or even a sack.

I liked Nagpur station when I discovered a retiring room with a modern, tiled bathroom with one of those odd loos that have a commode with a seat that enables it to be used either for standing or sitting on, and with a view of the sole narrow gauge line in Nagpur. Alas, it is no longer steam but you can watch, from the bathroom, the diesel loco hauling wooden rolling stock, built 30 years ago, in and out of the station.

Seventy-two trains a day pause a while at Nagpur. If you have to make a reservation here, there are no special facilities for foreigners but the SS will help. There is a magazine library (deposit Rs10) where you can get something to read while you wait your turn in the queue. If you are wait listed, there are booths on platform 1 where you can check seat/berth availability before boarding your train. Another feature that makes Nagpur a better station than many others, is its auto-rickshaw funnel at its exit. You give your name and destination to the despatcher and get assigned the first auto to pop out of the funnel. It's metered too.

NERAL

This station serves as a link between Central Railway's BG trains (main and suburban) from Bombay VT and the NG railway to Matheran. There are two BG platforms with the booking office at the courtyard entrance to the station. The office of the SS is on platform 2 which is platform 3 on its other side where it serves the NG line. There are four NG platforms with the booking office for Matheran on the island platform between BG and NG. Although a railcar service is promised in the notice, this is reserved for railwaymen only. (You'll see the car in the shed from the left side of the train as it pulls out of the station.)

The 1st Class lounge, opened on demand, contains some sturdy ancient wooden dressers of great value, as well as modern ones already collapsing. The hot potato cakes sold by the NV counter are delicious and sell as fast as proverbial ones.

PATNA

The original station was built in the 19th century but the current ugly building dates from 1939 with extensions added in the 1960s with the computerized reservations complex opened in 1992. As a junction its importance stems from the meeting of the Patna–Gaya branch line with the main and chord lines of Eastern Railway; trains both terminate and transit here. It has seven platforms and a combined veg/non-veg restaurant with a base kitchen that can prepare 1,000 casserole meals a day.

The retiring rooms are upstairs from platform 1. They are small, airless cells, some with AC. Two dormitories have 10 beds in each. A notice, which you can disbelieve, says 'Check out is at 1200 am'. A roof garden is opposite rooms 1 to 7 with the 2nd Class waiting hall (like an underground car park for human bodies) below. There is a Bihar Department of Tourism kiosk in the station with useful maps of Patna and information on the town's sights. The 7.5 km road bridge, opened in 1983 linking north with south Bihar over the Ganga, is one of them.

Buses to Raxaul, four km from the Nepal border, cross this bridge at the start of their six hour journey from Patna.

Patna is on the main New Delhi to Calcutta line and is served by the trains (except Rajdhani Express) linking those cities. It is 992 km from Delhi (about 15 hours train time) and 545 km from Calcutta (about nine hours).

Patna Jn station enquiries: Tel. 22012.

PONDICHERRY

The Union Territory of Pondicherry comprises four enclaves in three South Indian states: the seaside towns of Pondicherry and Karaikal in Tamil Nadu, Yanam in Andhra Pradesh and Mahe (qv) in Kerala. From 1814 the territory was French, merging with the rest of independent India in 1954. The new town of Auroville is 10 km from Pondicherry station.

The station, with its tall portico, was re-modelled in 1987. There are three retiring rooms in a separate building on the sole platform which sees only two (MG steam!) passenger trains a day, from Villupuram, arriving at 0610 and 1905, departing at 0805 and 2100. In the high-ceilinged lobby there is a booking-cum-reservations counter open 0900–1200; 1500–1800, where through tickets can be bought for the

0805 departure which might just connect at Villupuram with the Pallavan Express to Madras Egmore, but don't rely on it.

The railways seem to have a conspiracy to keep the rail links to Pondicherry a secret, despite providing a through 1st and 2nd Class sleeper coach from Madras Egmore on the 109/631 passenger train; it leaves Egmore every evening at 2140, arriving Pondy at 0610. It's not in *TAG* and the ITB doesn't know about it; check the small print in the through carriage section of Southern Railway's own timetable.

As Villupuram has rail links with towns in the south which are worth visiting (such as Trichy and Madurai) it would be possible to make a side trip to Pondicherry when you pass through Villupuram on the way to Madras Egmore, instead of from it.

The nostalgic will adore the Grand Hotel de Europe (rue Suffren) run by the equally old M. Maigre who, when I visited in 1989, proudly thrust what I thought was a lychee-type Indian sweet into my hand and told me it was a stone from his kidney. M. Maigre was born in 1913 and says after his death his pure-French hotel with French food will be no more, so go quickly. (It was still open in 1992.) Economy rate, six rooms with antique furniture, full board only, and only if M. Maigre likes you. The best French food in India, according to its fans, is to be had at the (licensed) Club Restaurant of Pondy's Alliance Francaise, open to non-members. For real crusty French bread, seek out the bakery Selvan.

PUNE

The approach to Pune by rail with its shanties close to the track doesn't prepare you for the spacious sweep of the station building, extravagantly designed and built in 1925. The black, marble-faced columns of the entrance lobby sparkle in the sodium lights at night. The station has won the Central Railway shield for General Appearance, Cleanliness and Tidiness nine times since it was first awarded in 1946. A statue of the unmistakable figure of Gandhi seen from the rear greets the traveller emerging from the station. Buses to the city and suburbs are available a few minutes walk to the right of the forecourt.

Pune has been computerized. The waiting rooms, with showers, are on the first floor. The non-veg restaurant has cowboy movie style swing doors, and antique wood and glass fronted almirahs serving as crockery cupboards. There is a dormitory ('Janata Room') on the same floor with hot water showers and eight beds. Included in the cost of a twin bed room are afternoon tea, shoe-shine and morning paper.

Pune (don't pronounce it to rhyme with prune; it's Poona still) is an agreeable town at 549 m above sea level. There is a tourist information centre at the station. Express and commuter passenger trains link it with Bombay VT. Fast trains such as the superb Deccan Queen (see Chapter 11) do the 192 km journey in 3½ hours, others like the

Sinhagad or the Deccan Expresses take over four hours. A separate service of EMU trains runs between Pune and Lonavla and there is also a Pune/Daund shuttle service. The Jhelum Express from Jammu Tawi (qv) terminates here, and the station is served by regular trains from Bangalore, Kanniya Kumari, Kolhapur, Madras, Nagpur, New Delhi, Secunderabad, Trivandrum and Vasco da Gama (via Miraj).

Pune station enquiries: Tel. 667333.

PURI

Puri is known for its annual chariot festival and as a seaside temple city lapped by the waters of the Bay of Bengal. Peak periods are during the winter months, and the summer and autumn vacations. The South Eastern Railway Hotel (Chakratirtha Rd, Puri. Tel: 2063) was established in 1925 and its traditional style has its admirers.   Rob Dobson reports modestly priced places to stay front the beach; a former royal home if now a little decadent is the Z Hotel with its own garden and friendly staff.

There are retiring rooms at the station, doubles and dorm beds. The sun temple at Konark is 28 km from the station, reached by road.

Reservations are computerized. Trains originating and terminating at Puri include the 2815/16 superfast Puri/New Delhi Express, the 8475/76 Neelachal Express and the daily 8477/78 Kalinga Utkal Express to H. Nizamuddin (2,142 km). There are daily expresses from/ to Howrah. Connections to Madras are made at Bhubaneswar (qv).

Puri station enquiries: Tel. 2065.

QUILON

People go to Quilon to get away from it, either by backwaters boat to Alleppey or by day or night MG train to Madurai and Trichy. (The boat trip departs 1030 to Alleppey, takes eight hours and makes about 70 stops. More fun perhaps is to make your river cruise instead to Kottayam from Alleppey, now Alleppey has its own rail station.)

Quilon has a long main platform serving BG on one side and MG on the other; there are unattractive refreshment rooms. There are five single and two double retiring rooms and a six-bed dorm; some rooms have balconies overlooking the pleasant forecourt. An advance reservations block is on the left of the forecourt; current bookings off the station lobby.

Quilon is a compulsory stop for BG expresses to/from Trivandrum and the beginning of the single track MG line that cuts inland to Sengottai. You can get here direct from many stations (see Chapter 9) and terminating trains include the 6105 Quilon MG Mail from Madras Egmore and the 6161 Quilon MG Express which wends its way overnight across the south via Madurai (qv) from Tiruchchirappalli (qv).

RAJKOT

Platforms 1 and 2 are metre gauge at this rural junction station where MG trains to/from the south of Gujarat originate and terminate. The other platforms are broad gauge with number 3 being the main one. A new passenger booking hall was under construction at the beginning of 1992. The retiring rooms are on the first floor but the sign at the foot of the stairs is in Hindi so you'll have to ask. You could ask at the enquiry counter but that sign is in Hindi too. The rooms, one AC, two non AC, one dorm with four beds, are among the neatest and cleanest I've seen. The waiting rooms are off the main platform where there is a cozy vegetarian restaurant; being Gujarat there is no Non Veg one.

As well as links by the daily 9015/16 and 9005/06 Saurashtra Express and Mail trains with Bombay Central via Ahmadabad, Rajkot has a daily link with Bhopal (1269/70 Express) and weekly links with Secunderabad (2731/32) and Trivandrum (2603/04). MG trains go down to Veraval.

RAMESWARAM

Although this station on an island at the tip of India was remodelled in 1986, the sea air, sand, dust and pilgrim traffic have given it a sad appearance. A passenger arriving here by ferry (currently suspended) from Sri Lanka would find it a depressing sight and unlike other stations of Southern Railway. There are 12 retiring rooms built in a block alongside the station and, according to the SS, they are the only rooms for tourists in Rameswaram which have water 24 hours a day. There is a waiting room for ladies on the station, kept locked and opened on request, and a large room for upperclass passengers. A combined fruit and non-veg stall sells quick meal packets and there is also a veg refreshment room.

There are four reservation counters (0700–1300, 1330–1800) on the right of the entrance lobby and a notice saying the Indrail Pass is on sale. When the ferry brings passengers from Sri Lanka, the SS reckons to sell 150 passes a year. There is a tourist office here with details of trips around Rameswaram. A devout Hindu who visits Benares (Varanasi) is expected to visit Rameswaram also for the culmination of his quest for salvation, hence its popularity with pilgrims. Buses are available from the railway station to various places on the island. Until the road bridge opened recently (and it is a magnificent sight from the rail crossing), train or boat were the only means of getting to Rameswaram. Direct train links are from Coimbatore and Madras Egmore, via MG stations in the south.

Although the ferry is suspended, I was able to hitch a ride on a shunting steam engine to Rameswaram Port station. This is a cluster of sheds and palm-thatched huts which on ferry days handles about 800 passengers. They can spend up to six hours in squalid conditions, watched by desperate-eyed residents, waiting to be processed for either the train or the boat to depart. Even when the ferry is operating again, I would advise foreign tourists to continue to fly between Sri Lanka and India instead.

RANCHI

Ranchi station, originally exclusively narrow gauge, had BG added in 1961 and is now subject to a 'modelization' programme. Fortunately, the one-storey Lego-like façade from the early years of this century is being retained, as are the candy-striped awnings of wood over the cages within which are the sole retiring room, the dormitory of four beds and the ladies waiting room, all with bathroom facilities. The veg and non-veg refreshment rooms which have an ancient look are to go and there will be new reservation and ticket offices. The present ones are open 0800–1330, 1430–2000.

At Ranchi station you can see the Highline Transhipment system of transferring freight from NG to BG. NG wagons loaded with bauxite are shunted up a ramp and onto a track built over a BG line. The BG wagons are shunted underneath then the floors of the NG wagons are opened and the bauxite falls into the BG wagons below. Hatia station (seven km away) is the main depot for Ranchi's BG trains.

There are direct services to Ranchi from Madras by the Bokaro Steel City Express which takes nearly 37 hours for the approximately 1670 km journey northwards, and from Howrah by the Hatia Express. There are also trains from Patna, and from Gorakhpur.

At Ranchi station there is a noticeboard with a list of places of interest in and around Ranchi, mostly hills, lakes and falls, and the tourist literature describes Ranchi as a 'popular hill station'. Whatever it may have been in the past, it is hardly that now. It has become an industrial centre without much charm, the change being wrought by bauxite and iron ore.

However, the hill station atmosphere (it's 629 m above sea level) is retained in the South Eastern Railway Hotel (Station Road, Ranchi, Bihar. Tel: 21945), one of only two railway hotels in India (the other is at Puri). It is reached by crossing the NG line and strolling through a garden of healthy lawns and shade trees to its bungalow verandah entrance. 22 rooms are grouped in cottage units with red tiled roofs and wide galleries, built in 1915. They are in the economy range. There are coal fires in the public rooms in winter. The bearers have resisted change and wear the uniform and brass cap badge of the Bengal & Nagpur Railway.

SALEM

Salem is the railhead for the quiet hill resort of Yercaud. It is on the main line from Madras to Trivandrum and Mangalore and can be reached in five hours from Madras. There are three retiring rooms in a house built on the island platform, 1 and 2, with individual steps up to each room from the roof. The station is busy throughout the night so the train noise can be disturbing. As well as BG main line trains, there is an MG link with Bangalore.

A map in the lobby shows the location of the main bus stand (for buses to Yercaud). The reservations office (open 0900–1300; 1500–1800) is off the lobby, current booking counter with separate queues for Ladies and Gents on the right.

Salem station is 280 m above sea level; Yercaud, at 1,515 m above sea level, is 32 km from the station. The hill road begins eight km from the town. It is an easy drive, despite the 20 hairpin bends, through lush coffee plantations and orange groves, watched by monkeys begging for scraps as vehicles slow down to negotiate the curves. I tasted the renowned Shevaroyan Hills coffee (black with a taste that lingered throughout the morning) at the Hotel Shevaroys (Yercaud 636601) close to Yercaud's lake. The hotel (economy rate) has new, marble appointed cottages complete with bath tubs, fridge and TV plus forest view.

SECUNDERABAD

Secunderabad is the HQ of the South Central Railway which serves six states: Andhra Pradesh, Maharashtra, Karnataka, Goa, Madhya Pradesh and Tamil Nadu (well, 8 route km of it). Its zone stretches from Kakinada in the east to Goa in the west, linking the Bay of Bengal with the Arabian Sea. The HQ building, Rail Nilayam, has a vintage 1905 NG locomotive called Sir Alec, on display outside it.

Secunderabad station has a tourist office run by the Andhra Pradesh Tourist Development Corporation on its main platform but most of the tourist attractions are in its twin city of Hyderabad (qv). To get a taxi at Secunderabad station for a tour, you must ask a traffic cop (they wear white shirts and khaki pants) since they are parked around a corner from the station entrance. An even more frustrating feature of this station is the location of its reservation office. From the station you turn right, walk to the bus station, then turn right again and enter a yard to find the building is close to the station platform, but there's no short cut. Don't try it with heavy luggage. However, once there, the token system cuts down queuing and computers process reservations speedily. Current bookings are made in the lobby of the station.

From the lobby a wooden staircase leads up to the first floor where there is the Kohinoor Restaurant, opened in 1978. It has fans and meals served on plates, not *thalis* or casseroles, but its atmosphere is gloomy and it seems a fancy name for a station restaurant. Adjacent are the retiring rooms off a flower-bedecked balcony. There is one AC suite, 13 double rooms and one single.

There are dozens of direct trains to Secunderabad from all parts of India, including Ahmadabad, Ajmer, Bhubaneswar, Cochin, Tirupati and Visakhapatnam. From Bombay VT, there is the daily 2101 Minar Express, 14 hrs 20 mins for the 800 km journey, and from New Delhi, the fast (27 hrs for 1665 km) daily 2724 Andhra Pradesh Express. The fastest service from Madras (784 km) is by the 6059 Charminar Express which takes 14 hours. From Howrah, the daily 8045 East Coast Express completes the 1581 km trip via Bhubaneswar in 31 hours.

SHIMLA

Shimla station is located at 2,075 m above sea level and has a charm to match its breathtakingly beautiful setting. As well as the fascination of getting there (see Chapter 11), Shimla is a welcome destination after the hectic heat of Delhi. Citizens and visitors stroll through the town for the sheer pleasure of it, watched by monkeys who think they own the place, and by residents gazing from the balcony of the outside of the Amateur Dramatic Club's Victorian theatre. With snow-capped mountains of the Himalayas in the background and lush green valleys below, the town is not only spectacular but rich in a magical atmosphere. In his wonderful *Guide to Simla* (obtainable from his own Maria Brothers bookshop, straight out of *Kim*, on the town's Mall), Mr O.C. Sud, the author, speculates that the town's name, really pronounced Shimla despite its occasional spelling of Simla, comes from *Shamla*, meaning 'Blue Female' another name for the goddess Kali.

Shimla has almost 150 hotels and guest houses but there is only one which captures its essence (and one of the few with a bar): the Oberoi Clarke's Hotel (The Mall, Shimla. Tel: 6091). The rooms have the comfortable feel of the 1930s with views of the forest-clad hills and the town. Rates are standard bracket including all meals, which are superb. Since cars are not allowed, you will have to walk from the lift that takes you from the lower part of the town, near the station, to the Mall. The air always seems clean here despite the concentration of houses and people. The main season is April to June, September to October, and Christmas. But foreigners, drawn by Shimla's spell, visit year round.

As well as from New Delhi, it is also possible to reach Shimla from Jammu Tawi and from Howrah, via Ambala (qv) and Kalka.

Shimla station enquiries: Tel. 2915.

UDAGAMANDALAM

This station will always be known as Ooty, short for Ootacamund, by its fans. A summer resort since the days of the Raj and 'Queen of the Hill Stations', the town nestling in the Nilagiris, or Blue Mountains, may have lost its dignity (there are video games at the lake) but it is still relaxed and rural. You sense it on arrival at the station (for the journey there see Chapter 11) which, until its threatened modernization takes place, preserves a forgotten, leisurely style.

The popular veg restaurant can be entered from the platform or the forecourt. When I was having lunch there one day, a horse calmly trotted through one open door and out the other.

Although, at 2,203 m above sea level, the station is at the end of the line, its loco shed is only for stabling engines and carriages, the main yard being at Coonoor on the way up. Any reservation requirements should be discussed with the affable SS. The station has quotas to Madras, Cochin, New Delhi, Bilaspur and Ahmadabad. Ooty is 2,833 km, via Coimbatore, from New Delhi, 1,924 km from Bombay VT, 394 km from Trichy and 578 km from Trivandrum.

If you intend travelling to Cochin or Trivandrum (the most popular destinations for foreign tourists from Ooty) try to get your reservations in advance before reaching Ooty, since the station has no quotas. The reservations office is open 1000 to 1200 and 1530 to 1630.

In the office of the SS is a photo of the very British Bob Hill, station master from 1909 to 1930. His clear blue eyes stare down sternly on the modern world, his handlebar moustache waxed to fearsome points. I hope he survives the remodelling which was underway in 1992 to create retiring rooms with ensuite bathrooms.

The town, bus station (for Mysore/Bangalore/Coimbatore) and race track are close to the station. Out of Ooty is better than in it, and what remains of the woods and downs can be enjoyed best by a stay (or at least a visit) to The Fernhill Palace Hotel now taken over by the Taj group.

In Commissioners Road (take an auto from the station, 6 minutes) is Shinkows, a Chinese restaurant, where two of us had an enormous meal of steaming-hot meat and fish dishes with fresh Ooty cauliflowers and sweet peppers substituting for bean sprouts and bamboo shoots, plus piles of rice and noodles, at amazingly low prices.

UDAIPUR

The Udaipur City station building is nothing special to look at, especially when compared with the lavish beauty of the marble and crystal palaces of the city. It was built in 1963 but its drab exterior gives way to a station that's well run and a pleasure to visit. The large booking hall has counters well labelled in English with an enquiry window open daily 0500–1300 and 1400–2200, and a reservation window beside it, giving reservations on that day's trains until 1230. The CRS and the SS actively look for tourists in need of assistance.

There is an embankment of steps up from platform 1 to the exit and the booking office. Steps lead from the lobby to the retiring rooms. The dormitory has wooden screens around each of the ten beds but its (very clean) bathroom is next door. The sole twin-bedded room has attached bathroom and a terrace. Next to the rooms is a veg restaurant like an English tea room; it specializes in breakfast. Downstairs on platform 1 are snack bars which sell bottles of chilled mineral water.

The friendliness of Udaipur City station gives way to a city of magnificent palaces, one of which is an extraordinary hotel. Photos of the Lake Palace Hotel (Pichola Lake, Udaipur. Tel: 23241) floating like a white marble wedding cake on the clear blue waters of Lake Pichola are instantly identifiable. Built on four acres of rock, in 1628, it was a royal retreat, converted by the Taj group in 1972 into a splendid hotel, reached by ferry five minutes drive from the station. It is a maze of courtyards, fountains, gardens, filigreed screens, marble pavilions, mirrors, inlaid ivory and pools. Luxury bracket and worth every rupee, even if it's your last.

This is Rajasthan, so choose your time to visit wisely; October to March is best. The easiest way to get to Udaipur by train is from Delhi (via Jaipur and Chittaurgarh), a distance of 739 km, by the 2915 Garib Nawaz Express three times a week (as a portion of the 2901 Pink City Express) or by the 9615 Chetak Express which leaves Delhi every day at 1300 and arrives in Udaipur at 0915 the following morning. Other connections, such as from Bombay, are via Ahmadabad (297 km) from where the 9644 Express leaves at 2315 and arrives at 0815. There is a fast passenger train overnight to/from Jodhpur.

Udaipur station enquiries: Tel. 23471.

VARANASI

The surprise at Varanasi is how it has changed since I wrote about its indifference in the first edition of this book. A Foreign Tourist Bureau (linked to ITB in New Delhi) has been opened to solve the travel problems of the many foreigners who use Varanasi (formerly Benares). The bureau is on the left as soon as you enter the station. The charming gentleman, Mr Qamruddin, running it in 1992 apologised for not being able to make reservations (but Varanasi is computerized) since he offers 'only guidance'. Not even the Indrail Pass can be purchased there and he complains of not many foreigners using his services. Those who do write glowing comments in his visitors book. His office is open 1000–1700, not on Sundays.

Upper class reservations can be made at the counter on the right of the booking office. There is an enquiry office (sign in English) in the hall and also a telecom bureau and a Uttar Pradesh Tourist Bureau. A sign warns 'Please be cautious to your luggage. Do not leave it unattended. Do not trust the strangers.'

I was given a station tour by the most helpful CRS I've ever encountered, Mr R.K. Mishra. With broad gauging of many lines, Varanasi Jn (also known as Varanasi Cantt) has only two MG platforms now, from where trains leave for Allahabad City. The main platform is an island one, number 2 and 3, where the ladies waiting room has an exquisitely tiled pink and green fireplace (not used).

Unfortunately, the retiring rooms that impressed me in 1988 have lost their glamour and been reduced in number. The towel size has shrunk too with only handkerchief size towels for guests in the AC room which does, however, have a fridge and TV. There are six rooms and a dormitory of 53 beds; the booking office for them is on the first floor.

The AC cafeteria there is gloomy, preserving an obvious dislike of customers. People and dogs sleep unchallenged in areas reserved for ticket holders and cows wander at will through the booking hall and along platforms.

The real joy of the station is in its exterior. Go outside and gaze up at it, or view it from platform 6 as a steam train chuffs past. It is art deco, Indian style, and a contrast to the frenzy of the city. In the lobby is a model of a diesel locomotive with the legend: 'Home Of Diesel Loco. Builders for the Nation.'

If you take an MG train from Varanasi Jn (or from Varanasi City, the town's exclusive MG station) to Allahabad City, it passes – after Bhulanpur station – through a beautifully landscaped park where at least two steam engines lovingly preserved are mounted on plinths in front of an administration building. This is Varanasi Diesel Locomotive Works (DLW), a factory colony where the general manager is like mayor to a community of 35,000.

The colony has a golf course, an Olympic size swimming pool, playing fields, schools and cinemas. 8,400 people work in the plant, manufacturing 150 BG and MG diesel locos a year, and spares for the existing fleet of 3,000. It takes 14 weeks from start to finish to produce one of these huge turbo-charged diesels whose generators could provide power for 200,000 people.

The most fascinating aspect of Varanasi is life on the river front at dawn. Hindu pilgrims inspired by their faith in life after death flock to the *ghats* (stepped embankments) on the river bank to perform ablution: a dip in the river and salutations to the sun. Sarnath, the venerated spot where Lord Buddha preached his first sermon after enlightenment, is 10 km by road from the station.

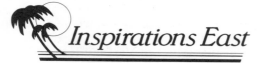

VASCO DA GAMA (GOA)

The main railway station from which to reach all parts of Goa is Vasco da Gama, known simply as Vasco and pronounced 'Barsco'. It's a mean looking station with few facilities although its atmosphere is friendly and the SS helpful. Its main neighbouring station is Madgaon (qv).

At Vasco there is a small reservation office with a counter for Indrail Pass holders and foreign tourists, shared with 1st Class passengers. Tickets can be paid for in foreign currency and the day's exchange rate is displayed. The office is open from 0800 to 1200 and 1500 to 1700. The general booking office has opening hours of 0800 to 1400 and 1500 to 2300 and closes ten minutes before the departure of a train.

There are clean, if musty, retiring rooms in an annexe to the station, reached by climbing stairs from the end of the platform to a balcony that overlooks the station forecourt. The dorm has six beds. There is no restaurant at the station, only a tea counter, but since the town abounds in food kiosks, wine shops and restaurants with a western ambience, meals can easily be obtained.

Panaji is the capital of Goa, 30 km from Vasco which is the best station for reaching it since the bus park is opposite the railway station. Limited rail reservations can be made in Panaji at the Railway Out Agency.

Goa's airport is at Dabolim and although there is a station at Dabolim, it is a rural halt with no bus/taxi service so passengers bound for the airport should alight at Vasco. With more international flights going to Goa, Vasco Station is a good starting point to begin a rail journey. The Indrail Pass is sold at the station.

Vasco's rail access to the rest of India is by MG trains via Londa to Bangalore or, via Miraj, to Bombay and H. Nizamuddin (Delhi). I prefer the link with Bangalore since no change of train is involved on the approximately 20 hour journey by the 6201/02 Vasco/Bangalore Mail/Passenger train. There is also a daily through carriage service (2nd Class sleeper only) from Vasco to Mysore by the same train.

However, connections via Miraj for the change over from MG to BG trains are good and the complete trip between Bombay VT and Vasco takes around 21 hours; it's 42 hours to Delhi. Trains serving Miraj and Bombay VT stop at Pune from where there is the daily Jhelum Express to/from Jammu Tawi via Agra Cantt and New Delhi.

Reports that the MG train is a boring/arduous way of getting to Goa are not to be believed if you enjoy mountain scenery and good company, but go 1st Class for comfort (there's no AC coach). The atmosphere livens up when the train crosses the Goa border and vendors swarm aboard selling beer and Goa's special tipple, *feni*, a cheesy smelling *eau de vie* made from the fruit of cashew nuts.

Goa is famous for its three fs: fish, football and, say the Goans, the third is left to your imagination. Actually, it's feni.

All trains going to Goa pass through Londa, and then the ghats begin: a range of magnificent green hills through which the train gropes along tunnels, or meanders over bridges with streams plunging below. After Caranajol station, you're in Goa and the hills soar into the distant clouds. Dudhsagar has a lookout tower to scan the lush depths of the valley and river below. Then after tunnel Number 11, the train emerges into heavy spray as it crosses perilously close to the Dudhsagar waterfalls. The track doubles back on itself giving a heart-wrenching glimpse of the moss covered railway bridge that spans the rush of the falls and seems so fragile beside the force of the water gushing under it.

The journey back through the ghats from Vasco is, if anything, more spectacular, since an ancient steam engine is attached at Kalem to push the train up the hill. At Castle Rock it is detached while passengers have tea, if it's been ordered in advance.

In the season, a chair car is added on the daytime departure from Vasco and the train makes a halt alongside the falls. You can spend the day there and return on the evening train. The shelter at the falls is 241 m above sea level with the falls plunging down from far above that.

Although Vasco da Gama is the terminus of the line, there is a 4 km extension to Mormugao Harbour where a train goes every morning and evening. Accommodation at all rates is plentiful around Vasco. The nearest star-class hotel to the station and to the airport is the Oberoi Bogmalo Beach. Despite looking like a concrete monolith astride a sandy cove, it's comfortable and convenient.

Vasco da Gama station enquiries: Tel. 2398. Panaji Agency: Tel. 5620.

Chapter 11

Great Trips

Great trips by rail in India can be on the country's fastest train, by a maharaja's special, on a crack intercity express, on a trunk route, by a hill railway, in a private coach or on an ordinary 2nd Class passenger train chugging through magnificent scenery. Such is the diversity of Indian railways.

SHATABDI EXPRESS

This is India's equivalent of Japan's bullet train. It began service between New Delhi and Jhansi in July 1988 and has a speed potential of 140 km an hour, which makes it the fastest train in India. The train's electric loco, designated WAP-3, was made by the Chittaranjan Locomotive Workshop and the coaches by the Integral Coach Factory in Madras. The locomotives are of 4704 horse power fitted with six traction motors of 784 horse power each.

There are three Shatabdi Express trains from New Delhi and plans have long been considered for a Shatabdi service between Secunderabad and Vijaywada and between Madras and Bangalore.

Meals are included in the ticket price. Reservation necessary. Indrail Pass (1st Class) holders travel without extra charge but 2nd Class holders must pay a supplement as the train is all AC Chair Car accommodation.

These trains also have an Executive Chair Car at double the regular Shatabdi fare; the 1st AC Class Indrail Pass is valid, but other kinds of IRP attract a supplement.

The Shatabdis are prestige trains showing how Indian Railways can transport passengers in speed and comfort. The 2001/02 New Delhi/ Bhopal train could be of benefit to early risers who want to spend a day (10 hours) in Agra. At New Delhi station the train conductors in tailored light grey suits with blue ties invariably look smarter than their passengers.

The ordinary AC coaches have 69 grey rexine covered seats which recline by lever control and have lots of leg room. There is a magazine pocket in the back of the seat in front and a table which drops down for meal service. You expect to be told to fasten your seat belt; instead Indian music comes through the loudspeakers, and continues for the whole of the journey.

TIMETABLES FOR SHATABDI EXPRESSES

2002 (Daily)	
New Delhi	0615
Agra Cantt	0810/0815
Gwalior	0930/0933
Jhansi	1039/1047
Bhopal	1400

2001	
Bhopal	1440
Jhansi	1750/1758
Gwalior	1858/1903
Agra Cantt	2013/2021
New Delhi	2220

2004 (Except 6,7)	
New Delhi	0620
Kanpur	1110/1130
Lucknow	1255

2003	
Lucknow	1515
Kanpur	1640/1700
New Delhi	2150

2005 (Daily)	
New Delhi	1625
Ambala Cantt	1852/1854
Chandigarh	1934/1945
Kalka	2040

2006	
Kalka	0530
Chandigarh	0615/0636
Ambala Cantt	0719/0721
New Delhi	0945

Each seat is numbered. The layout is 3 × 2, three seats on one side of the aisle and two on the other. The aisle links up with the other carriages, but the passage between coaches has an awkward step up and the doors are clumsy to open.

The coaches are air conditioned, often too cold, and also have fans. Smoking is not permitted. A lighted sign in the coach indicates when the toilets are occupied. These are western style with fan, toilet paper and liquid soap, but no hand towel or tissues.

There is a galley in each coach, opposite the toilet, equipped with gadgetry for boiling water and keeping food hot. Meals are served to passengers in their seats.

On a trip to Agra, breakfast is included in the fare. Served from a trolley, it is presented on a tray. The foil dish contains an omelette and croquettes, or a potato patty with peas. There is also a plastic cup with

Fares (in Indian rupees) for Shatabdi Expresses

	1st AC Executive Class	AC Chair Car Class
New Delhi–Lucknow	660	330
New Delhi–Kanpur	620	310
Lucknow–Kanpur	210	105
New Delhi–Kalka	460	230
New Delhi–Chandigarh	420	210
New Delhi–Ambala	400	200
Ambala–Chandigarh	200	100
Ambala–Kalka	230	115
Kalka–Chandigarh	170	85
New Delhi–Bhopal	840	420
New Delhi–Jhansi	600	300
New Delhi–Gwalior	510	255
New Delhi–Agra Cantt	400	200
Agra Cantt–Gwalior	230	115
Agra Cantt–Jhansi	330	165
Agra Cantt–Bhopal	650	325
Bhopal–Gwalior	550	275
Bhopal–Jhansi	480	240
Jhansi–Gwalior	220	110

(Half fare for children between the ages 5 and 12.)

a tea bag, sachets of sugar and creamer, and of tomato ketchup, salt and pepper, and a roll and butter. Plastic cutlery.

A veg or non-veg dinner, included in the fare, is served from Agra to New Delhi; usually soup and two vegetable curries, dhal, rice and roti, a kind of pancake, with curd, or chicken masala. Snacks between Agra and Jhansi have to be paid for.

Seating in the Executive Coach is 2 × 2 and very comfortable in reclining, cloth upholstered chairs. Food is supposed to be better in this class but it isn't. Juice is offered about 45 minutes after journey's commencement but neither tea nor coffee are served until after breakfast, so you'll be left gasping if you haven't been able to get a cuppa before boarding at such an early hour.

The windows of the train are darkened so people can't see in and this gives a brownish hue to the outside world as you speed through it. The Shatabdi Express is a travel machine, an Indian land plane; clean, fast and comfortable. It's a great trip that will impress you. Pity about the music.

TAJ EXPRESS

For long the favourite way of getting from New Delhi to Agra by train, the Taj Express has been downgraded to just another train in favour of the Shatabdi Express, even though it has kept its romantic name. It has no AC and is all chair seating. The 1st Class coach has 60 chair seats, in 2 × 2 layout. The other coaches are 2nd Class with 90 bench type seats in 2 × 3 format. There is a pantry car, with snacks and meals available from bearers passing along the aisle. There is a box for posting complaints and suggestions in the side of the guard's van at the front of the train. A nice touch.

The Taj Express leaves New Delhi every day at 0705 and arrives at Agra Cantt at 0950 on its way to Gwalior, returning from Agra Cantt at 1845 and reaching New Delhi at 2200.

PINK CITY EXPRESS

The Pink City Express (2901/02) may sound exotic and the carriages are indeed pink (so are the tea flasks in AC class) but this is an ordinary MG train running between Delhi and Jaipur, the pink city. However, being MG, the accommodation is compact. There are two 1st AC coupés and four 2nd AC four-berth cabins (instead of a 2nd AC dormitory as in BG coaches) in one carriage. The 1st Class, non-AC, chair car has 48 seats in 2 × 2 layout while the 2nd Class carriages have upholstered bench type seats for 80 in 3 × 2 layout, or for 64 in 2 × 2.

The train leaves Delhi at 0600 after which tea is offered throughout the train from units placed in each coach. As it has a pantry car breakfast and, on the return journey, other meals are available chair-side. The journey of five hours passes pleasantly, especially into Rajasthan with its intriguing scenery of desert-like landscape, white walled, single-storey houses and – a touch of the exotic at last – camels.

For six days a week, not Sundays, this train is also called the Garib Nawaz Express (9015/16) as a portion of it goes on to Udaipur from Jaipur. A steam loco is used to shunt the carriages that remain at Jaipur, waiting for the return trip to begin at 1615.

PALACE ON WHEELS

The romance of rail travel does still exist, for a price, in a train confusingly named *Palace On Wheels*. It's confusing because the name conjures up palatial luxury and that's not what passengers get for the

OUTWARD ROUTE ►►
RETURN ROUTE ▷▷

PALACE ON WHEELS

N

fare of at least US $200 per person per night. No, you can't use the Indrail Pass. Tickets must be purchased from a travel agent in the UK through the GSA, S.D. Enterprises (see Chapter 3) or as part of a holiday in India package, or from the Rajasthan Tourist Development Corporation.

As a way of seeing the palaces of Rajasthan on wheels, this is the perfect train. Elephant, camel, bus rides and guided tours are included and for a week there is no need to change trains or worry about accommodation.

At 1900 hours every Wednesday evening from August to April, some 90 passengers gather at Delhi's Cantonment station and receive the first of many flower garlands at the beginning of an unforgettable week of touring by rail to some of the legendary sights of India. Two metre-gauge steam engines, one dubbed *Desert Queen*, both freshly hosed down and looking terrific, are waiting to haul the 21 cream coloured coaches to Rajasthan. The passengers dine on board then retire to their cabins for the 2245 departure to Jaipur.

Inaugurated in 1981, this train has become renowned. Many people, usually those who have not been on it, speak in awe of its luxury, superb food and attentive service. The Palace On Wheels, whose passengers are described by station masters *en route* as POWs, when it began was composed of renovated coaches once used by maharajas as their palaces on wheels. Since the wooden coaches were in danger of falling apart and were not really suitable for the demands of the modern tourist, they were retired in 1991.

The Palace On Wheels is now a brand new train especially built in six months at the Integral Coach Factory in Madras, the same one where ordinary Indian Railways coaches are made, but there the connection ends. It is superbly designed and decorated, with each passenger coach consisting of four air-conditioned bedrooms (two beds in each), two bathrooms, a non-AC saloon (where you can open the windows) and a galley with fridge and toaster. Don't be disappointed that these are not the maharaja's carriages of old, a maharaja himself would love them.

Each cabin is cleverly laid out with lots of little storage cupboards and drawers, and even a dressing table. A bunk, upholstered in velvet, hangs down over one of the beds for a third person and this can be used for luggage or pushed up and recessed out of the way. There are shaver sockets in each cabin and a control to turn off the piped music but then you miss the announcements. Unfortunately, there is no individual AC control so you have to put up with the AC as cold, or as mild, as the coach captain or fellow passengers want.

Breakfast and cold beer can be served in the cabin or in the lounge at the end of each coach although more than six people in there make it crowded. There is a TV and video player in each saloon/lounge, rather an unnecesary refinement when the train goes through such exciting scenery and the tour itself is packed with so much to do, there is hardly enough time (or inclination) to watch videos. One passenger told me she had no time even to write her postcards.

Forget the hype and look on Palace On Wheels as a unique and enjoyable and troublefree way of seeing Rajasthan in the manner of a sea cruise. You can even arrange to have your laundry done while travelling. Because of the limited space, service is limited too, but it's fun. Each carriage has a staff of two who somehow manage to live in the small galley which also has a crew toilet/shower. The passenger bathrooms are located in the centre of each coach, between two pairs of cabins; they are not *ensuite*. They both contain a shower.

Although this train has a vestibule that runs its length, the doors between carriages are only opened when meals are served while the train is moving so passengers can get to the restaurants. There are two of these, the Maharaja and the Ghana, with covers for 40 guests in each at tables for four. The bar (the only one on a train in India) is plush and a popular place; adjoining it is the non-smoking library and parlour.

The decor throughout the train is opulent, the service obliging, the food – actually cooked on board in two tiny pantries – is pleasant and the tour managers dedicated to seeing their guests (who come from many different countries and cultures) enjoy themselves. No easy task.

I lost count of the number of palaces, forts and temples we were taken to, and of the number of garlands, coach rides (plus an elephant and a camel ride) and cultural shows. It was, indeed, an experience of a lifetime.

Although the train begins its journey from Delhi Cantt station hauled by two MG steam locos, these are detached at Bandikui during the first night's run to Jaipur, and replaced by diesel traction. During the last night's run back to Delhi Cantt, the Desert Queens take over again.

The train's itinerary where passengers join buses for various tours is Jaipur, Chittaugarh, Udaipur, Jaisalmer, Jodhpur, Bharatpur and Agra.

Plans are in hand to start a version of the train in the south of India, taking in various historical temples, mountain scenery and possibly going to Goa. If you are determined to ride in a Maharaja's carriage, the only chance seems to be in those of the Maharaja of Jodhpur (see Jodhpur entry in Chapter 10).

RAJDHANI EXPRESS

The quickest way of travelling between Bombay or Calcutta and New Delhi by train is on one of the Rajdhani Expresses which reduces the journey time to under 18 hours. Fares are at least 25 per cent higher than on ordinary expresses, so you expect a great trip. But you are mainly paying extra for the speed which, together with the elimination of lots of stops, cuts several hours off the usual journey time.

The train is open only to passengers with reservations and no interlopers are allowed. There are three types of accommodation, all AC. Chair car consists of 70 seats in a 2×3 format. These are rexine covered and recline, with a foot rest, a table dropping down from the seat in front, and a magazine pocket. Ten chair cars are on the typical Rajdhani Express which testifies to their popularity. Personally, I would rather travel in a sleeper on an ordinary express than be confined to one of those seats for 18 hours.

Sleeper class on the Rajdhani Expresses is like the AC two tier coaches of ordinary expresses. The layout is the same although the outside berths have been designed with a table between facing seats. The carriages hold 45 passengers; their toilets are the same as on ordinary expresses.

There is a difference in 1st AC Class which have the most luxurious toilets of any long distance train in India: rubber tiled floors, real washbasins and liquid soap in a dispenser. There is even toilet paper in some. For sleeping, there are 18 berths in three cabins of four, and three of two. During the day, these are converted to sofa style seats with woven upholstery. There are flowers in the cabin and a small washbasin and mirror. At night, the beds are made up with crisp linen.

Fares for Rajdhani Expresses (and AC Expresses)

	1st AC Class	2nd AC (2-tier) Class	AC Chair Car
New Delhi–Howrah	2070	1195	590
New Delhi–Dhanbad	1830	1060	520
New Delhi–Mughal Sarai	1435	800	435
New Delhi–Kanpur	950	580	310
New Delhi–Allahabad	1260	550	385
Howrah–Kanpur	1645	975	490
Howrah–Mughal Sarai	1290	770	390
Howrah–Dhanbad	650	415	220
Howrah–Allahabad	1440	840	430
New Delhi–Bombay Central	2030	1170	580
New Delhi–Vadodara	1605	915	465
New Delhi–Ratlam	1390	780	420
New Delhi–Kota	990	595	320
New Delhi–Sawai Madhopur	865	520	285
New Delhi–Surat	1765	1035	510
Bombay Central–Kota	1510	870	450
Bombay Central–Ratlam	1280	765	390
Bombay Central–Vadodara	885	540	290
Bombay Central–Sawai Madhopur	1660	980	495
Bombay Central–Surat	690	430	280

(Half fare for children between the ages of 5 and 12.)

Music is piped throughout the train but in 1st Class this can be switched off. There is a stern announcement before departure warning that it is an offence to drink alcohol on the train and threatening 'detrainment' and prosecution for anyone caught doing so.

When I travelled on the Rajdhani Express from Howrah to New Delhi in 1992, the crew was led by a young train superintendent cum catering inspector in a red blazer and a chief steward clad in a charcoal grey suit. Both were adept at handling passengers' requests. A staff of 55 looked after 870 passengers.

Food for 1st AC Class passengers is prepared on the train; passengers in other classes are given meals from base kitchens. The meal I had, and the dignified way it was served, was of top hotel standard.

Fellow passengers in 1st AC on the Rajdhani are likely to be fascinating Indians of importance whom you would normally not expect to meet. I found myself sharing a sofa seat with a Marxist

member of parliament on one side and a war-mongering right wing
Indian army colonel on the other. Sparks flew until both men agreed,
to my relief, that although their outlooks were opposed, they were
both patriots.

A reader commented: 'Even though liquor is forbidden on Indian
trains, on the Rajdhani Express to Bombay, not only were my cabin
mates able to order liquor with their meals, they had their choice of
several different types of Scotch.'

You can travel with your Indrail Pass on the Rajdhani Expresses, in
the designated class, if your pass is valid for seven days or longer. The
one-day 1st AC Class IRP is only valid for 2nd AC Class and the one-
day 2nd AC Class IRP can only be used for travel in the AC Chair Car.

In mid-1992 it was planned to introduce a Rajdhani link between
New Delhi and Secunderabad/Bangalore.

DECCAN QUEEN

The Deccan Queen is known as the pride of Maharashtra State. As
train number 2124 it leaves Pune at 0715 every morning for Bombay
VT where it arrives (after stops at Lonavla and Dadar) at 1040. Every
evening, as the 2123, it returns from Bombay VT at 1710, stopping at
Karjat and Lonavla before arriving at Pune at 2035.

During weekdays, the Deccan Queen is packed with commuters so it
is better to travel on a Sunday when the service is just as good.
Although it operates on a reserved seat basis only, in 2nd Class the
gangways can be jammed.

There is a supplement payable on top of the reservation fee and
fare; no extra for Indrail Pass holders.

1st Class accommodation is in reclining armchairs with woven
upholstery. Seats are in a 2 × 2 pattern with an aisle between. 1st Class
season ticket holders have compartments of their own which are less
luxurious. Modern carriages have rexine seats.

2nd Class has seats in a 2 × 3 format and these are hard upright
bench style. In some carriages they are wooden, and cost the same
price. There are 90 seats in a typical second class carriage. Sometimes
the train has a double decker coach. Both classes have fans, no AC,
and the windows in 1st Class have curtains. A carriage, reserved for
ladies, has two uniformed lady constables travelling in it. Armed
railway security guards also ride the train.

What makes the train so special, as well as its decor, is that 1st Class
passengers can have breakfast or dinner in the 28-seat restaurant. Tea
is served in real pots, not plastic flasks; meals are on china plates and
some of the silver-type cutlery bears the crest of Air India. The menu
is imaginative with such dishes as baked beans on toast for breakfast.
The tiny pantry produces 10,000 items a day on its trip to Bombay
and back. Snacks are also served to passengers at their seats.

The train's electric engine is emblazoned with its name and the coaches are painted white and grey with a bold red stripe along their length. Pictures and posters adorn the walls inside the coaches, and in the restaurant car there is a fish mobile hanging in a glass case used as a partition.

The Deccan Queen rides above the mist-filled valleys of the western ghats in the morning. Monkeys gambol around the train when it halts at brake-testing points and scoop up food tossed to them by passengers. The train provides a gentle approach to the congestion of Bombay, as trees give way to forests of power pylons and rural shacks lead to tenement blocks. It is a great train in which to arrive, or leave, Bombay.

PANDYAN EXPRESS

The Pandyan Express is a crack metre gauge overnight train linking Madras with Madurai. As number 6717, it leaves Madras Egmore nightly at 1900 and arrives in Madurai, 556 km distant at 0615 the next morning. As the 6718 it returns nightly at 1930 and arrives in Madras at 0645.

Apart from the charm of its name, recalling the ancient Pandyan kingdom whose capital over 2,000 years ago was Madurai, the Pandyan Express appeals to passengers for its dainty comfort. The track permits speeds of 100 km per hour and the train glides along smoothly at 75 kph. It comprises three carriages for 1st Class passengers and seven for 2nd Class. There are also three unreserved carriages (three tier berths) and one seat-only carriage as well as a ladies compartment as part of the guard's coach.

The train is an example of the better accommodation in some metre gauge expresses compared with broad gauge ones. Instead of the 46-berth AC dormitory carriage of a BG train, the Pandyan Express offers berths in cabins for two, three or four people. The 1st Class AC sleepers are comfortable cabins with a wash basin and serviced by attendants who make up the bed and bring tea in the morning.

DARJEELING TOY TRAIN

Considering the time it takes (nearly nine hours from New Jalpaiguri, plus 13½ hours overnight from Calcutta) you might wonder if travelling on the Darjeeling toy train is worth the trouble.

Two guide books I consulted had different opinions. One calls the train ride 'a superb experience which shouldn't be missed'. The other says, almost sacreligiously for train fans, 'I really wonder about all the fuss made over it,' and advises travellers to go by bus. (But see Hugh Ballantyne's comments, page 96.)

An authority that should know, the Northeast Frontier Railway which runs the train, says in its timetable: 'A journey over the Darjeeling Himalayan Railways by "toy trains" is an unforgettable experience. Starting from New Jalpaiguri or Siliguri Jn in the plains, the railway winds its way along mountains and valleys to reach Darjeeling. On the way, one can break the journey at Kurseong, another hill resort at an altitude of 1,458 metres. The Batasia loop and Tiger Hill on the way are favourite spots'.

The Darjeeling Himalayan Railway (DHR) began as a steam tramway in 1880 from Siliguri to Darjeeling following a cart road built by military engineers in 1861. It was the first hill railway to be built in India. The line consists of 82 km of narrow gauge (0.610 m or 2 feet wide) track which climbs to 2,135 m in 65 km. The gradient in one place is actually 1 in 19 and the ruling gradient is 1 in 25.

To cut down on having to build tunnels, a system of loops and reverses was devised. This has the track circling around and passing over a gradient by means of a bridge, thereby obtaining a higher elevation. The reverse part is when the track runs diagonally upwards for a short distance and later uses a parallel alignment to the original, higher up the mountain. No wonder it takes so long.

The tank engine which pulls the train, and locals strolling beside it as it dawdles alongside the road, make marvellous photos and contribute to the fame of this railway. It is unique. It is also frequently closed through bad weather, breakdowns and political problems. If it is operating, the best time to go is September to November, before it gets too cold, or in the spring of mid-April to mid-June.

The conventional way is to take the 3143 Darjeeling Mail from Calcutta Sealdah station, daily departure at 1900, which arrives at New Jalpaiguri (NJ) station at 0830 the following morning. The train has 1st and 2nd Class AC berths, AC Chair Car and ordinary 1st and 2nd Class berths. Bed rolls are available.

It connects with the 1D passenger train (1st and 2nd Class coaches) which leaves NJ station at 0900. The train stops at a dozen stations on the way, as well as elsewhere when it pauses for breath. It should arrive at Darjeeling at 1730 but it is often late.

The return journey to Calcutta is by the 4D, at 0825, or 2D, at 1000, from Darjeeling which arrive at NJ station at 1620 and 1745 respectively. The 3144 Darjeeling Mail leaves there at 1950 and arrives at Sealdah at 0845 the next day.

There is an earlier departure scheduled from NJ for Darjeeling at 0715 (the 3D). To catch that you will have to arrive at NJ the day before and you could stay at NJ station where there are four double rooms and three dormitory beds.

Check with railway sources before planning to visit Darjeeling by train to avoid disappointment in case the train isn't operating.

MATHERAN HILL RAILWAY

Less than two hours from Bombay there is a great rail trip by another toy train, the one that goes to Matheran. The name means 'jungle head' or 'forest on the top' and it still applies to this place, discovered in 1850. It is the nearest hill resort to Bombay, 108 km away, situated in the western ghats at 803 m above sea level.

The narrow gauge railway was opened to traffic in 1907 and was, until a few years ago when a road was built, the only way to reach Matheran. Motor traffic does not penetrate beyond the resort's car park from where walking, pony riding or rickshaw is the only means of getting around.

The toy train begins its 21 km journey from Neral, pulled by a cute diesel locomotive. Although the climb of 610 m is slow (it takes two hours) time passes quickly because of the breathtaking scenery. The ruling gradient is 1 in 20 as the track zigzags upwards gradually revealing the full beauty of Matheran Hill.

There are usually six coaches, one 1st Class, on this narrow gauge train. In 1st Class the window seats are numbers 1, 4, 5 and 8; upholstered bench seats facing each other with four places on each bench. The new 2nd Class coaches have glass panes to the roof for super views, but wooden seats; sit on the right for the best views going up. The boys travelling on the running board are cheerful vendors of soft drinks, on the way down they help the brakesmen. There are no toilets on this train but Jumma Patti (242 m above sea level) and the aptly named Water Pipe (at 484 m) are convenient stops. An unnerving sign in the coaches says: 'Do not crowd on one side of the coach – it is dangerous.'

It is possible to visit Matheran on a day trip, but many people (especially Bombayites escaping from the city) stay longer in this lush, traffic free town. The railway is closed from mid-June during the monsoon season and only opens again at the end of September or early October. There are no retiring rooms at Matheran station, nor at Neral, but the town has lots of places to stay. The fare to Matheran from Neral is calculated on a distance of 126 km instead of the 21 km actually travelled.

The first train of the day, the 601 passenger, leaves Neral at 0840 and arrives at Matheran at 1040. There are other departures at 1100 (the 603) and 1700 (the 605) with an extra train (the 607) leaving at 1015 in the season of mid March to mid June. To connect with these departures the 1007 Deccan Express leaves Bombay VT at 0645 and arrives at Neral at 0819 in time for the 601 departure. The 7307 Koyna Express leaves VT at 0845 and arrives at Neral at 1032 in time for the 603 departure.

Trains from Matheran are the 602 leaving at 0545, arriving at Neral at 0745; the 604 at 1310 arriving at 1450; the 606 at 1435 arriving at

1620; and the 608 (season time only) at 1620, arriving at 1803. There is no convenient connection back to Bombay unless you try a suburban train on the Karjat to Bombay line such as the S24 leaving Neral at 1645 and reaching VT at 1840. Another option is to leave Matheran at 0545 so you can catch the Deccan Express at 0819 to Lonavla or Pune.

NILAGIRI MOUNTAIN RAILWAY

The broad gauge Nilagiri Express from Madras terminates at Mettupalaiyam station and passengers change over during the 30 minute wait before the fabled Blue Mountain train departs for Ooty.

During the wait, vendors pass along the platform selling coffee and breakfast snacks, and the 1920s steam engine shunts into position at the back of the train. The station has the look of a frontier with the modern overnight Nilagiri Express, hauled by a huge diesel and with AC sleeper and 3 tier carriages, on one side of the platform, and the old wooden coaches of the metre gauge mountain train on the other.

Although the idea for a railway from Mettupalaiyam to Coonoor, a distance of 27 km, was first mooted in 1854, it wasn't in operation until 1899. The problem had been how to get the train up the steep gradients of the mountains and how to stop it running too fast on the way down.

The rack and pinion system was devised. Special rack bars were laid between the track rails where the line slopes to form a kind of elongated ladder. The train pinions itself onto the rack for the climb up, pushed by the engine. The rack section commences just after Kallar and continues up to Coonoor. Maximum speed on that section is 13 kph. The line was extended to Ooty in 1908.

The train is pushed by one of the eight X class steam locos remaining out of seven introduced in 1925 and five put on the line in 1952. One of those eight has recently retired to the Rail Museum in Delhi.

The train's coaches are as old as the engines. Made of wood, they are painted dark blue and a grubby yellow on the outside and pale blue inside. There are two 1st Class cabins at the front of the train, furnished with coconut fibre and foam bench cushions covered in green rexine. Both cabins seat eight passengers, or more, with the best seats on the way up being in the front cabin facing the way the train is going. Since the engine pushes from behind passengers have a glorious view of the jungle, mountains and valleys. Sit on the left side facing the window for the best views.

2nd Class carriages with wooden bench seats form the rest of the train, with a guards van and luggage box at the rear. Each of the coaches and wagons is crewed by a brakesman who stands on the open gallery at the front of the carriage and independently operates the wheel and rack brakes on whistle codes from the driver.

After the train leaves Mettupalaiyam, its first stop is at Kallar, a phantom station since it is not in the SR timetable, but this is where the rack and pinion system is engaged. The next stop is at the entrance to tunnel number 3, for the engine to take on water. At every tunnel the kids on the train erupt with hoots of excitement as the train passes through it, and look down aghast when the train emerges to cross vast chasms on spindly bridges.

Elephants and rock-falls are hazards on this run. At Hillgrove station where the train stops to take on waterr again, passengers flock to the refreshment stall. Wild monkeys perform on the station's roof for bananas. There are no toilets on the train but those at Hillgrove are new and good.

Coonoor, a little over half the way to Ooty, is surrounded by mountains and fringed with buildings. Its station was built in 1897 out of granite blocks and is painted bright blue and pale yellow. There are three retiring rooms, a refreshment stall, newly built and clean toilets, a fountain, and a pretty umbrella shaped shelter.

An attraction at Coonoor is the loco shed, the base for all the locomotives on this line. It is close to the station and has a hand-painted scene of a steam engine as its signboard. The engines are maintained and overhauled here with the oldest (number 37384, built in 1920) still in operation. The station bell is an old metal toothed wheel of the pinion system which is hammered with an iron bar to announce the last five minutes before a train's departure. It is possible to break the journey at Coonoor and catch a train later, or another day, up to Ooty.

The military base station of Wellington comes soon after, with an occasional glimpse of soldiers practising on the target range beside the track. At Aravankadu there is a cordite factory opposite the station and the railway retiring room has a view over it. The climb to Ooty broadens as the train chugs gently through forests and hills. On the evening run from Coonoor, skeins of mist hang in the valleys below the track and men wander along the line wrapped in blankets. It is chilly in Ooty in the summer, and cold in winter.

Four kilometres before reaching Ooty is a station named Lovedale, at 2,192 m above sea level. It is set in the forest and has a post office for neighbour, so there must be some residents but they are not to be seen. Lovedale lives up to its name; peaceful and romantic. The station, like an English country cottage, has two retiring rooms.

The train crosses 250 bridges on its way to Ooty and passes through 16 tunnels. The ruling gradient is 1 in 24.50 but it is 1 in 12.28 from Kallar to Coonoor. The total length of the line is 45.88 km and the journey time is 4 hrs 25 mins going up and 3 hrs 20 mins coming down.

The line is subject to landslides and is often closed for weeks during the monsoon season. Every day the track is inspected and the train only leaves Kallar when it is safe to proceed. Elephants have attacked station buildings which is why some have been closed.

'Travel by rail and spend longer among the hills' reads a slogan painted on a retaining wall close to the tea growing area before Runnymeade, one of the closed stations.

After its arrival at Udagamandalam, as Ooty is now called, the train is shunted over a service trench where an engineer examines it underneath. For its descent, the loco leads (but in reverse) with the brakesman of each coach watching carefully to prevent too fast a run down hill.

The usual itinerary for independent travellers involves taking a bus from Ooty to Mysore since Ooty is the end of the line. It's a shame to do this and miss the descent, which is just as dramatic as the ride up.

The conventional way of getting to Ooty by train is from Madras on the 6005 Nilagiri Express which departs nightly at 2105, arriving at Mettupalaiyam at 0720 the next day. This connects with the 562 leaving Mettupalaiyam at 0750, arriving Coonoor at 1040 and at Ooty at 1210. An additional train, (564) operates during periods of extra demand, such as the April/June season. There are also departures from Coonoor for Ooty at 0725 and 1635.

For the return, the 561 leaves Ooty at 1450 and arrives at Mettupalaiyam at 1830 to connect with the 6006 Nilagiri Express, departing at 1915 and arriving in Madras at 0555 the next day. That train gets to Coimbatore at 2000 from where there are many connections to other parts of Southern India.

Fares on the Blue Mountain Railway are charged according to a calculated distance rather than actual distance.

Distances:

Station	Remarks	Actual km	Charged km	Elevation Metres
Mettupalaiyam	Rooms	0		326
Kallar		7.46		404
Allderly	Closed	12.27		731
Hillgrove	Snacks	17.26	50	1092
Runneymede	Closed	21.97		1407
Kateri Road	Closed	24.35		1547
Coonoor	Rooms	27.03	77	1711
Wellington	Rooms	28.54	80	1769
Aravankadu	Rooms	31.34	86	1812
Ketti		37.19	98	2092
Lovedale	Rooms	41.76	108	2192
Udagamandalam	Rooms	45.88	116	2203

KALKA SHIMLA RAILWAY

The best way to appreciate the grandeur of the 96 km of 0.762 m narrow gauge track as it climbs through the foothills of the Himalayas, is by Rail Motor Car. It makes you aware of the extraordinary feats of engineering that created this line with great arched viaducts spanning chasms, and over a hundred tunnels bored through the mountains.

The Rail Motor Car (No. 101) leaves Kalka at 0630. It's possible to take an overnight train, the Howrah/Kalka Mail, from Delhi station at 2245, and arrive at Kalka at 0525. The Rail Car waits at the end of the platform where the Kalka Mail terminates. The sight of it, like a light blue 1920s Ford truck that's escaped from a museum, will make you rub your eyes in disbelief. There are actually four cars in service, built in 1927 and reconditioned in 1982.

The car has space for two next to the driver's cab and behind are four bench seats, all comfortably upholstered, for five passengers each. Upgrading of tickets to ride in this extraordinary vehicle, which has been in operation for over 60 years, is done by a ticket inspector at the empty, marble-topped snack bar counter close to where the Car is parked.

The driver engages gear and the Car leaps forward for the journey through 103 tunnels (the longest is number 33 at Barog, at a height of 1144 m) and over 869 bridges, climbing from 656 m above sea level at Kalka to 2,075 m at Shimla. The views are stunning and, seated in the Rail Car, you miss nothing.

The Car will stop at any station en route, if the request is made at Kalka or to the driver himself, but usually it sails right through the tiny picturesque stations. There is no toilet in the Car but the driver will stop if your need is great and even reverse if he passes your station and you forget to tell him.

A 15 minute halt is made at Barog where the restaurant is one of the nicest of any station in India. It is above the platform with a flower-bedecked veranda, a hillside view, service that is friendly and fast, and food that is freshly prepared. You should order meals in advance through the railway staff before leaving Kalka or Shimla.

Every one of the 18 stations on the journey to Shimla seems an attractive spot to linger, but none has retiring rooms. Above Solan station there is something called a 'Relieving Lodge' and Solan Brewery station is actually in the middle of a heady-smelling brewery. Shimla station has five retiring rooms, with plans for more. The rooms are on the first floor over the station and all have attached bathrooms with hot water. A deluxe room has a TV and fridge.

Shimla station has a magnificent view down the mountains and is kept clean (lots of blue paintwork) and well run. There is no foreign tourist quota for reservations at the station (which seems strange in view of Shimla's popularity with foreign tourists) but the SS and his staff try their best to arrange bookings. Computerization is planned. There are two waiting rooms, a tea stall and a restaurant.

The line was built in 1903 on a rising gradient meandering through the Shivalik Range, the steepest one being 1 in 33. The ruling gradient is 1 in 67. About 70 per cent of the track is on curves. The Rail Car is permitted a maximum speed of 29 khp, and the diesel hauled passenger train is restricted to a maximum of 25 khp.

One of the passenger trains (no. 251) leaves Kalka at 0710. The 1145 departure waits for the 4095 daytime Himalayan Queen which leaves New Delhi at 0600 and arrives at Kalka at 1115.

On the Kalka to Shimla train, 1st Class seats are in a chair car with one seat on one side of the aisle and a pair of seats on the other, total 18. The seats are reversible to face whichever end of the train is the front. Another type of 1st Class carriage has a coupé and a lounge with seats along the side of the carriage.

Seats in 2nd Class are wooden, with slats, and are rather hard for the journey which usually takes between five and six hours. Departures from Shimla are at 1055, 1325, 1645 (rail car) and 1800.

The 1645 Rail Car gets to Kalka in time for the 2330 departure of the 2132 Kalka/Howrah Mail. On arrival at Kalka, there are connections to Ambala and from there to Jammu Tawi or eastwards. The Shatabdi Express provides a new link between New Delhi and Kalka.

BUTTERFIELD'S INDIAN RAILWAY TOUR

'I was pretty apprehensive about India and spending so much time on a train with a group of unknowns,' wrote Australian Lynne Barraclough to Jane and Ashley Butterfield. 'But thanks to you both I would happily return to India for another trip.'

Jane and Ashley Butterfield run rail tours in India from September to March by a specially converted railway carriage which is attached to scheduled trains. From their HQ in Yorkshire, they send out fact-filled brochures describing their tours so that potential passengers have a good idea of what's in store. All tours are accompanied either by the Butterfields, or by two experienced and equally enthusiastic guides. The cost (around £800) includes train travel, all meals on board and some hotel accommodation and excursions. Air fares to India are extra.

Their brochure states: 'Our carriage accommodates up to 26 people and comprises two large sitting rooms, a small dining room/library, a pantry, a kitchen, two wash rooms with showers and four Asian style toilets. It is equipped with electric lights and fans ... At night the sitting rooms convert into dormitories, and then you can choose between sleeping on benches, upper berths or camp beds'.

The Butterfields have been running the only comprehensive railway tour of India using a private railway carriage for years. Their experience of getting around India by rail is unique and their tours are ideal for those who want to try train travel but not alone. Londoner Barry, 25, wrote in the Butterfield comments book: 'If I had tried to do India on my own, I suspect that I would still be in Delhi arguing about seat reservations'.

A Butterfields' tour lasts for 23 days. It begins in Delhi with the 'bogie' – the private carriage – being attached to a train to Haridwar. Then it's eastwards to Lucknow and Varanasi, south to Hyderabad, Mysore, Ooty and Cochin, and north to Bombay. Guests can spend an extra week in the south at the end of the tour and are given details on how to get around as well as a choice of suggested routes. There is also a 24-day tour of south India starting in Madras, ending in Bombay, which covers the area in depth with nights in hotels and a leisurely pace. The cost (around £1,800) includes flight to India from London as well as train travel, meals on full board basis, hotel accommodation and excursions.

Jane and Ashley Butterfield have written a 50-page booklet called *The Bogiewalla's Guide to Enjoying India – And Helping India Enjoy You!* which can be purchased through their Yorkshire address.

Based on the Butterfield's experience during years of touring India with foreigners, the booklet's hints are worth taking seriously, especially since even the most sensitive short-term visitors would not have the time, let alone the patience, to garner such invaluable knowledge for themselves.

There are fascinating sections on religion, caste, language and the extended family as well as on behaviour and etiquette. The Butterfields say 'it is a fallacy to think that learning follows automatically from being in a new place.' Follow their advice and you will indeed learn, as well as avoid causing offence by behaving 'normally'.

The Butterfields tell passengers: 'Although we live together on board, when we stop you are free to be as independent as you please'. It is a formula people enjoy, as they can travel safely by rail in convivial company without having to worry about the arrangements, and yet can wander off on their own to explore when they want.

Address: Burton Fleming, Driffield, East Yorkshire, YO24 OPQ. Tel: 0262 470230

Chapter 12

Super Trains

India has some trains that really are super: fast, comfortable and with a pantry car and bearer service. The best are the Superfast Trains, although they do not all share the same standards of accommodation and service. Some are exclusively 2nd Class and some have no refreshment facilities at all. In this section I have included a list of the main superfast trains, indicating with 'R' where a pantry car or on-board refreshment is available. However, even where there is no 'R', meals/refreshments could still be obtainable through station halts.

Express and mail trains are also good; a separate list of those having 1st Class AC sleepers is given here. There are over 200 express and mail trains with AC 2 tier (2nd Class) sleeper accommodation and the number is increasing; too many to include accurately here. However, unless it is an all 2nd Class (3 tier) 'Janata' train, most expresses will have a non-AC 1st Class carriage if there is no AC 2 tier sleeper. A separate list is given of trains which have AC Chair Car coaches.

Superfast express and mail trains

A supplementary charge (see Chapter 3) is levied for travel on the trains listed here. Not all are daily. MG = Metre Gauge.

Number	Express	Service between
1269/70	Express	Bhopal–Rajkot
2001/02	Shatabdi (R)	New Delhi–Bhopal
2003/04	Shatabdi (R)	New Delhi–Lucknow
2005/06	Shatabdi (R)	New Delhi–Kalka
2101/02	Minar	Secunderabad–Bombay
2113/14	Indrayani (R)	Bombay VT–Pune
2119/20	Konark	Secunderabad–Bhubaneswar
2123/24	Deccan Queen (R)	Bombay VT–Pune
2133/34	Pushpak	Bombay VT–Lucknow
2135/36	Natravati	Bombay VT–Cochin
2159/60	Chambal	Gwalior–Howrah
2161/62	Lashkar	Dadar–Agra
2165/66	Express	Bombay VT–Varanasi
2167/68	Saket	Bombay VT–Faizabad
2179/80	Taj (R)	New Delhi–Gwalior
2181/82	Chambal	Agra–Howrah

Number	Express	Service between
2301/02	Rajdhani (R)	Howrah–New Delhi
2311/12	Kalka Mail (R)	Howrah–Delhi–Kalka
2373/74	Himgiri (R)	Howrah–Jammu Tawi
2381/82 & 2303/04	AC Expresses (R)	Howrah–New Delhi
2391/92	Magadh – Vikramshila (R)	Patna–New Delhi
2401/02	Sharamjeevi	New Delhi–Patna
2403/04	Sharmik	Varanasi–Kanpur
2405/06	Express	New Delhi–Ludhiana
2415/16	Ganga Gomti	Allahabad–Lucknow
2417/18	Prayag Raj	Allahabad–New Delhi
2419/20	Gomti (R)	Lucknow–New Delhi
2427/28	Varuna	Varanasi–Lucknow
2449/50	Express	Muzaffarpur–Delhi
2455/56	Tinsukia Mail (R)	Delhi–Guwahati
2461/62	Mandor (MG)	Delhi–Jodhpur
2473/74	Shaheed	Muzaffarpur–Delhi
2459/60	Express	Amritsar–New Delhi
2497/98	Shane–Punjab (R)	New Delhi – Amritsar
2521/22	North East (R)	New Delhi–Guwahati
2547/48	Purvanchal (R)	Gorakhpur–Howrah
2553/54	Vaishali (R)	Barauni–Gorakhpur–New Delhi
2557/58	Kanchanjunga (R)	Sealdah–Guwahati
2587/88	Express (R)	Jammu Tawi–Gorakhpur
2601/02	Weekly Express (R)	Trivandrum–Guwahati
2603/04	Weekly Express (R)	Trivandrum–Rajkot
2605/06	Pallavan (MG) (R)	Madras Egmore–Tiruchchirappalli
2609/10	Express	Cochin–Patna
2611/12	Express	Howrah–Bangalore
2615/16	Grand Trunk (R)	Madras–New Delhi
2621/22	Tamil Nadu (R)	Madras–New Delhi
2625/26	Kerala–Mangala (R)	Trivandrum/Mangalore–New Delhi
2627/28	Karnataka (R)	Bangalore City–New Delhi
2635/36	Vaigai (MG) (R)	Madras Egmore–Madurai
2637/38	Express (R)	Ahmadabad–Cochin
2639/40	Brindavan (R)	Madras–Bangalore City
2641/42	Navjivan (R)	Ahmadabad–Madras
2649/50	Weekly Express (R)	Cochin–Guwahati
2651/52	Express	Cochin–Howrah
2673/74	Weekly Express	Bangalore–Guwahati
2675/76	Kovai (R)	Madras–Coimbatore
2701/02	Goa	H. Nizamuddin–Miraj
2723/24	Andhra Pradesh (R)	Secunderabad–New Delhi
2731/32	Express (R)	Rajkot–Secunderabad
2815/16	Express (R)	Puri–New Delhi
2821/22	Dhuli (R)	Howrah–Bhubaneswar
2825/26	Mahanadi	Bilaspur–Bhopal
2841/42	Coromandel (R)	Madras–Howrah
2853/54	Amarkantak	Bhopal–Durg
2859/60	Gitanjali (R)	Howrah–Bombay
2901/02	Pink City (MG) (R)	Jaipur–Delhi
2903/04	Frontier Mail (R)	Bombay Central–Delhi–Amritsar
2905/06	Ashram (MG)	Ahmadabad–Delhi

Number	Train	Service between
2907/08	Surya Nagari	Ahmadabad–Jodhpur
2915/16	Garib Nawaz (R)	Udaipur–Delhi
2921/22	Express (MG)	Jaipur–Agra Fort
2925/26	Paschim (R)	Bombay Central–Amritsar
2951/52	Rajdhani (R)	New Delhi–Bombay Central
2953/54	AC	Bombay Central–New Delhi
2971/72	Express	Bombay Central–Jammu Tawi
2981/82	Sarvodaya (R)	Ahmadabad–Jammu Tawi
2993/94	Karnavati	Ahmadabad–Bombay Central
2977/98	Express (R)	Happa–Jammu Tawi
7575/76	Express	Guwahati–Bangalore

First Class AC Sleeper Trains

Trains with 1st Class Air Conditioned Sleeper coaches are listed here. Usually there is one coach per train, sometimes combined with other accommodation. 1st Class AC berths are not necessarily provided daily, even though the train may run daily. R = Pantry Car.

Number	Express	Service between
1037/38	Punjab Mail	Firozpur–Bombay VT
2301/02	Rajdhani (R)	New Delhi–Howrah
2311/12	Kalka Mail (R)	Howrah–Delhi–Kalka
2381/82 & 2303/04	AC Expresses (R)	Howrah–New Delhi
2391/92	Magadh Vikramshila (R)	Patna–New Delhi
2401/02	Sharamjeevi	New Delhi–Patna
2403/04	Sharmik	Varanasi–Kanpur
2417/18	Prayag Raj	Allahabad–New Delhi
2419/20	Gomti (R)	Lucknow–New Delhi
2497/98	Shane Punjab (R)	New Delhi–Amritsar
2547/48	Purvanchal (R)	Gorakhpur–Howrah
2553/54	Vaishali (R)	Gorakhpur–New Delhi
2615/16	Grand Trunk (R)	Madras–New Delhi
2621/22	Tamil Nadu (R)	Madras–New Delhi
2723/24	Andhra Pradesh (R)	Secunderabad–New Delhi
2901/02	Pink City (MG) (R)	Jaipur–New Delhi
2903/04	Frontier Mail (R)	Bombay Central–Amritsar
2905/06	Ashram (MG)	Ahmadabad–Delhi
2907/08	Surya Nagari	Ahmadabad–Delhi
2925/26	Paschim (R)	Bombay Central–Amritsar
2933/34	Karnavati	Bombay Central–Ahmadabad
2951/52	Rajdhani (R)	New Delhi–Bombay Central
2953/54	AC	Bombay Central–New Delhi
3003/04	Mail	Howrah–Bombay VT
3005/06	Mail	Howrah–Amritsar
3015/16	Shantiniketan	Howrah–Bolpur
3031/32	Express	Howrah–Danapur
3143/44	Darjeeling Mail	Sealdah–New Jalpaiguri

Number	Express	Service between
3317/18	Black Diamond (R)	Howrah–Dhanbad
4033/44	Jammu Mail	Delhi–Jammu Tawi
4041/42	Mussoorie	Delhi–Dehradun
4057/58	Kashi Vishvanath	New Delhi–Varanasi
4095/96	Himalayan Queen	New Delhi–Kalka
4229/30	Lucknow Mail	Lucknow–New Delhi
4517/18	Unchahar	Kanpur–New Delhi–Ambala
4893/94	Mail (MG) (R)	Jodhpur–Delhi
6003/04	Mail	Madras–Howrah
6005/06	Nilagiri	Madras–Mettupailayam
6007/08	Mail	Madras–Bangalore
6023/24	Express	Madras–Bangalore
6103/04	Pearl City (MG)	Madras–Tuticorin
6177/78	Rock Fort (MG)	Madras–Tiruchchirappalli
6717/18	Pandyan (MG)	Madras–Madurai
7007/08	Godavari	Visakhapatnam–Hyderabad
7047/48	Gautami	Secunderabad–Kakinada Port
8001/02	Mail (R)	Bombay VT–Howrah
8005/06	Express	Howrah–Sambalpur
8007/08	Express	Howrah–Puri
8011/12	Ispat (R)	Howrah–Rourkela
8013/14	Steel (R)	Howrah–Tatanagar
8015/16	Express	Howrah–Ranchi–Hatia
8543/44	Samta	Visakhapatnam–H. Nizamuddin
9001/02	Gujarat Mail	Bombay Central–Ahmadabad
9011/12	Gujarat (R)	Bombay Central–Ahmadabad
9019/20	Dehradun	Kota–New Delhi
9027/28	Express	Bombay Central–Vadodara
9055/56	Sayaj Nagari	Bombay Central–Vadodara
9901/02	Mail (MG)	Delhi–Ahmadabad

AC Chair Car

In this list of trains that have air conditioned carriages with seating accommodation, some only have a few seats available in carriages combined with 1st Class AC Sleepers. R = Pantry Car.

Number	Express	Service between
1007/08	Deccan (R)	Bombay VT–Pune
2001/02	Shatabdi (R)	New Delhi–Bhopal
2003/04	Shatabdi (R)	New Delhi–Lucknow
2005/06	Shatabdi (R)	New Delhi–Kalka
2113/14	Indrayani (R)	Bombay VT–Pune
2301/02	Rajdhani (R)	Howrah–New Delhi
2381/82 & 2303/04	AC Expresses (R)	Howrah–New Delhi
2401/02	Sharamjeevi	New Delhi–Patna
2403/04	Sharmik	Varanasi–Kanpur

Number	Train	Service between
2419/20	Gomti (R)	Lucknow–New Delhi
2427/28	Varuna	Varanasi–Lucknow
2497/98	Shane Punjab (R)	New Delhi–Amritsar
2547/48	Purvanchal (R)	Barauni–Gorakhpur
2553/54	Vaishali (R)	Gorakhpur–Barauni
2587/88	Express	Jammu Tawi–Gorakhpur
2605/06	Pallavan (MG) (R)	Madras Egmore–Tiruchchirappalli
2635/36	Vaigai (MG) (R)	Madras–Egmore–Madurai
2639/40	Brindavan (R)	Madras–Bangalore
2675/76	Kovai (R)	Madras–Coimbatore
2723/24	Andhra Pradesh (R)	Secunderabad–New Delhi
2821/22	Dhuli (R)	Howrah–Bhubaneswar
2925/26	Paschim (R)	Bombay Central–Amritsar
2951/52	Rajdhani (R)	New Delhi–Bombay Central
2953/54	AC	Bombay Central–New Delhi
3143/44	Darjeeling Mail	Sealdah–New Jalpaiguri
3317/18	Black Diamond (R)	Howrah–Dhanbad
4095/96	Himalayan Queen	New Delhi–Kalka
5001/02	Krishak	Varanasi–Gorakhpur
5003/04	Express	Allahabad–Gorakhpur
6301/02	Venad (R)	Trivandrum–Shoranur
6303/04	Vanchinad (R)	Trivandrum–Ernakulam
6307/08	Express	Ernakulam–Cannanore
6349/50	Parasuram (R)	Trivandrum–Mangalore
7033/34	Bhagyanagar	Secunderabad–Sirpurkagaz Nagar
7201/02	Golkonda (R)	Secunderabad–Guntur
8011/12	Ispat (R)	Howrah–Rourkela
8013/14	Steel (R)	Howrah–Tatanagar
9031/32	Kutch	Bombay Central–Ahmadabad

Some trains with pantry or refreshment cars
(in addition to those indicated with 'R' in train lists)

Number	Train	Service between
1001/02	Panchavati	Bombay VT–Manmad
1009/10	Sinhagad	Bombay VT–Pune
1015/16	Express	Bombay VT–Gorakhpur
4067/68	Malwa	New Delhi–Indore
4789/90	Express (MG)	Delhi–Bikaner
5313/14	Marudhar (MG)	Jodhpur–Lucknow
5609/10	Avadh Assam	Guwahati–Delhi
5645/46	Weekly	Guwahati–Dadar
5659/60	Kamrup	Guwahati–Howrah
5815/16	Express (MG)	Guwahati–Allahabad
5905/06	Kamrup (MG)	Guwahati–Dibrugarh
6017/18	Himsagar	Kanniya Kumari–Jammu Tawi
6039/40	Ganga Kaveri	Madras–Varanasi
6043/44	Express	Madras–Patna

Number	Express	Service between
6501/02	Express	Bangalore–Ahmadabad
6687/88	Navyug	Mangalore–Jammu Tawi
8101/02	Express	Muri–Amaritsar
8237/38	Chattisgarh	Bilaspur–Amaritsar
8475/76	Neelachal	Puri–New Delhi
8477/78	Utkal Kalinga	Puri–H. Nizamuddin
9021/22	Flying Ranee	Bombay Central–Surat
9023/24	Janata (2nd Class)	Bombay Central–Firozpur
9931/32	Aravli (MG)	Delhi–Ahmadabad
1BM/2BM	MG	Barmer–Munabo
1RM/2RM	MG	Ratangarh–Merta Road
1SB/2SB	MG	Samdari–Bhildi
251/252	MG	Jodgpur–Phulera
265/266	MG	Jodhpur–Ahmadabad

Chapter 13

Help

Onboard emergencies
For health and security problems contact the train superintendent or conductor immediately. There are emergency cords in every compartment to stop the train. Trains carry books in which complaints can be made.

At the station
Contact the Station Superintendent in person, or if the station is too small to have one, then the station master, if you experience problems at his station. Many stations have police posts at which reports can be made, and public grievance booths. There are also complaints books available on demand; complaints are taken seriously and investigated. The SS will have a list of doctors who can be called on in an emergency.

Consul
The UK Foreign & Commonwealth Office have a leaflet available called *Consular Assistance Abroad* which contains invaluable advice that applies to travellers of all nationalities. Don't expect your consul to get better treatment for you in hospital (or prison) than is provided for local nationals, or to interfere in local judicial procedures. However, the consul can provide a list of lawyers, interpreters, and doctors, and sometimes arrange for messages to be sent to relatives or friends if you are arrested.

The leaflet recommends that, as soon as you arrive, you jot down the address and telephone number of your local embassy, high commissioner or consul to carry with you; check the local telephone directory for it. Carry your passport with you at all times in India.

Mail/Messages
Holders of American Express travellers cheques or credit cards can use the local American Express office as a mail drop. If you have a reservation to stay at a reputable hotel at some stage during your tour of India, have your mail sent there, with arrival date marked on the envelope. Mail can be sent to stations (see Chapter 2) but you might never get it. Telegrams can also be sent to you at stations.

Homesick

If you are feeling homesick, or perhaps simply overwhelmed by India and too much travelling, don't bottle up your misery. Talking to fellow passengers can help. In a town, turn to the telephone directory, or hotel management, or even the SS, for addresses of social organizations or professional associations with which you have some connection at home, such as Lions, Rotary, trade unions, sports clubs, hobby groups.

Foreigners who have an interest shared by Indians are likely to be given a splendid welcome which banishes feelings of loneliness. Some towns have clubs where visitors can become temporary members. If the club has a western style menu, that can help cure homesickness.

Elephants are still used on the railways. They were helping lay new railway lines in the Northeast Frontier zone in 1992 although the sight of elephants shunting as used to take place at the Rajgangpu station cement factory is rare.

Chapter 14

Endpiece

A summary of how to get the best out of travelling in India by rail.

- Travel on an Indrail Pass, preferably bought from an overseas GSA so he can make your first reservation in advance.

- Go for at least 21 days.·

- September to March is the best time.

- Make full use of the facilities for foreigners by booking your subsequent reservations through the ITB at New Delhi station, or through the Foreign Tourist Bureaux at the other main stations.

- If you intend buying rail tickets in India from the Foreign Tourist Quota, have foreign currency or travellers cheques to do this; especially as it saves a trip to the bank to change them.

- Make train reservations well in advance and allow time to do so; if you have problems, ask the CRS or the SS for advice and help.

- Travel upper class: 1st or 2nd AC or 1st Non-AC.

- Sleeping on trains and in station retiring rooms saves money for memorable nights in classic hotels in Rajasthan and major cities.

- Use *Trains At A Glance* to plot your own itinerary.

- Choose trains which arrive/depart during daylight.

- Avoid tight connections.

- Allow days in your itinerary for doing nothing; you might need spare days in the event of delay.

- Take your full quota of duty-free liquor into India.

- On long distance trains, let the bearer be your friend since he can be a source of advice and extra comforts.

- Drink lots of liquid but not station water unless you've purified it yourself.

- Travel light but include a padlock (to secure your luggage to something in the train or waiting room and to lock the retiring room door), a pocket knife/bottle opener, a hand towel, a water bottle and purifying tablets.

- Wear loose cotton clothing and underwear; buy plastic sandals in India to wear in train or station toilets and showers.

- Keep travellers cheques and travel documents on you, never in your luggage; have change handy for purchases from platform vendors.

- Do not alight from a train that has not properly stopped but, if you must, then face the way it's going so you don't fall flat on your own face. Always check up and down a track before you cross it.

- Have proper and adequate insurance cover for accident, illness and theft.

- When dealing with railway people, be patient and polite; know what you want and ask for it intelligibly.

FOR YOUR OWN SAFETY **BE CAUTIOUS** WHEN NEGOTIATING A RAILWAY LEVEL CROSSING.

CENTRAL RAILWAY

SAFETY ORGANIZATION

Remember AGAINST A RAILWAY ENGINE YOU STAND **NO CHANCE**

Appendices

FURTHER READING

Since this book is intended as a guide to India by rail and not as a general guide to India, you will need maps and books that tell you about the places and ways of the country as well. There is no point in travelling by train to, say, Madurai unless you know something about all those temples you'll be gazing at.

Maps
India (Bartholomew) 1:4,000,000.
A good general map.

Nelles Verlag Maps 1:1,500,000.
A series of five regional road maps of the Indian subcontinent, with shaded relief, railways, tourist information, and insets of city plans. The most comprehensive coverage of India at a consistent scale.

Guide books
India: a travel survival kit (Lonely Planet).
The book I, and thousands of other visitors to India, depend on. Very comprehensive (over 800 pages).

South Asian Handbook: India (Trade and Travel). Updated annually, this hefty book (±1500 pages) also covers six neighbouring countries.

Other guides to India include:

Into India (John Murray).

India (Hildebrand).

The Cadogan Guide to India (Cadogan Books).

India Discovered (Collins).

Local guides are available at bookshops or railway book stalls in India.

Rail enthusiasts will delight in tracking down these books (try at the Delhi Rail Museum) by a distinguished railwayman, R.R. Bhandari:
  Rail Transport Museum (Railway Board, 1980)
  Locomotives In Steam (Railway Board, 1981)

Jodhpur Railway (Northern Railway, 1982)
Kalka–Simla and Kangra Valley Railways (Northern Railway, 1983)
Exotic Indian Mountain Railways (Railway Board, 1984)
Western Railway Metre Gauge System (Western Railway, 1987)
The Blue Chip Railway (South Eastern Railway, 1988)

Highly recommended is *A History Of Indian Railways* by G.S. Khosla (Railway Board, 1988), and *The Bogie-Walla's Guide To Enjoying India – And Helping India Enjoy You!* by Jane and Ashley Butterfield (see page 226).

SPELLING

Many stations and train names have two or more ways of spelling them in English, such as Hardwar/Haridwar, Nilgiri/Nilagiri, and Shimla/Simla. I have tried to use the spelling which appears in the zonal timetables although sometimes even those sources are not consistent.

GLOSSARY

Indian Railway bureaucracy is riddled with initials and abbreviations used freely in conversation among railway men as well as in signs intended for foreign tourists. For instance, at Agra Fort there is a sign which tells tourists to contact 'the CRS'. You'll frequently be asked for your 'PNR'. Above a door at a station I saw a sign which said VLRRMTP. I pushed it open to find it meant 'Vegetarian Light Refreshment Room, Mettupalaiyam'.
    Terms used in this book are as follows:

AC	Air conditioned
ACC	Air Conditioned Class
ACCC	Air Conditioned Chair Car
BG	Broad gauge
CCTV	Closed Circuit TeleVision
CR	Central Railway
CRS	Chief Reservations Supervisor
CRS	Computer Reservations System
Crore	100 lakhs, ie: 10,000,000
DHR	Darjeeling Himalayan Railway
Direct	'Without any change of train'
DRM	Divisional Railway Manager
EMU	Electric Multiple Unit
ETA	Estimated Time of Arrival
GRP	Government Railway Police
GSA	General Sales Agent (for Indrail Passes)
IRP	Indrail Pass

ITB	International Tourist Bureau
Jn	Junction
Lakh	100,000
MG	Metre Gauge
ND	New Delhi
NER	North Eastern Railway
NG	Narrow Gauge
NJ	New Jalpaiguri station
NR	Northern Railway
NV	Non-vegetarian (restaurant/meal)
PNR	Passenger Name Record (ie: number on a computer generated reservation coupon)
R	Refreshments available
RAC	Reservation Against Cancellation
Rexine	Artificial leather
RPF	Railway Protection Force
SER	South Eastern Railway
SM	Station Master
SR	Southern Railway
SS	Station Superintendent
TAG	*Trains At A Glance*
TC	Ticket Collector
TS	Train Superintendent
TTE	Travelling Ticket Examiner
V	Vegetarian (restaurant/meal)
VT	Bombay Victoria Terminus station

UPDATE

For this book to maintain its value for travellers, it needs to be updated. As much as I would like to spend a few months each year travelling in India by rail, it would take me a long time to ride every train, visit every station, and discover every change. So if you have any new information, tips for other rail travellers or reports on new developments which could be included in the next edition of *India by Rail*, please send them to me:

Royston Ellis,
INDIA BY RAIL,
c/o Bradt Publications,
41 Nortoft Road,
Chalfont St Peter,
Bucks SL9 0LA,
England.

Contributions which are used will be acknowledged in the next edition, as well as being of great help to other rail travellers.

THE GLOBETROTTERS CLUB

An international club which aims to share information on adventurous budget travel through monthly meetings and *Globe* magazine. Published every two months, *Globe* offers a wealth of information from reports of members' latest adventures to travel bargains and tips, plus the invaluable 'Mutual Aid' column where members can swap a house, sell a camper, find a travel companion or offer information on unusual places or hospitality to visiting members. London meetings are held monthly (Saturdays) and focus on a particular country or continent with illustrated talks.

Enquiries to: Globetrotters Club, BCM/Roving, London WC1N 3XX.

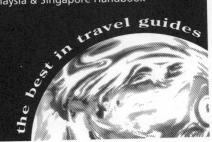

Index of Place Names

For places with recommended hotels, see page 121; for stations with retiring rooms, see page 124. See also Destinations, page 159.